DATE DUE

D0744152

639.3
~~S912~~ STR
Straughan
The salt-water aquarium in the home

1

THE SALT-WATER AQUARIUM IN THE HOME

BY THE SAME AUTHOR:

Exploring the Reef

Sharks, Morays, and Treasure

THE SALT-WATER AQUARIUM IN THE HOME

Second Revised Edition

By Robert P. L. Straughan

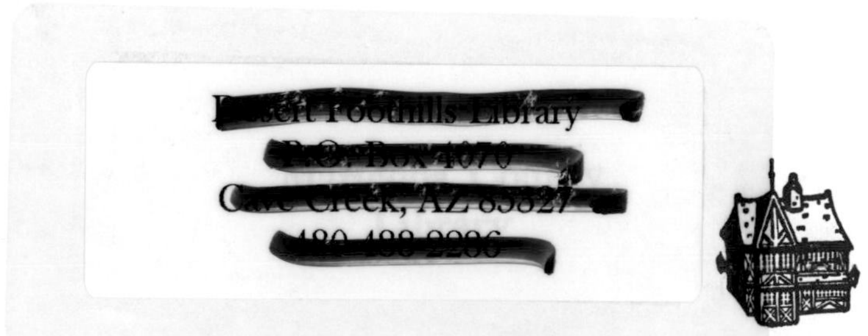

South Brunswick and New York: A. S. BARNES AND COMPANY
London: THOMAS YOSELOFF LTD

© 1959, 1964, 1970 by A. S. Barnes and Company, Inc.
Library of Congress Catalogue Card Number: 69-15785

A. S. Barnes and Company, Inc.
Cranbury, New Jersey 08512

Thomas Yoseloff, Ltd
108 New Bond Street
London W1Y OQX, England

Second Revised Edition October, 1969
Second Printing April, 1970
Third Printing May, 1971
Fourth Printing February, 1972
Fifth Printing November, 1972
Sixth Printing July, 1973

ISBN: 0498-07476-5
Printed in the United States of America

639.3
S912
c1 43

Contents

Hocho 7.98 6/76 (003)

Foreword

The wonders of the sea may be kept alive in your own home in a salt-water aquarium the maintenance of which offers a wide open field of exploration and discovery. Here is a home hobby where everyone becomes a scientist and where the compiling of notes and free exchange of ideas will broaden this fascinating hobby into one of the nation's greatest home enjoyments.

To bring a bit of the ocean into your home is a marvelous thing, for what could be more interesting? We know the sea is the last great unexplored area on earth. Only in the past few years has man ventured below its surface to any extent and it is the invention of the face mask, the aqua-lung, and other marvels of this age that has led man to explore the last frontier on this planet. It is a vast frontier and is like the land upon which we live. It has its mountains, its prairies, its valleys, and its jungles. And it has life in such strange and weird forms that the imagination is left far behind.

Keep a part of this fascinating world alive in your own living room and you will have a reason for the salt-water aquarium.

Acknowledgments

This salt-water book has been in preparation for a long time and probably would still be in that state without the constant prodding by many of my friends. In particular I would like to mention Clair Holloway, a marine hobbyist and collector who assisted me in some of my work and who constantly stressed upon me the need for finishing the book. It was her sincere efforts in urging me to complete the book rather than work on more projects that led me to the final publication.

I would also like to thank Dr. Paul Zahl, of *National Geographic* magazine who kindly read through the entire book in its unfinished form with a critical eye for any major errors in science or biology and who further encouraged me with his comments on the book.

Introduction

A book of this type can never be complete. The author has intended this one as a guide and beginning towards further experiments and achievements in keeping the endless variety of colorful and amazing creatures of the sea alive and content in small home-type aquariums.

As a full-time collector of all types of marine life, the author has had the opportunity to observe and study hundreds of thousands of salt-water specimens, both in the sea and in his own aquariums. He has had at his disposal, nearly every type of fish or crustacean that could conceivably be kept in an aquarium for any length of time. This book deals mainly with the hardier specimens that have been found to do quite well in the confinements of a small aquarium.

The author in his early literature also pioneered the use of the subsand filter with marine aquariums, and has done considerable work with marine plants, fish diseases, and feeding problems. He has also disproved many of the old taboos about sea-water aquariums and has proven that with proper understanding and knowledge, marine fish may be expected to live happily and contented in the home aquarium.

The fish photographs in the accompanying text were taken of living specimens by the author either in his home or in his experimental shop in Miami. None were taken in large public aquariums, which has been the case with most marine literature in the past. Since this book is aimed primarily at the self-sustained aquarium completely alienated from the sea, all experiments were based upon these conditions so that the inland aquarist, far from the ocean, could still keep a part of this fantastic world in his own home.

All the specimens with the exception of the Pacific fish were collected by the author and maintained in his aquariums for research and study. The author's findings and discoveries in this book are by no means infallible, but they are based on first hand observation and actual experiment. Altogether they encompass several thousand hours of pains-taking labor and investigation.

Even then it is only a beginning. The magnitude of the Seven Seas leaves a million lifetimes of fascinating discovery ahead of the marine aquarist.

R.P.L.S.

THE SALT-WATER AQUARIUM IN THE HOME

1

The Salt-Water Aquarium

The salt-water aquarium is in itself, a miniature ocean brought into your home. It can be a marvelous thing of growing, unending interest, and a fine source of learning about the wonders of the sea around us.

The basic problems of keeping salt-water fish in home aquariums have been solved. Pollution of the water, at one time the major obstacle, has been practically eliminated and with proper knowledge and aquarium procedure it will seldom occur. The feeding problem, next in importance, is rapidly being solved and at this writing so much has been learned about it that it is no longer a serious problem. Already many of the salt-water fish diseases have been discovered and treatment made available to the aquarist so that, all in all, the future looks bright for this interesting hobby.

The ideal salt-water aquarium is of all glass construction with a piece of glass across the top to slow down evaporation. Unfortunately, the only such vessels commonly sold on the present day market are small, having a capacity of only three gallons. This small size makes them fine for dwarf sea horses, small hermit crabs, neon gobies, coral shrimp, or any number of the smaller aquarium specimens available. The square all-glass battery jars are also fine, but they are difficult to obtain. They are larger in size. This makes them ideal for most of the regular-sized fish and, with them, almost perfect control of the marine tank may be obtained. Needless to say, they must be washed thoroughly before use as they originally contain an acid solution.

The glass bowls are good for one or two choice specimens, but as they give a certain amount of distortion, their general use is limited to lamps, table centerpieces, or other special effects. The flat-sided drum bowls are also good for a small marine exhibit.

Homemade aquariums of heavy plywood with a glass front are excellent for salt-water exhibits especially if a large aquarium is desired. These may be covered inside and out with the new fiberglass

Fig. 1. *Clear Plastic tanks are ideal for research or the class-room as they are uniform in size and are leakproof. They may be moved without leakage problems simply by draining out half the water. The author uses many of them for experimental tanks in growing marine plants, or for control tanks in various testing procedures. The tanks are manufactured by Aquariums Inc. of Maywood, N.J.*

Fig. 2. *An eight-foot long plywood tank with a glass front. Plywood is nailed together with monel boat nails and joints are sealed with silicone rubber. For large aquariums it is usually more practical to use plywood rather than all glass.*

Fig. 3. *A complete salt water aquarium with outside filter containing activated carbon and adjustable siphon stem which reaches all the way to the bottom. It also has an undergravel filter. Sea fans and whips are in back of the aquarium in a specially built box.*

material which will not only strengthen them, but also make them almost inert in salt water. They must be constructed very carefully and seasoned several weeks with a strong rock salt solution before use. Great care must be taken when fitting the glass so that it won't leak or break when the aquarium is filled.

In view of the discovery of the new all-glass aquariums, it becomes difficult to determine whether or not it would be more practical to make even a large aquarium of plywood instead of glass. When one must consider that heavy plywood is not really cheap, perhaps all-glass tanks would be on a nearly equal par so far as cost is concerned when compared to a tank constructed of plywood. The plywood itself is not the main cost in building a wood tank. One must also consider fibreglass cloth if it is used, epoxy paint, monel nails and a great deal of labor as well as maintenance over the years. Plywood sometimes does warp or buckle. We have made all-glass tanks up to six feet long with no problems. Even some eight footers have been made. With all-glass tanks, there is no worry of toxic reactions with epoxy or fibreglass. There is also little or no wear

Fig. 4. *This all-glass aquarium containing salt water in the front section and fresh water in the rear portion, allows for many trick designs such as this Sea Horse exhibit. The plants shown here are* Vallisneria, *a fresh water variety. Note the rare Short-Nosed Pipe fish at left.*

Fig. 5. *The ordinary fish bowl is the simplest container for the Dwarf Sea Horse. With aeration, as many as a dozen Dwarf Horses may be safely kept in this container.*

and maintenance. It would, therefore, appear logical to suggest that unless one wishes to make a plywood tank for its beauty and decor, it would be better to construct the tank of all glass. However, for those who wish to make a large plywood tank, particularly in the six- to eight-foot size, which would be the minimum size where plywood would prove less costly than glass, the author recommends three-quarter inch exterior plywood for the bottom, sides and back and half-inch to three-quarter inch glass depending on the height of the tank. If the tank has any length to it (over four feet) then a cross brace should be run across the top to keep the tank from bulging when it is filled. Large plywood tanks are actually very easy to construct. You simply order your plywood cut to size, then nail it firmly together with pleated, monel boat nails. Run a bead of silicone rubber along each edge just before you nail it so that it will form a rubber cushion which should be waterproof if it is applied properly. When the tank is finished, an additional bead of silicone rubber may be evenly applied to all the seams as an added assurance against leakage. Allow the sealer to dry overnight and the tank will be ready for painting. Contrary to popular opinion, it is usually not necessary to use glass cloth at all, unless one wishes to apply it to the seams for added strength. The author makes his plywood tanks without it and has had some for over ten years, still in good condition. The tanks are simply nailed together and then are painted with three coats of good epoxy paint. A light blue, comparable to a pale blue sky, is a good color for the inside as it simu-

Fig. 6. *Molded plastic aquariums are very desirable for salt-water displays as they are leak-proof and corrosion-free. This attractive model was designed as a coffee table.*

Fig. 7. *Clear plastic vegetable crisper makes a small, leak-proof marine aquarium. This inexpensive container is available in most five and dime stores and may be fitted with a sub-sand filter. Note tiny Angelfish and miniature marine plants.*

lates the ocean to a certain degree. The author uses a half and half epoxy mix; half paint and half hardener, rather than the epoxy paints which require drops of hardener, as it is easier to get the proper mix with a half and half solution. The paint should be allowed to "work" for an hour or so after it is mixed before it is used so that the catalyst will react properly. Follow instructions on the can before use. After the tank is painted it should be allowed to dry for about a week before the front glass is inserted. The glass may be sealed in place with the silicone rubber. It is best to lay the tank down when inserting the glass so that the glass will lie flat against its frame when it is placed on the sealer. A few small bags of sand may be of help to apply small pressure if needed to make contact all the way around. Simply place them on the glass where needed. Allow the silicone to harden for a few days, then right the aquarium and let it set for a week before filling with water. It should be rinsed well and then filled with a salt brine solution to cure the paint. Depending on its size and depth, the tank should be reinforced with a frame of two-by-four inch or four-by-four inch lumber which should be bolted together at the top and bottom of the tank. It is better to be safe than sorry and the author would certainly recommend a heavy wooden frame at the top and bottom of a large tank.

Clear plastic or lucite tanks are rapidly gaining popularity in the country for marine aquariums. They are nearly ideal as a container for salt water as they don't rust or corrode, can seldom leak, and

Fig. 8. *This two-and-a-half gallon plastic aquarium is especially suited for the salt-water display. It harbors five small marine fish including the Black Angelfish, Butterfly fish, Beau Gregory and two Gobies. It will also make a fine home for a dozen Dwarf Sea Horses, a single Sargassum fish, a sea anemone; or one or two large Sea Horses. Sub-sand filter and inexpensive vibrator air pump operate the unit efficiently. Light bulb is concealed under hood.*

Fig. 9. *A salt-water aquarium in the author's home. Large lettuce coral in center provides secure home for Royal Grammas and spectacular Rock Beauty while a mated pair of Neon Gobies live under the shell. Cured sea fans add to the decoration.*

Fig. 10. *The salt-water aquarium should have a close-fitting glass cover suspended by plastic or glass holders inside the aquarium a quarter to a half-inch down. This will slow evaporation, keep fish from jumping out and prevent salt water from dripping along the outside of the aquarium. One corner of the glass should be cut out to insert an aquarium heater and facilitate feeding. Note that the glass protrudes above stainless steel rim, thereby eliminating contact with salt water.*

will not give aquarium cement trouble. They are appearing in various shapes and sizes; some designed as end tables, coffee tables, etc. Others are made to standard aquarium specifications and are undoubtedly the marine aquarist's dream come true. The only drawback is that they scratch easily. However, if care is taken when they are set up and coral used only in the center, this can be of little significance and they will give years of pleasurable service. The many advantages they have far outweigh their one main disadvantage.

This now leads us to the stainless steel aquarium which is by far the most popular medium for exhibiting fish in the home. Its fine, attractive finish, its clear glass construction (which gives little distortion), and the fact that it may be purchased anywhere in the country make it the standard unit for display. It may be purchased in nearly any desired size or shape and has a price range suitable to all. It has many fine virtues and only two drawbacks so far as marine aquariums are concerned.

A. The cement holding the glass in place sometimes reacts harmfully with salt water and may poison the fish.

B. Salt spray tends to collect along the top edge of the tank causing rust and corrosion which may seep back into the aquarium with harmful results.

Both of these drawbacks no doubt will soon be eliminated as the growing need for better marine tanks arises, but at present they must be seriously regarded.

The cement factor is the more serious of the two as it is more difficult to detect or control. Some aquarium manufacturers use cement less toxic than others to marine fish, consequently much better results are obtained when using their products. Since marine fish are costly, this experimenting should be done by your dealer who supplies you with your salt-water fish and supplies. If the fish are living in his tanks, it is a good indication that the cement in the aquariums he carries is nontoxic. However, if your dealer is not interested in marine fish, then you will have to tackle the problem alone. At any rate, it is always best to sterilize the aquarium with a strong salt solution for several days before use. This helps to neutralize the cement and often no further trouble is encountered. The corrosion at the top of the aquarium is rather easily controlled and is described in detail in the maintenance section of this book.

Caution for Inland Aquarists

Aquarists who live far inland must use extreme caution in choosing an aquarium for their salt-water venture. Just any aquarium will not do, and since it is likely to be somewhat costly, as both marine fishes and the fresh sea water in which they live are difficult to obtain inland, the hobbyist should consider these factors when purchasing equipment for salt-water use. If the aquarium is to be relatively small, from five to fifteen gallons, an all plastic aquarium either of the molded type or a custom-built tank of clear plastic will prove to be quite trouble free and the aquarist can keep the most delicate fish, plants, and even live coral without worry about metal tank rim or tank cement poisoning the precious sea water. In addition, the aquarium light should be made of plastic and a sheet of clear plastic or glass should be suspended beneath the light so that salt spray won't hit the light socket and drip poisoned water back into the tank. It wouldn't be too practical to buy a special plastic aquarium and fail to guard against all forms of contamination.

Inland aquarists may still use a stainless steel aquarium for salt water if it is chosen with discretion. There is no doubt that a glass-sided aquarium allows for clearer viewing than plastic, and in some instances this is not only more desirable but for some purposes, such as photography or close laboratory study, is a necessity. At first glance, most stainless steel aquariums appear to be quite similar but, like all products, some brands are better than others. The old adage, "You get what you pay for," still holds true. Good stainless steel aquariums are not cheap and the superior workmanship is usually evident upon close examination. First inquire about the quality of the stainless steel and the thickness of the glass. Then examine the inside of the tank and note how much space there is between the end pieces of glass and the sides. Best results for salt-water use will be obtained when the tank is of tight construction with little space between the end pieces. Many aquariums today have as much as a quarter-inch to a half-inch space on each side where the end pieces fit together. This is carefully filled with aquarium cement and trimmed off flush, so that it is not noticed except upon close examination. These tanks are designed primarily for fresh-water use and this type of construction is not harmful for fresh water, but in a self-contained salt-water aquarium it is likely to cause endless trouble.

There are some manufacturers who make a "tight" tank in which the glass fits closely, but it may require a little shopping around to locate a suitable tank. Most manufacturers will be happy to construct a special salt-water tank with glass bottom and glass protruding above the metal rim at the top, which will prove far superior to the standard tank for marine use. Make certain to specify that the glass is tight fitting with a minimum of cement exposed. The author originally designed this type aquarium for salt-water use and is convinced that it is well worth the extra cost or trouble that may be required to obtain it. It will prove especially useful to aquarists who want a large tank for spectacular fish like the adult Townsend Angelfish or Lion fish and who require or prefer the extreme clarity offered by glass. An aquarium of this type, if properly cured and maintained, will sustain even the most delicate invertebrates, live corals, marine plants, and fishes.

In recent years, plastic frame aquariums have appeared on the market. These have glass sides like the stainless steel tanks, but the frames are made of plastic, which of course is better for salt water. The Oscar aquarium, which holds eight gallons, is constructed this way and the frames are available in several colors. It makes a fine yet inexpensive salt-water tank. There are reports that larger plastic-frame tanks will be manufactured soon, and if the companies follow through and make the glass fit tightly together at the ends and bottom, these tanks should prove highly successful to the marine hobbyist and to the public aquariums as well. Maintenance on the plastic frames would be reduced to practically nothing, whereas with stainless steel tanks this can represent considerable work.

Make Certain Cement Is Thoroughly Dry

Whether you use a standard stainless steel tank, a special salt-water one, or a plastic-frame tank, make certain that the cement is thoroughly dry and hardened before the tank is filled with water. It

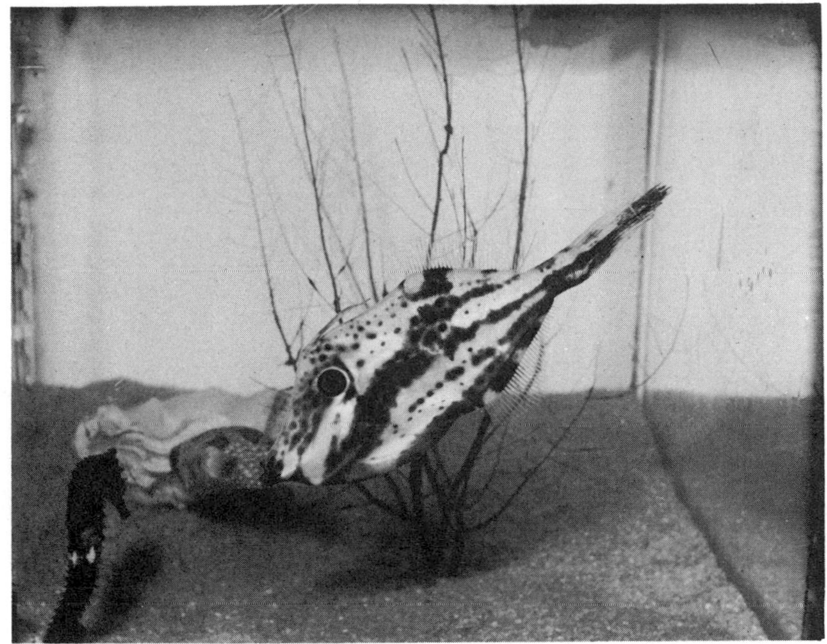

Fig. 11. *The strange orange File fish or Unicorn File fish is so thin and bony it appears to be emaciated, but this is its natural condition. It feeds on blades of turtle grass and also eats tiny crabs and shrimps that it extracts from seaweed with its delicate mouth.*

is preferable to use a tank which has been sitting on the dealer's shelf for six months or more, so that the cement is well dried. This will allow the minimum penetration and reaction of the salt water with the cement and will prove much more successful than a freshly constructed tank, especially to the inland aquarist who must use the same water over and over. Do not use an aquarium in which the cement is soft or oily, as this will result in rapid deterioration of the sea water and will usually kill the more delicate and beautiful specimens. It will cause endless trouble, for the sea water will gradually dissolve the cement and form large pockets where gas and poisonous compounds will form and eventually make the water lethal to most forms of marine life.

The New All-Glass Aquariums

Now at last, we have all-glass aquariums that are easy to construct and are inexpensive. They are virtually trouble free and should be for sale in most cities or you can make your own. The author feels that he was among the first to discover this new process after trying many products in an attempt to make an all-glass aquarium. The first all-glass aquariums, as mentioned in the early edition of this

Maricopa County
Cl Library

Fig. 12. *As modern as tomorrow, Ellis Skolfield designed this fabulous all glass aquarium which won the Straughan Annual Award in* Salt Water Aquarium Magazine. *The modern all glass aquarium of silicone rubber opens up new horizons in aquarium manufacturing as limitless as the imagination.*

book, were not successful. These were bonded with epoxy resin which held temporarily but they eventually let go and the process was abandoned. After trying many products, the author came across a rubber-type bathtub caulking material known as silicone rubber. It seemed reasonable that if it worked around bathtubs, it should work in aquariums. The author purchased a tube and made a small all-glass tank. It was a phenomenal success. The tank was tested under a variety of conditions which included placing it in the refrigerator to see if changes in temperature would effect it. This was the problem with the earlier epoxy tanks which would crack when the temperature changed as there was no give to the epoxy. The silicone rubber tank held and met every test. The author published an article in his salt water aquarium magazine and to his knowledge this is the first published material in making a tank in this manner. He wrote to the manufacturer of the silicone rubber telling of his discovery. The idea spread across the country like wildfire and soon everyone was building all glass tanks. A friend of the author's, Ellis Skolfield, was the first to build a large tank with the silicone rubber and he constructed fabulous tanks some of which were over six feet in length. Neither the author nor Mr. Skolfield was given credit for the discovery of the all glass tanks. Although the possibility exists

Fig. 13. *Danger Areas in a stainless steel aquarium. White areas under the glass are caused from separation of the cement from the glass and unless the glass is resealed, they will cause endless trouble in the aquarium.*

that others may have discovered this method of tank construction before us, it seems more than coincidental that if the company making the rubber sealant had a working, all glass aquarium, then they would have promoted it before I began my correspondence with them instead of several months later. But at any rate, the all glass aquarium is now a reality and we have had many tanks (some five and six feet long) in use for more than three years. There has not been a single failure in any of the aquariums and none are forseen. Even the original tank is still in use.

The all-glass tanks are easy to construct. Those who cannot purchase one at their local pet shop can make' their own. Just get the glass cut to the proper size and you may glue it together yourself. Use quarter-inch or three-sixteenth-inch glass for tanks up to thirty gallons and three-eighth-inch for larger size up to forty or fifty gallons. Fifty gallon and up should be made with half-inch glass. Sheet glass is suitable for most tanks and very often a glass company can sell you salvage glass at a considerable savings over new glass. It is actually new glass that is left over from a job and is usually long narrow strips. Your local glass cutter can also advise you on thickness of glass needed for an aquarium. Keep in mind that height governs the thickness needed, rather than gallon capacity; the higher the tank, the thicker the glass. Tanks up to fourteen inches high can use the quarter-inch or three-sixteenth-inch glass. Tanks taller than this should go into a heavier glass.

To make your aquarium, first wipe the edges of the glass where the cement is to be applied with a clean paper towel so that all grease or cutting fluid is removed. Start with the bottom sheet of glass and place this on the floor near a wall so you can use the wall for support. Squeeze out a bead of the silicone rubber along the entire top edge of the glass on the side nearest the wall. Next, carefully place the back piece of glass down on top of the sealer, taking care that it does not slide off the edge. You can let the glass rest against the wall while you check the bottom to see that the glass is resting evenly on the bottom piece. When it is evenly in place, you may push a large book or box up against the upright glass so it won't fall forward. Wait about a half hour for the cement to partially set before going on to the next piece. The next piece to be added is the end piece. Run a bead of the cement along the edge of the bottom glass and a bead along the edge of the side glass. Then push the end glass into place, making certain it is even before you allow the cement to harden. Wait another half hour or so and add the other end. Now you are ready for the last piece. Just run a bead of the cement along the remaining edges and set the front piece in place. Let it harden for a few days and your aquarium is all finished. It's as simple as that! You can actually make an aquarium in ten minutes as the author did in his original article, but it's easier to go more slowly because if the glass slides off one edge while you are adding a sheet of glass, it makes a mess. It's best to do one side at a time and get it even and straight before going on to the next piece. Of course if you are going to make many tanks you can make a jig or wood frame to hold the glass so that you can go into real production. Each tank maker will of course come up with his own innovations and time savers.

It is best to let the tank stand empty for a week before filling it with water. Tanks up to fifteen or twenty gallons can be all glass so long as they are not over fourteen inches tall. Long tanks should have a double brace across the top, going from front to back, so that the tank won't bulge when it is filled. A simple wooden frame at the top and bottom of the tank will protect the glass edges and give added strength to the tank. This is not needed on the small tanks up to fifteen or twenty gallons unless it is desired as an added safety

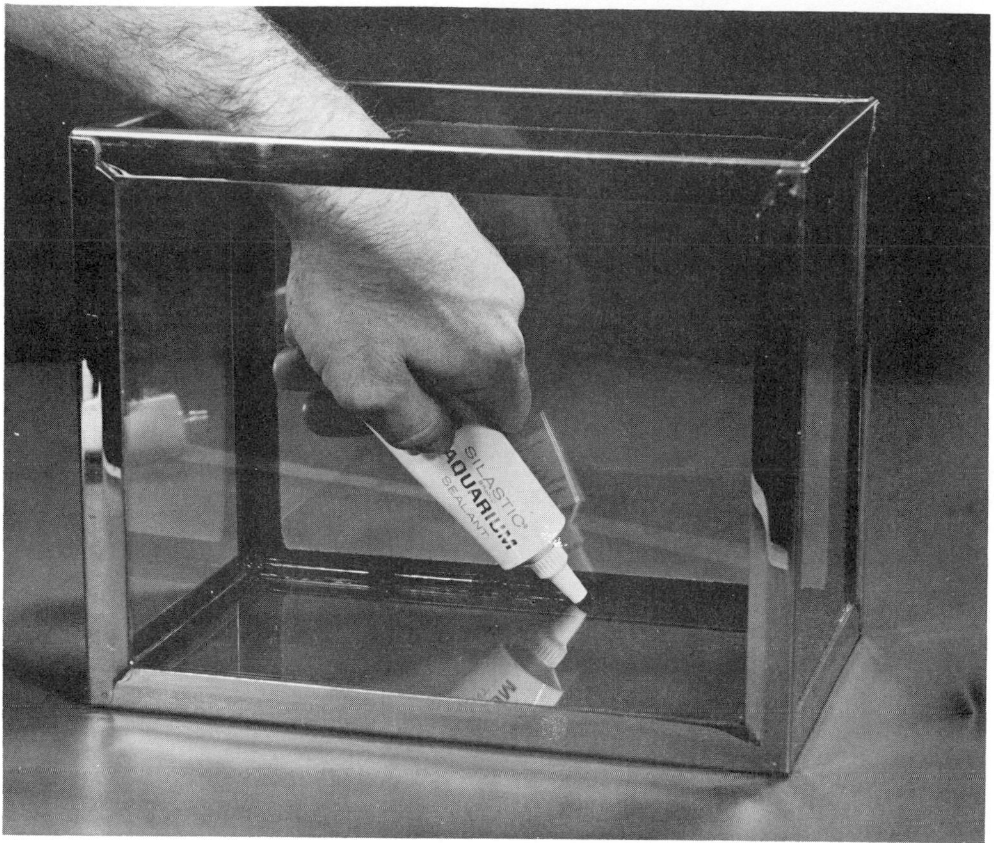

Fig. 14. *Sealing a stainless steel tank with silicone rubber sealer is accomplished by carefully applying a bead of sealer to each seam as shown here. The metal frame at the top should be well covered so that salt water won't come in contact with the metal.*

factor or to hide the water line. It is recommended for larger tanks however. The glass tanks must have a strong, smooth stand to support them. It is best to place a sheet of plywood on the aquarium stand so the glass will have a smooth, even support. On large glass tanks over three feet long, it is further helpful to place a sheet of quarter-inch or half-inch styrofoam on top of the plywood. This will further take up shock and unevenness and is an added safety factor. All glass tanks are so easy to construct that they are destined to eventually revolutionize the entire aquarium field. Already many spectacular aquariums have been made, for the new method lends itself to unlimited design and decor. Those venturing into the salt water hobby should get an all-glass tank if at all possible for it is far superior to all other aquariums. It requires little or no maintenance and you may concentrate your efforts on the fish and other aspects of the hobby. The glass tanks require little curing since the sealer is practically inert. Just fill them with water overnight, rinse them out well and they are ready for use. If there is a great deal of rubber sealer exposed, soak them in salt water as explained in next chapter.

It will be up to the individual to decide which type of container he will use for his salt-water aquarium. A lot will depend on how much he wishes to spend and how large a project he wishes to undertake. The serious hobbyist who wants to use fresh sea water should consider the cost and weight of having fresh sea water flown in from Florida when he orders his live specimens. An aquarium of from five- to twelve-gallon capacity is economically feasible if a hobbyist wants to use real sea water in his tank, for with modern air transportation the cost of shipping this quantity by air is not prohibitive, especially if live fish are ordered at the same time. Most air lines have a fifty- and hundred-pound rate, and if the shipment of fish does not weigh this much the customer will be charged a certain amount regardless; so that by adding a few gallons of sea water the additional cost is often little or nothing. In recent years, more hobbyists have begun to realize this; so at this present date aquarists living far inland may still have a real ocean-water aquarium. An eight-gallon aquarium measuring eighteen inches long by eight and a half wide by twelve inches high makes a nice sea-water display and since about a gallon or more of space will be taken up by sand and coral the seven gallons required to fill the tank would not cost a fortune if shipped along with an order of fish. Two tanks of this size would allow a diversified exhibit for the aquarist who might wish to keep live coral and invertebrates in one tank and the exotic marines in the other. At any rate, a word of caution here. Don't leap before you can swim! Start small with the hardiest specimens. Then, with experience, go on to that twenty-five or fifty-gallon aquarium.

2

Setting Up Your Exhibit

There are several methods of setting up and maintaining a salt water aquarium and each will be discussed in the following text. However, most emphasis will be upon the sub-sand filter method as it is by far the simplest, the most economical, and the most efficient. The author has been experimenting with this unique device for nearly a decade and was perhaps the very first to realize its value in the marine aquarium.

Unless a person is living by the sea and can obtain his own sea water and specimens, the first marine aquarium should be relatively small. A recommended size is from five to ten gallons or twenty if finances permit. In the author's opinion, the ideal salt-water aquarium is the fifteen gallon show size which measures twenty-four inches long by ten and one half inches wide by fourteen inches high. This popular size is easily decorated and can hold a fine assortment of the most beautiful marine specimens. The salt-water hobbyist must remember that not only are marine fish expensive, but the sea water itself, whether natural or artificial, is also expensive especially if shipped a long way. Therefore it is best to start small with your first marine aquarium.

Selecting the Marine Aquarium

If a standard stainless steel aquarium is to be used for salt water, it should be new, as old aquariums usually have hidden "pockets" between the cement and the steel frame which soon become a major source of trouble. The salt water settles in these obscure places, becomes stagnant, and emits harmful gases and bacteria into the aquarium with disastrous results. The aquarium should have a glass bottom rather than slate. Salt water attacks slate and since most manufacturers can supply either type at approximately the same price, the glass bottom should be preferred.

The author has designed a special salt-water aquarium in which the glass protrudes above the top of the stainless steel rim. This eliminates all possible contact of the sea water in the aquarium from the metal frame thereby eliminating metal poisoning. The design was used successfully in "Aquarama," a huge travelling aquarium which is touring the United States and which was originally outfitted with coral and salt water fish by the author. Also, several manufacturers have produced this aquarium for their salt-water customers at slightly higher cost than the standard tank. Its chief advantage is that it lacks the conventional metal rim which hangs down inside the regular aquarium, and helps in maintenance especially when there are many salt-water aquariums in use. However, it is not a necessity and was merely designed as an improved model for salt water. When fitted with a close-sealing glass cover it becomes virtually an all-glass aquarium which of course is the ideal salt-water container.

If this type of aquarium cannot be obtained, the top metal rim of the aquarium must be given special care or it will soon dust and corrode. It may be painted with the new epoxy-based plastic paint which will give it permanent protection or it may be protected by washing and rinsing it once a week with fresh water. Either method is quite effective except if the latter is used, care should be taken not to drip the metal-contaminated water back into the aquarium. It may be worthwhile to mention here that there are many grades of stainless steel used for aquarium manufacture and of course the better grades resist rust and corrosion to a greater extent. Regardless of what some manufacturers may claim, there are no stainless steel frames that will not rust in salt water. Also, don't be misled by manufacturers claiming their aquarium is the *only* tank recommended for salt water because of some special cement they may claim to use. This may be true in some instances but quite often it is merely a sales gimmick to sell their product. There are many good aquariums manufactured in the country and if your local dealer is keeping salt-water fish successfully then no doubt the aquariums he is using are satisfactory for marine use.

The Sub-Sand Filter

The next important item beside the aquarium is the sub-sand filter. This ingenious device should be used with every marine aquarium as it will insure greater success with your salt-water display. The sub-sand filter is a flat piece of plastic which covers the bottom of the aquarium. It acts as a false bottom and allows water to circulate under the sand eliminating stagnation in this critical area. Placed beneath the sand, it removes microscopic particles of food and dissipates fish excretions which otherwise would decompose into harmful

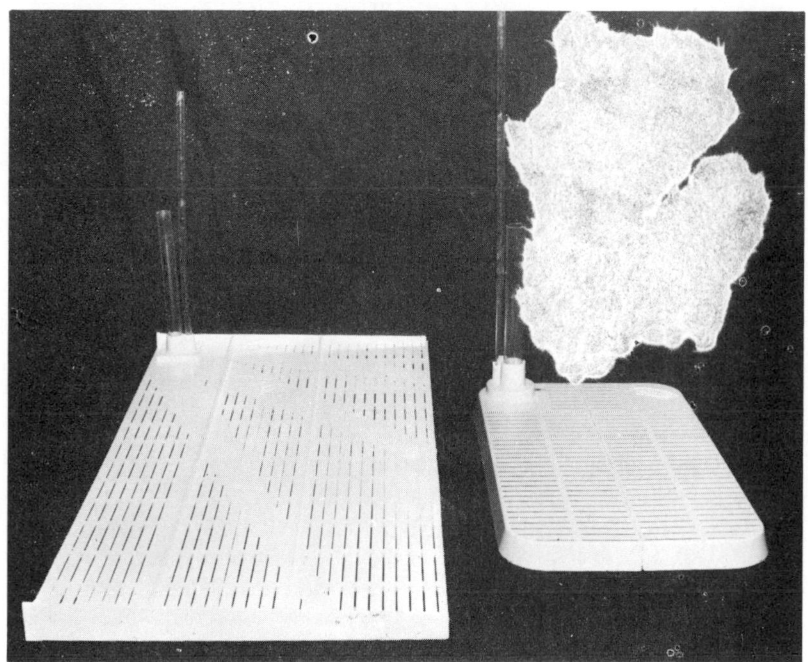

Fig. 15. *Modern under-gravel filters are made of non-toxic plastic with fine slots or holes, which allows water to circulate beneath the sand.*

Fig. 16. *One of the first undergravel filters tested by the author was this extremely flat model. It was very effective. Undergravel filters or sub-sand filters as they are also called, are a boon to the marine hobbyist for they allow the use of sand in the aquarium which not only gives the tank a natural look but allows the water to circulate beneath the sand, making the sand itself a filter.*

gases causing a breakdown of the entire aquarium. When the author first began experimenting with this device, there were only one or two on the market, now nearly all the filter companies are making them. An aquarist who would oppose the sub-sand filter is one who apparently had never tried one for the filtering capacity of this amazing invention is truly phenomenal! When used properly, it will clear up the largest aquarium overnight and will out-perform all other types of filters some costing many times more. The author considers it the greatest advance in the aquarium hobby since the air pump. It is used in conjunction with a small air pump and with just these two items, the marine aquarium can be kept sparkling clear for many months. It will both aerate and filter the aquarium unless it is very crowded, in which case the simple addition of an air stone or two will remedy the situation. Probably the chief advantage in using the sub-sand filter is that it allows the use of sand in the aquarium without the worry of toxic gas. Without sand, it is quite difficult to make a marine aquarium look natural or attractive. Now, thanks to this wonderful device, sand may be used profusely without any danger. Not only will this beautify the display, but it will also make the fish feel at home and they will be able to make snug little excavations beneath the coral where they can retreat whenever necessary. Also, if

Fig. 17. *Proof of the efficiency of the sub-sand filter method is this aquarium with spectacular Lion fish. The aquarium has had only one change of water and one sand washing in three years. It is aerated and filtered only by the Miracle sub-sand filter and a small vibrator pump.*

marine plants are desired, they may be safely planted in the sand without the constant fear of toxic gases forming in their roots. The sub-sand filter may also be used in conjunction with inside or outside filters containing activated carbon or spun nylon or orlon but this is only necessary under special conditions which will be discussed in the following text. Test aquariums using the sub-sand filter as the sole filtration unit have proved that it will keep an aquarium clear and healthy for periods of a year or more with little maintenance other than occasionally washing or replacing the sand.

There are many sub-sand filters on the market at the present time. For the small aquariums they come in one piece but for the larger tanks, the unit is made in two sections with a bubbler stem at each end. Choose a sub-sand filter of good, rigid plastic quality and a type with holes or slots small enough so that no glass wool will be needed to keep the sand from penetrating through to the bottom. Sub-sand filters with very large holes should be avoided as these would necessitate the use of pea-size gravel which is quite unsatisfactory. A regular coarse aquarium gravel or silica sand with grains approximately a sixteenth of an inch long works best on the sub-sand filter. Filters which would allow this sand to pass through should not be used.

Location

Choose a location that is comparatively draft free and that will get a small amount of sunlight in one corner of the aquarium at some time of the day. Do not place the aquarium in strong daylight or sunlight as it will rapidly turn the water green and make maintenance extremely difficult. An ideal set-up is where the aquarium is located so that it receives an hour or two of early morning or late evening sun. This is not strong enough to cause excessive algae and may be easily controlled by shading the aquarium when necessary. In large northern cities, where dense smoke and haze weakens and filters the sunlight, it is sometimes possible to place the aquarium in the brightest part of the room without getting excessive algae. A little experimenting will soon tell you which location is best.

How to Sterilize the Aquarium

After selecting a location for your exhibit, the next step is to sterilize the aquarium and sub-sand filter and any additional equipment that is to be used in the aquarium. The inside of the aquarium should be carefully inspected and all excess cement should be trimmed off so that it is flush with the glass. Then the aquarium should be filled with fresh water to which has been added three tablespoons of

Fig. 18. The salt-water procedure. STEP NO. 1 *Sterilize aquarium and all equipment which is to be used in the aquarium, such as sub-sand filter, plastic tubing, air stems, etc. Fill aquarium to one-fourth inch from the top with salt brine solution.*

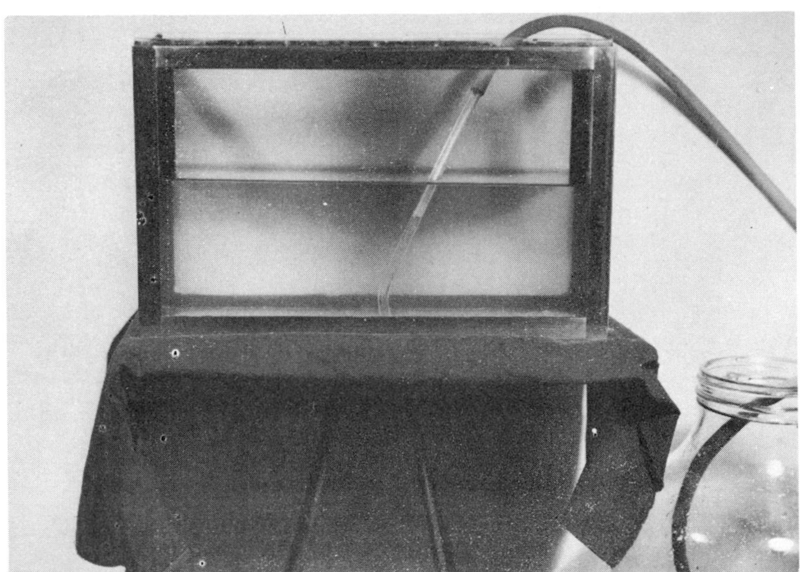

Fig. 19. The salt-water procedure. STEP NO. 2 *Remove filters etc., from brine solution and wash them thoroughly in fresh water. Siphon brine from aquarium and rinse aquarium well in fresh water. Do not tip aquarium to empty it as this will make it leak. When aquarium is clean, it may be filled with sea water in which the fish are to be kept.*

ordinary table salt for each gallon of water. Place bottom filter, etc. in aquarium and fill it to the top so that all the cement will be submerged. Allow it to soak for several days. This removes surface oils from the cement and cures the tank.

Next, after soaking the prescribed time, siphon off the solution and rinse the aquarium and filter with fresh water. Fill the aquarium again with fresh water to soak up any remaining salt and drain again, rinsing the sides of the tank as the water goes out. A small cellulose sponge, purchased specially for this purpose will be useful for cleaning the glass and soaking up the last of the water from the bottom of the tank. It should be set aside and used only for your marine aquarium. Never tip an aquarium to pour the water out as this may cause it to leak.

The aquarium is now ready for use and the actual finish work may begin. First, rinse your hands *thoroughly* in fresh water to be certain that there is no trace of soap. This is very important, for soap, even in minute quantities, is deadly in marine aquariums. Be especially careful that there is none under the nails and rinse the hands and arms up past the elbows as they will be submerged in the coming task.

Next, fill the aquarium two thirds full with fresh, pure sea water and insert the sub-sand filter slowly into the aquarium with bottom toward you so that you can see and shake loose any bubbles that may

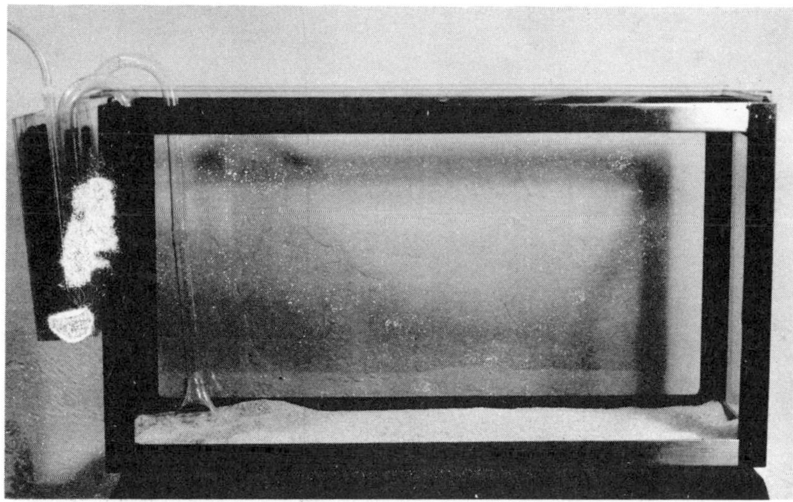

Fig. 20. The salt-water procedure. STEP NO. 3 *Add sand to aquarium. Hold sub-sand filter down so that no sand will get under it, then spread about one inch of coarse silica sand evenly over the bottom of the aquarium. Part of sub-sand filter was left uncovered here in order to show its position in the aquarium. Hook up air tubing and attach outside filter if one is to be used.*

form. Large bubbles should be removed or they will destroy the action of the filter. Jarring the filter against the sides of the aquarium quickly dislodges the small bubbles and the filter may then be placed on the bottom. Fasten the bubbler stems securely in place and then add the sand.

Preparing and Adding Sand

Coarse silica sand or regular aquarium gravel with grains about one sixteenth of an inch should be used on top of the sub-sand filter. Beach sand should be avoided as it usually contains oil and surface scum which has been washed ashore, and since sand is very inexpensive only the best should be used. The sand should be washed thoroughly so it is sparkling clean when added to the aquarium. It may be washed by stirring in a *clean* enamel bucket filled with fresh water. Pour the water off so that sand stays in the bottom and repeat this procedure several times, or until the water remains clear when mixed with the sand in the pail. Then pour off the remaining water and the sand is ready for use.

The sub-sand filter should fit the aquarium and cover nearly the entire bottom. If it is slightly smaller, push it toward the back of the

Fig. 21. The salt-water procedure. STEP NO. 4 *Place coral in aquarium. When properly arranged, coral provides good hiding places for the fish as well as masking any aquarium apparatus. Too much coral is worse than not enough for it leaves areas where uneaten food can collect. However, a few choice pieces greatly reduce the cleaning problem. Sea fan has been specially cured for use inside the aquarium.*

Fig. 22. *Lettuce coral with its pockets and crevices provides many hiding places for the fish. Here, a Butterfly fish finds safety under a dark ledge while a Neon Goby looks out on top. Striped fish at left with spot on its tail is a young Porkfish.*

tank so that the front area which will not be filtered, may be watched. If the filter has a tendency to float, it may be necessary to hold it down with one hand until you have added the first handful or two of sand. A clean saucer will be helpful in scooping up the sand and easing it into the aquarium. Spread it out to a depth of an inch to an inch and a half, and be careful that none gets under the filter. It may be spread in artistic mounds making it slightly higher in back, so that it does not come above the bottom rim of the aquarium at the front, unless it is necessary to cover the filter.

Arranging Coral

A few choice pieces of coral and a shell or two, if properly selected, will give the marine aquarium its basic beauty. Avoid loading your aquarium with excessive coral as this may cause much trouble. Coral in itself, is one of the marvels and masterpieces of nature's handiwork under the sea. Chosen wisely, it will enhance your aquarium and even without fish, the salt-water aquarium artistically decorated with beautiful coral and cured sea fans is a magnificent thing. When properly lighted it will handsomely decorate the finest of homes. The coral should be arranged so that it will provide hiding places for the fish so that they will feel secure. Rather than crowd the tank too much with coral, a few well-chosen shells will furnish a snug, safe home for your pets. One or two choice pieces of coral, with a shell or two, should be sufficient for most aquariums, depending on the

Fig. 23. *Large shelving pieces of Elkhorn coral make a spectacular display when one piece is placed on top of the other as shown here on the right. The large Elkhorn coral is especially useful for fifty to five hundred gallon tanks. A giant formation of finger coral at the left is also useful for decorating a large tank, although it is difficult to obtain. A large Queen Angelfish looks small in comparison to the huge corals in the tank. Sea fans are outside the tank.*

size of the tank. Then it will be a simple matter to siphon out uneaten foods without disturbing the fish.

All coral, shells, etc. must be *absolutely* clean and sterile before placing in the aquarium. Just because an object is snow white does not mean that it is cured. It might be, but it is best not to take the chance. Coral should be soaked in fresh water at least two or three weeks before use. Then, it should be rinsed thoroughly and, if completely free of decaying odor, it may be dried, preferably in the sun. Then it may be used but with discretion. If your first marine aquarium was a failure it was probably due to improperly cured coral. Coral taken directly from the sea must be cured much longer. A minimum safety time would be from one to three months or longer depending on the size and type of coral being cured.

The only type of shells which should be used are the shallow, bivalve or clam shells. These are quickly cleaned and seldom cause harm. The baby giant-clam shells of the *Tridacna* family are ideal as they make perfect homes for the marine fish. Pushed part way into the sand, they will leave several openings for the fish to enter or escape and it will furnish them with a dark, snug home. These shells

Fig. 24. *A nicely decorated aquarium contains a piece of Elkhorn coral at left, a large Brush or Sunflower coral in the center, small cluster coral at right, and two tridacna shells. The shells are arranged so that they provide a snug home for demoiselles or gobies. Such an arrangement is easy to clean and maintain with a minimum of effort.*

Fig. 25. *A tank crowded with coral, although beautiful, is difficult to clean. But it has its good points in that the large amount of coral tends to buffer the water, keeping it more on the alkaline side. In addition, if one keeps a great many fish in the same aquarium, it is necessary to provide a great deal of coral so that the fish may find protective homes in the many crevices. A densely crowded tank should have good aeration and filtration. The new motor driven magnetic drive filters are excellent for this as they remove hidden waste.*

Fig. 26. *A beautiful formation of Atlantic Staghorn coral which is easy to clean and cure for the marine tank. Spotted Reef Trunkfish at top.*

Fig. 27. *Brilliant red Pipe Organ coral, hollowed out with a knife, makes dark, secure homes for the smaller marine fish. Tridacna shells at right also provide excellent cover. Blue Neon Gobies cavort contentedly about the coral structure.*

may be obtained in any size, from an inch and a half to several feet long so they will fill the needs of any type specimen.

The best coral to use is the Staghorn, Elkhorn, Lace, or Cluster coral as these types are usually available and they are easily cleaned. They come in a wide variety of sizes and shapes and will fill nearly every aquarium need. The cluster coral is white with a beautiful brown base and it makes an attractive combination. Most of the corals will be snow white, when cleaned, with the exception of the Organ Pipe coral which is brick red. This type of coral is much in demand for it gives the desired color to an otherwise all white display. It is constructed of tiny hollow "pipes" which gives it an interesting appearance. However, because of its construction, it should be used with caution. Not more than one or two pieces should be used in the aquarium and these must be soaked and washed for at least a month to be certain that all decayed matter is removed from their interior. This type of coral is relatively soft so that it can be easily hollowed out with an ordinary table knife, to make superb homes for your salt water pets.

Lettuce coral, Brain coral, Rose coral, etc. also may be used and they are extremely beautiful and interesting. However, because of their dense structure, they are quite difficult to cure and to be safe, they should be soaked in fresh water for at least six months before

Fig. 28. *Atlantic sea fans and coral. Left to right, Staghorn coral, sea fans, rare type of Brain coral, Mushroom coral, sea fans, Staghorn coral, common Brain coral, and delicate Finger coral.*

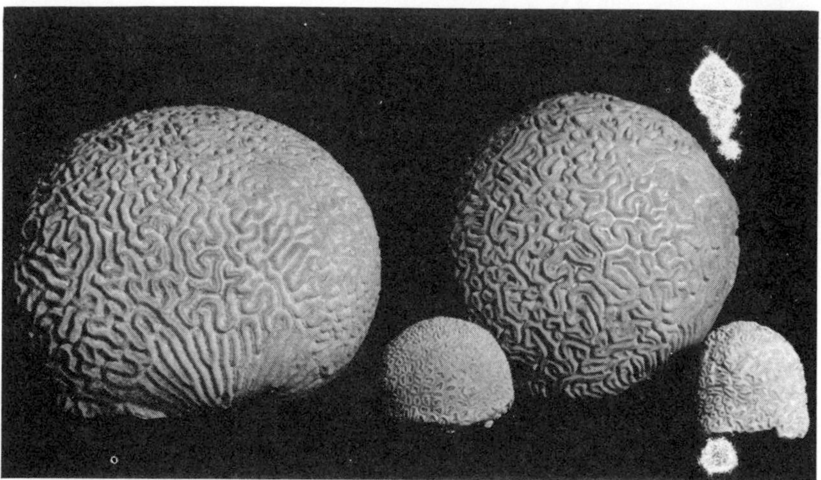

Fig. 29. *Exquisite Brain coral is difficult to cure for general aquarium use and is best kept in the background. With care, the inside of this coral may be chiseled out leaving the outer shell which makes it easier to cure.*

use. Then they must be inspected closely for decay and if there is still a foul odor present, they must be soaked even longer. The author has cured some exquisite specimens of Brain coral for as long as two years before finally considering them safe for the aquarium. Don't let this discourage you however. If you have a favorite piece of Lettuce or Brain coral and would like it for your aquarium, by all means cure it! You can always set up your aquarium with one or two smaller pieces while waiting for it to cure. But don't take a chance on it and put it in your marine aquarium until it is absolutely spotless and free from odor. You may lose your entire display.

The Nose Test

The most accurate method for determining if coral is safe for the aquarium is the nose test. If the coral smells clean, most likely it is clean. However, if it smells terrible, then it must be washed thoroughly with a strong stream of water and soaked for another few weeks before use. Generally small pieces of snow white coral purchased from your dealer or curio stands are about two-thirds cured and need only be soaked a week or two as a precautionary measure. It is best to soak all coral, regardless of claims that it is cured to be on the safe side. Bad coral is a sure killer in the salt-water aquarium. Soak coral in an enamel bucket or glass container if possible, keeping it out of direct sunlight except to dry after it is cured.

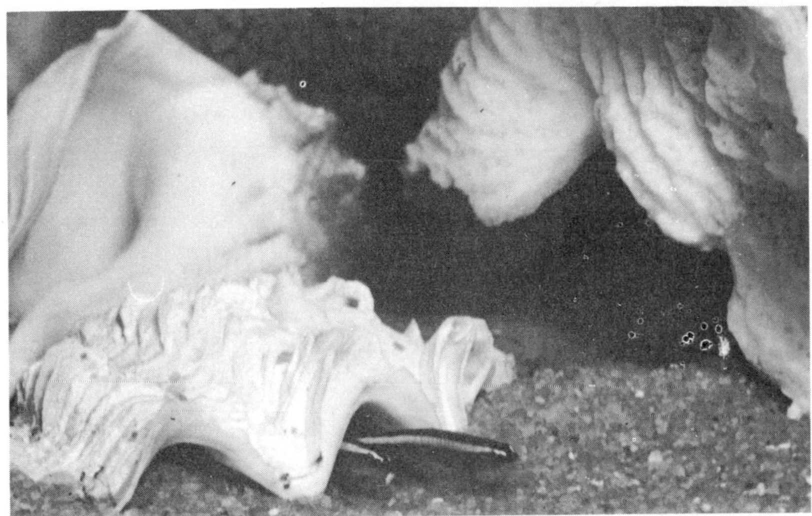

Fig. 30. *The Tridacna shell makes a good home for the marine fish and is easily cleaned. Here, a pair of Neon Gobies find refuge under the shell. Gastropod shells, like the one in rear, are also fine if they are thoroughly cleaned so that none of the animal is left inside.*

Fig. 31. *Lump coral which grows from ten to twenty-foot diameters, may be obtained in sizes suitable for most aquariums but is difficult to cure. It must be hollowed out inside before it can provide a safe retreat for Squirrel fish or Cardinal fish.*

Fig. 32. *Dead coral rock formations, if properly cured, give the aquarium a natural look. This interesting formation, hollow inside, resembles a miniature volcano. Note Sea Horse and algae at left.*

Fig. 33. *A superb home for the strange Mantis shrimp can be made by inverting a small piece of Elkhorn coral and placing a cluster of lace coral on top for looks. This is also excellent for Octopus, Moray eels, and other specimens who like a dark cave.*

Live Coral

If you are going to use live coral in your aquarium instead of the white, bleached coral, it should not be treated, bleached, or cured in any way, which of course would kill it. It should be handled just like a live fish, and may be taken directly from the ocean and placed in the aquarium. While en route from the ocean to your home the coral should be kept shaded and in clean sea water, with aeration if needed. When it is placed in the tank, sufficient fresh sea water should be added to insure the health and proper chemical balance of the water. Sea water varies greatly with each location; so when gathering live coral for your aquarium it is best also to bring back enough fresh sea water to fill the tank, if possible. Remove any slime from the aquarium, if any is present, after you place the corals in your tank. The slime can easily be taken out with a fine mesh net or siphoned out with a plastic hose. Live coral should be watched closely the first few days, and if it appears to be dead and is turning white it should be promptly removed. If you are not certain that it is dead, place it in a fish bowl or other container of sea water and observe it for a few days.

Although the distribution of live coral to aquarists away from the ocean is limited, it is being successfully shipped by air at the present time and small heads up to six inches across, complete with live tube worms, may be ordered from collectors in Florida or the Bahamas. (See Chapter 8).

Fish Introduction

Now that the sand and coral have been added and arranged so they look their best, the aquarium may be filled nearly to the top and the pump turned on so that the filter will operate. The pump should furnish sufficient air so that there is a strong surge of bubbles emerging from the bubbler tubes at each end of the aquarium as this aerates and filters the aquarium and does all the work.

You should now have before you a miniature ocean lacking only life. The next step will be adding the salt water fish and other specimens to your aquarium.

Most failures with marine fish occur during the first week after they have been placed in the aquarium. If the aquarium has been set up properly, the coral is well cured, then any immediate failure can usually be traced to improper introduction of the fish to the aquarium or to bad sea water itself.

When you arrive home with your marine fish, the first step is to open the box carefully and insert an air stone if fish appear crowded and in need of air. Do not excite them unnecessarily at this point.

This can be fatal to them. Just take a quick glance to see if they are alright and then start the transfers. Use a one gallon wide-mouth jar for the transfer and be certain it is clean.

Next, dip up half a jar of water from their container and place several fish in it. Float this in the aquarium for a half hour or so and tip the jar slightly allowing a little water from the aquarium to enter the jar. DO NOT LET ANY WATER FROM THE JAR SPILL BACK INTO THE AQUARIUM. This may introduce disease to your aquarium. If the jar looks like it might sink, attach it to the side of the tank with a clothespin as it must not tip over in the aquarium. Every ten or fifteen minutes, tip the jar slightly and allow a cupful or so of water to enter it. When the jar is nearly full and you are satisfied that the temperature in the jar is the same as that of the aquarium and the fish appear alright, carefully scoop up each fish with a net and drop it into the aquarium. Remove the floating jar from the aquarium being careful not to spill any of it into the aquarium. Save this water and the water in which you carried them home for at least a day or two. If the fish act strangely when first introduced to the aquarium, as though they are paralyzed or in shock, remove them immediately and return them to the jar in which you floated them. If they do not recover in this water, place them in the box of water in which you carried them home. It may be necessary to hold them in a net and move them back and forth in the container so that water circulates through their gills until

Fig. 34. The salt-water procedure. STEP NO. 5 *Add fish to aquarium. These should be floated in a glass or plastic container and gradually introduced to the aquarium especially if it contains artificial seawater.*

Fig. 35. *Introducing fish to an aquarium is best done by floating fish in a plastic container as shown here. This way, the water from the aquarium may be slowly added to the water in the floating bucket. When water has been well mixed, the fish should be lifted out with a dip net and carefully dropped into the aquarium. If fish show signs of shock, simply return them to floating bucket. Clothespin holds bucket in place so it won't tip. No water from floating bucket should spill into aquarium to avoid disease.*

they get back to normal. Then they should be introduced much more slowly after re-checking the salinity and general conditions of the aquarium to determine if everything is all right before introducing them again.

If it is not practical to float the fish, either because they are too large, or there are too many of them, then they can still be introduced to the aquarium gradually by placing their shipping box near the tank, inserting an air stone to give them air and pouring a small amount of water from the aquarium into the shipping box. Repeat this every ten or fifteen minutes until you feel that the water in the box is well mixed with water from your aquarium. Then lift out each fish with a net and drop it gently into the aquarium. Do not mix any of the water in the shipping box with the water in the aquarium but save the water for a few days in case fish act in distress as mentioned above. If you wish to be extra cautious at this point, you may add a half dosage of copper sulfate solution to the shipping box before you start the transfer. But remove a portion of the water and keep this separate so that if the fish react violently to the copper you will still have some of their original water in which to place them. Fish should show little or no reaction to properly mixed copper solution with the exception of the delicate butterflys, but the author recommends a half dosage as a precautionary measure. See chapter five for proper mixing of copper solution.

Do not transfer too many fish at one time as they will not have enough air in the jar as you float them. If you must transfer quite a few at one time, use several jars and place an airstone in each one, but be certain that you do not excite the fish too much at this point.

If you are using artificial sea water in your aquarium rather than the natural sea water, extra caution must be used. The fish must be transferred extremely slowly from the container to the man-made solution. They should hardly notice the transition from natural sea water to artificial. This may involve a time lapse of from one hour to as long as five or six hours during which time the fish must not be frightened unnecessarily. A hydrometer and thermometer both will prove useful here to determine how much difference there is between the water in the carrying container and the water in the aquarium.

After fish are in the aquarium, observe them closely. If they act peaceful and contented you have done a good job in transfering them. Don't expect them to feel at home immediately however. Usually they will try to hide or retreat to the farthest end of the aquarium and will remain there until they get up enough nerve to swim around and explore their new home. Approach the aquarium slowly at first until they get to know you for a sudden movement on your part could send them speeding into the sharp coral with harmful results. They may be fed a light feeding of live brine shrimp for the first day and a little dry food if they will eat it. You will now have completed your first marine aquarium.

Checking New Arrivals

Newly acquired fish should be checked carefully for signs of disease as it is easier to cure or control a disease if it is caught before it has become established and weakened the specimens. Such diseases as salt water "Ick," fungus, tail rot, and white patch disease are fairly common in the marine field and usually go undetected. (See Chapter 5 for treatment and diagnosis)

Frayed or torn fins often occur in transfer and should not be regarded seriously unless the fish is bleeding. Generally the fish will nip each other's fins in their shipping or carrying box and it is fortunate that most fish dealers foresee this and pack their fish accordingly.

If fish show any signs of disease, place them in a separate aquarium or other container for a week or two until they are cured. If there is

Fig. 36. The salt-water procedure. STEP NO. 6 *Aquarium is completed and fish are contentedly swimming about their new home. Sub-sand filter furnishes both aeration and filtration but for special purposes an outside filter may be used in addition to the sub-sand filter. Trigger fish is on left, Cubbyu in the center and young Black Angelfish on the right.*

Fig. 37. *Aquarium with outside filter only. When a sub-sand filter is not used, a fine layer of sand should be sprinkled on the aquarium bottom and one or two air stones used to give additional aeration. This set-up is recommended for temporary displays or special purposes. If air stones are not used, the filter should be operated quickly to insure adequate circulation of the water. The new type "Power Filters" can be used successfully for this.*

Fig. 38. *Inside bottom filter, preferred by aquarists who do not like filters hanging on the outside of the aquarium. This type fits snugly in the corner of the aquarium and can be hidden with a piece of coral if placed on the floor of the aquarium.*

any doubt of their health, do not put them in an already established aquarium as they may infect your prized pets with some disease and you may lose both your old and your new specimens.

Types of Filtration

Although the sub-sand filter is a marvelous invention, it cannot perform miracles and there are times when an additional filter will be needed to keep the aquarium in the best of condition. If an aquarium is very crowded with fish or if it contains large specimens such as moray eels, porcupine fish, spiny boxfish, or other fish that are rather messy in their eating habits, an additional outside or inside filter may be necessary.

This filter should be filled with the new synthetic orlon or nylon filter floss material and it is operated independently from the sub-sand filter. Its purpose is to remove suspended uneaten particles of food or fish excretions, which because of its quantity, would over-tax the efficiency of the sub-sand filter. Glass wool, which in the past has been a popular filtering medium, is not generally recommended for salt-water aquariums as it deteriorates and crumbles, sometimes filling the aquarium with fine glass fragments which of course are very harmful to the fish.

Probably the very best filtering material in the aquarium field is activated carbon. It will keep the water so clear that it will be virtually invisible. However, it must be used cautiously or it will quickly kill your specimens. If used improperly, it will change the pH of the water too fast and this is difficult for the fish to withstand.

Activated Carbon

If an aquarium has been set up for several months, the sudden use of activated carbon may prove disastrous unless it is introduced to the filter and aquarium with extreme care. The carbon should first be washed thoroughly to remove fine particles of dust. Then it should be soaked for a few days in salt water before adding to the filter. The filter should be operated slowly and only for an hour or two each day for the first two weeks and then, if the fish show no signs of discomfort, the running time may be gradually increased so that after a month or so it may be operated continuously.

If fish show extreme discomfort when the aquarium is filtered with carbon, replace half the water in the aquarium with fresh sea water and revert back to the sub-sand filter for clearing the water. Your fish may not be able to stand the strain of the carbon. The safest procedure is to start using carbon when the aquarium is first set up. This way, the fish become accustomed to it and will suffer little ill effects.

Heavily stocked aquariums containing sharks, moray eels, large porcupine fish, sea turtles, etc. will require approximately one pound of carbon for each five gallons of water. Aquariums with just a few fish use one fourth pound of carbon to each five gallons of water.

Activated carbon may be neutralized almost completely by simply soaking it for a few weeks in fresh sea water. It should then be rinsed thoroughly in fresh water before use. Once the fish have become accustomed to it they will swim contentedly in water that is unbelievably clear, and if the filter containing the carbon is rinsed once a month the carbon should keep the water clean and odor free for possibly years. Contrary to popular belief, activated carbon does not lose its filtering capacity after a few weeks or months. In fact, it becomes better with use, for after a few months it becomes so saturated with elements from the sea that it can be used in complete safety. If the carbon is cleaned and washed regularly it may be reactivated once or twice a year by placing it in a Pyrex baking dish and drying it in an oven for an hour or two at regular baking temperature. Then it may be rinsed well and used again.

Activated carbon removes all traces of color, odor, and gases from the aquarium. It is especially useful in an aquarium in which the same water must be used continuously, as it will remove the impurities from the water. There are things about it, however, that are still in the experimental stage as regards its use in marine tanks. Sometimes fish adjust to it without trouble; at other times it makes the fish restless and they stop feeding; in some instances it can kill the fish. At present, the safest way to use carbon is to place it in an outside filter and operate the aquarium for a week or more before adding the fish. Then introduce the fish slowly to the aquarium so they are gradually introduced to the carbon-filtered water. Or, if the aquarium is already set up, it should be introduced to the filter in small amounts and the filter operated very slowly, so that the fish become adjusted to it over a long period of time. Either way, the carbon should be rinsed well and soaked in sea water or salt water as long as possible to age it before use. Aquarist Dick Boyd has recently introduced activated carbon with an acid absorbing resin to the marine hobby, and although there have been conflicting reports about it the author feels the product has considerable merit and certainly should be investigated further. There cannot be enough praise for activated carbon as a filtering agent. It gets water so clear that it sparkles. The author first began experimenting with it more than a decade ago and recommended its use in conjunction with the under gravel filter in an early pamphlet copyrighted in 1954.* All experiments were centered on Reef Activated carbon, as this was found to be a very pure and stable brand. No doubt there are other equally fine brands but testing each one is a long and arduous task. The carbon may be placed in an outside filter and the siphon tube of the filter should reach to the bottom of the tank so that it will pick up uneaten food, fish excretion, and other debris that settles to the bottom. It may also be used in an inside filter with good results.

As pointed out earlier in the text, fish sometimes cannot adjust to activated carbon, especially if the tank has been set up for a considerable length of time. Fish become conditioned to the water and any change can prove harmful to them. But when fish are freshly caught and in good health, they can usually adapt to change better than fish which have been confined; so that by using the carbon right from the start, while the water is very alkaline, and allowing it to circulate through the aquarium for a few days or a week if possible, it becomes so saturated with the many elements of sea water that it has little or no effect on the fish. It can make the difference between an aquarium with dull, dingy water and a tank of sparkling, gin-clear water in which the fish glisten like jewels and in which their colors will show off to best advantage. Sea water or artificial sea water often becomes dull, yellowish, or off color after a few months of use in the self-contained aquarium. This is no problem for the aquarist living near the ocean, as he can get new water whenever he chooses; but the inland aquarist must take special care of his sea water as it is quite valuable. If the water becomes

* *Simple, Precise Instructions for Marine Aquariums,* by the author.

dull or brownish in color, he has no alternative but to filter it and attempt to restore it to its original brightness. But it is easier to keep the water clear from the start with the carbon than it is to clear up the water several months after the aquarium has been set up.

Continued research with activated carbon by the author indicates that most or *all* aquariums would benefit greatly by using activated carbon either in an outside aquarium filter or an inside filter because it keeps the water clean and healthy right from the start. The following article on activated carbon by the author, is reprinted from Salt Water Aquarium Magazine.

"Activated carbon gets the water so clear that fish seem suspended in space! This was one of my early statements on this fantastic filtering medium, and decades later I am even more enthusiastic about the fabulous filtering qualities of activated carbon. In my opinion it is without equal in the aquarium field, and to do without it is to do without a sparkling clean aquarium where the water becomes invisible and the living jewels of the sea sparkle in water that is not only scrupulously clear but chemically and biologically clean. What more could be asked of a filtering medium?

Yet activated carbon is not well understood in the aquarium field—particularly in the salt water world. Improperly used, it can wipe out a tank of expensive fish overnight. Properly used, it can keep a tank full of fish in healthy condition for years without a single change of water. In fact, with the advent of the all glass tanks, a good undergravel filter with silica sand and a good outside filter that reaches all the way to the bottom with the siphon stem, it appears possible that a salt water aquarium could remain healthy and in good condition for a period of ten years without a single water change, provided, of course, activated carbon is used prperly in the filter and good aquarium maintenance is observed at all times. Herein lies the solution to the successful use of activated carbon in the aquarium. You must know what you are doing! Otherwise you will have little or no success with the carbon.

Success with activated carbon depends upon several factors chiefly of which is the carbon itself. Like everything else, there is a great difference in carbons. Some are very cheap, others costly. Some are made of animal bones, wood, and various other materials. We use a product made from coconut shell, which we feel is consistently more pure and chemically inert than other products. It may or may not be the best, but I personally have tested it over many years in well over a thousand salt water aquariums under all types of conditions. It does the job and does it well, which is good enough for me. Until I find a product that works better, I am well satisfied with it. I have tried other brands of carbon of course. Some worked good; others were lethal. Activated carbon is a powerful filtering agent.

They use it in cigarettes, space ships, and deep sea submarines. It removes practically everything from the air, and in our instance, from the water. Because of its ability to extract gases, odors, fumes, etc., from the air, it can pick up poisonous substances from the air simply by being stored near them. In the case of chemical houses or pet stores, an opened case of carbon could absorb lethal doses of insecticides, paints, and dangerous chemicals, which could eventually cause problems in the aquarium. This sometimes causes unexplained failures with carbon when used in the aquarium. It also points out that activated carbon should be handled and stored with great care in air tight bags, especially if it is stored in a room with highly volatile substances. Otherwise it will be contaminated and unfit for use. As pointed out above, there are many grades of carbon. Choose a known brand and one that is used by your local dealer if he is using it, or order a good quality carbon. The better grades of carbon will average in price from $1.50 to $3.00 per pound, depending upon whether it is cured or fresh. At this price it seems expensive, but it will last a long while. Contrary to popular opinion, carbon does not lose its efficiency after a few hours in the aquarium. Quite to the contrary, it improves vastly with age! Well aged carbon is completely safe to use, for it is neutralized by its constant use. It can be used over and over again, even for years if it is not contaminated with oils or dangerous chemicals. Those who would state that carbon is not an effective filtering medium should try it sometime. I don't know where they obtained their information, but it's a fact that carbon five years old will turn a dull, dingy, brown colored aquarium into a thing of sparkling clean water as clear as distilled gin. Well, perhaps it's not the carbon that gets the water clean when you place it in the filter. It must be the spirit from the great beyond! Or perhaps these people don't know what they are talking about. I'm inclined to believe the latter.

The safest way to use activated carbon is to cure it in salt water for a few weeks before placing it in the filter. Then rinse it well in fresh water. It is best to start it in the filter when the tank is first set up and the fish have not yet been added. Let the filter operate for a week or two with the water, and then add the fish, floating them in a container and introducing them gradually to the aquarium. Carbon filtered water is different from unfiltered water. Salt water fish cannot take ANY sudden change from one type of water to another. The same is true when they are being introduced to a carbon filtered tank or when their aquarium is to have carbon added to it for the first time. It must be done very gradually so that the fish can slowly become adjusted to it. If a tank has been set up for several months, the sudden use of carbon can prove disastrous. In this case, a small amount of carbon, say a teaspoonful to a tablespoonful, should be added to the empty filter once or twice a week, gradually building up the carbon until the filter is full. But the carbon should be aged before use. This is most important. Many people write inquiring whether or not glass wool or nylon, should be used in conjunction with the carbon. This is a matter of choice. If you have a good filter, you can use just the carbon, but if the filter has wide slots in the bottom, a little nylon or orlon will keep the carbon from passing through the slots. We don't recommend glass wool, as the synthetic floss is safer to use in the aquarium and easier to handle besides. A little of it placed above the carbon will help trap additional dirt and is easily removed when dirty, which will help keep the carbon clean longer. We also get many inquiries about resins for keeping the water clean. To date, we have not seen any resins that would keep the aquarium water clean, and we have tried some of them. The only time we recommend them is when aquarium water needs softening, in which case they probably do help. We have used the activated carbon all by itself with nothing added to it for most of our experiments, and the results have been phenomenal to say the least. It will get the water unbelievably clear and keep the fish in perfect condition. We have even reclaimed chemically colored water almost the color of coffee, which was discolored by adding copper sulfate and sulfathiazole sodium to the same tank for disease control. We had to change the carbon a couple of times, but it did the job. It got the water so clear you couldn't see it, and the water was perfectly healthy even though it was nearly two years old! We put in a large variety of both Atlantic and Pacific fish and they flourished in the peak of health and splendor. Activated carbon can't do everything. It can't cure a sick fish. It can't keep an aquarium clean if you aren't using enough of it or if you overfeed or put some bad coral in the tank. Everything has its limitations. But if you use it correctly, a half pound to a pound for ten gallons depending upon other filtration, number of specimens, etc., and use it in a good filter so it can do its job properly, it will give you the cleanest water you have ever seen. You'll have to wash it when it gets dirty and dry it in the sun every now and then, but this is a small task and takes but a few minutes. Use good carbon and use enough to do the job. Your reward will be the cleanest water you can imagine, as clear and sparkling as a mountain spring. The colors of your fish will be pure poetry."

Turbine Pumps and Power Filters

In the past few years, turbine pumps and power filters have been introduced to the aquarium field. These powerful motor-driven devices are capable of moving large quantities of water through the aquarium. In recent years, they have been aimed largely at marine aquarists with the argument that marine fish must have rapidly circulating water in the aquarium as they are accustomed to this in their natural environment.

This is partly true. Many marine fish come from water that is quite active, particularly the outer reef fish. However, some manufacturers attempt to mislead the novice by boldly stating that he will have no success whatever in the marine field unless he uses a power or turbine filter in his aquarium. Of course this is not only nonsense, but is deceptive and is aimed solely at selling a product rather than meeting an aquarist's needs. The marine fish by themselves are expensive enough without the addition of a very costly power filter, especially since it is absolutely unnecessary. An inexpensive vibrator pump and a sub-sand filter will suffice.

The author has personally collected over a million marine specimens and consequently is quite aware of the water conditions in which they are found. While many marine fish do come from water that is quite active, even more come from water that is rather placid with little or no current. Even in the areas where there is a strong current the small, colorful fish come out of hiding mostly at slack tide when the current has almost stopped. This certainly indicates that marine fish as a whole don't need to be swirled around the aquarium in a vicious current. They need oxygen and a moderate current but many other things such as feeding, etc. are equally important.

However, the power filter or turbine filter does have much value and merit when used properly, especially when one is keeping large quantities of fish in the same aquarium. It will sweep up uneaten food and other debris from the bottom and is especially useful for pet dealers who may have to handle large quantities of salt-water fish at one time. It can be moved from tank to tank as required for cleaning and will prove quite useful if one wishes to invest in this expensive item. Like other aquarium accessories, it can be used for special purposes.

Douglass Filtration System

A new type aquarium filter which pumps water through a fine plastic cartridge has been sent to the author for testing and shows good promise, especially in disease control. The filter contains a motor driven water pump which sits outside the aquarium. The filter rests on the bottom of the aquarium and is connected to the pump by a length of heavy plastic tubing. The water is drawn through the filter at very high speed which both filters and aerates the aquarium. It picks up all uneaten food and other debris that settles to the

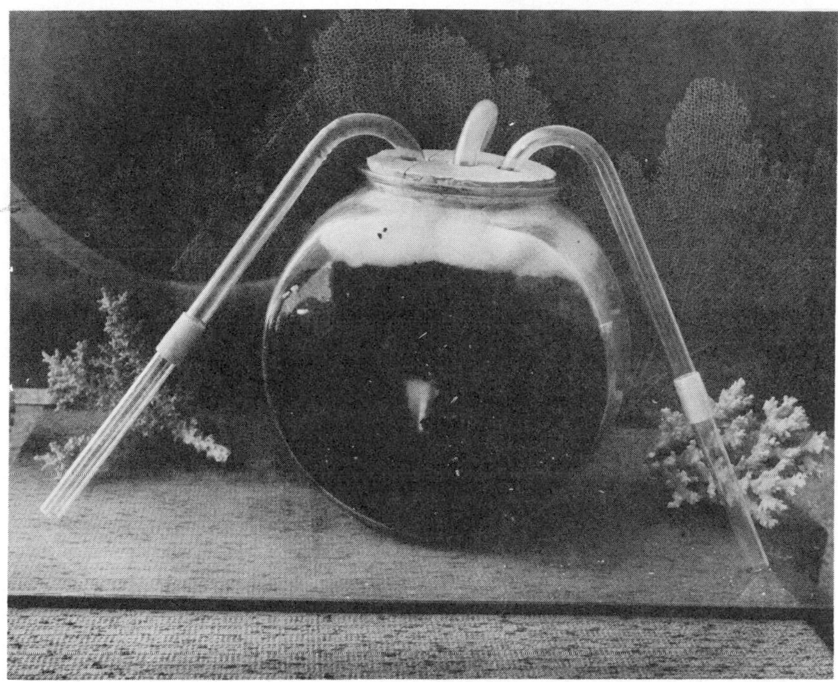

Fig. 39. *The author adopted the Douglass Filter to salt water by placing the filter cartridge in the bottom of a bowl and filling the bowl with carbon. Nylon floss keeps carbon in place. A styrofoam cap fits over top of bowl and two siphon stems are inserted. These are the intake siphons, and reach to bottom outside the bowl. The entire bowl is placed in a large aquarium. Adapted this way, the filter will get even a 200-gallon tank crystal clear in hours, as all water must pass through the carbon and cartridge in order to circulate through the water pump provided with the filter. The author has also adapted a gallon plastic measuring container to the filter with equally good results.*

bottom and deposits it on the plastic cartridge, which is made of a very fine material. Although tests at this time by the author are inconclusive, since the filter has just been acquired, already it has shown remarkable results in removing disease from the aquarium. A Rock Beauty heavily infected with a strange, flowing white fungus and in the throes of death was placed in an aquarium operated by the filter and in just one day, practically all signs of the disease had vanished and the fish was swimming about normally. The filter is said to remove "Ick" from the water, as well as other diseases and in the short time the author has tested it, it seems to have done this successfully. The principle of the filter is that it moves the water through the filter material at such a fast rate that all the parasites, bacteria and disease producing organisms are removed from the water as the water is forced through the fine plastic cartridge cylinder. It is said to cure many and most fish diseases even without medication but chemicals can be added to hasten the cure and the filter will remove the chemicals from the water as well as the disease. This can certainly be a boon to hobbyists or dealers who are sometimes plagued with a wide variety of diseases, especially fungus. The new filter could be utilized to operate a special tank which could be used as a hospital tank and sick fish could be placed in it until healed. This would be especially useful to dealers who have many aquariums and do not have the time to pamper their fish. Fish with torn fins, fungus or other diseases could be transferred to the special filter tank and kept there as long as needed. No doubt when the Douglass Filter comes on the market, it will find its useful place in the aquarium field. This type of filter appears to be most beneficial in very large aquariums where there is a need for rapid circulation of the water. It is of particular use in large tanks where regular filters cannot be attached due to the fact that the water line is not high enough or that the aquarium frame is not adaptable to a standard filter. The Douglass filter motor sets at the bottom of the tank outside the aquarium and water is siphoned down into it so that the water level inside the tank need not be right at the top as with most filters. The author has adapted this powerful filter to a large drum type fish bowl which was filled with activated carbon. The filter cartridge was placed at the bottom of the bowl and the carbon was covered with dacron filter floss to keep it in the bowl. With this arrangement, the two-gallon bowl of carbon became a giant inside bottom filter and all the water in the tank had to circulate through the carbon and then through the fine filter cartridge. It cleaned a huge six foot long tank to sparkling clear water in just a day or two. No doubt further modifications of the filter will be presented in the future.

The Diatom Filter

Another revolutionary new filter for aquariums is the diatom filter which uses diatomaceous earth as the sole filtering agent. This is one of the finest filtering mediums known. A powerful water pump circulates the water from the aquarium through a large jar which contains the diatom powder. The powder collects on a fine nylon screen and the water is filtered as it passes through a thin layer of the filtering material. The author has tested this unit on many aquariums and although the unit is slightly complicated, if one follows the instructions to the letter, it will work remarkably and actually filter out even milky-colored water. It is especially useful in clearing up bacteria-clouded water which it does very efficiently if the unit is operated properly. It will make the water in the aquarium actually sparkle, it gets it so clear. The diatomaceous powder is inexpensive, and when the filter needs cleaning it is simply washed down the drain by running fresh water through the filter. At present the unit is slightly cumbersome but it need not be kept on the aquarium for more than a couple days, after which it may be cleaned and put away. In many aquariums, it probably would be used once or twice a month to clear up the water, or if one had many tanks, it could be moved from tank to tank as needed. It shows good promise in the marine field for it positively will clear up bacteria-clouded water if operated properly. It is not intended to replace the standard filters on the aquarium and they may be left in place while it is in operation or, according to the recommended procedure, they may be removed for cleaning while the diatom filter is doing its job. The present diatom filter will clear up even a very large tank.

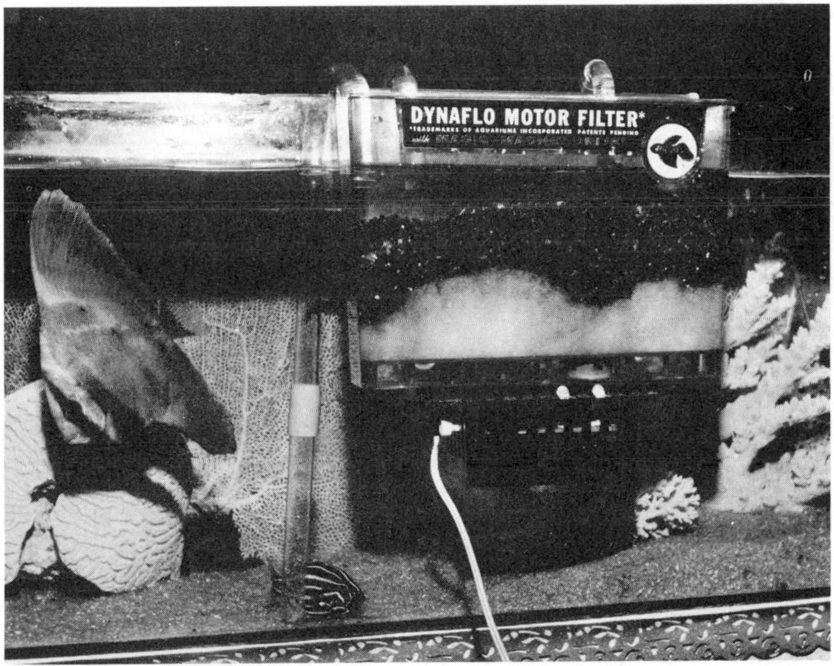

Fig. 40. *The Magnetic Drive Motor Filter brings the power filter within the price range of all aquarists. This powerful filter moves a large amount of water and works well when used with or without the sub-sand filter. Here it is adapted for use with sub-sand filter in a tank containing very large fish. It kept the water sparkling clear. Activated carbon and nylon wool are used in the filter.*

Magnetic Drive Power Filters

Although in the past, most power filters have been quite expensive, the new magnetic driver filters are quite inexpensive. They are very efficient and give good filtration, particularly for a ten to twenty gallon tank. As with all outside filters, make certain that at least one, preferably both siphon stems reach ALL THE WAY TO THE BOTTOM so that they will pick up dirt and debris instead of just exchanging water. This is very important. These filters have an all-plastic box and a magnetic drive power system which presents a minimum of metal contact with the water. In fact the only piece of metal in the entire filter that touches the water is a small, half-inch long shaft which the manufacturers have made of highly resistant metal. The author has tested these for over a year in continuous use and is very pleased with them. An important thing to remember when using them is to anchor the siphon stems firmly in place,

Fig. 41. *The most important part of any outside filter is the siphon stem. It should reach all the way to the bottom as shown here so that it picks up bottom dirt instead of just clean water. Note the sand swirling up inside filter tube, showing that it is picking up fine dirt. A better modification of the pick-up at the bottom would be a T-shaped attachment which would run the entire length of the tank. This would be slotted along its top edge and would attach to the siphon stem. It would clean a tank very effectively. A golden Striped Bass poses here.*

either with coral or some type of holding device. If a fish bumps into them and moves them they may lose their siphon and the filter will run dry. Perhaps some sort of suction cup will eventually be made to hold them in place. At any rate, it is usually best to have an undergravel filter in the tank in conjunction with the power filters so should the filter stop working, the fish will still have aeration. The filters are made in two sizes and since the price is only slightly higher for the larger size, it is more practical to get the big one which will give far better filtration in most instances. The author has tried many of the so-called power filters, some especially made for salt water, but many rust badly in just a short while. They also have metal shafts inside them which could present problems. The magnetic drive filters eliminate both the rust problem and the metal shaft and should prove a real boon to the marine aquarist.

The Ultra-Violet Filter and Sterilizer

There has long been a need for a good ultra-violet sterilizer and at last one has appeared on the market that is both good and inexpensive. It combines a specially made outside filter with a strong

Fig. 42. *An ultraviolet sterilizer in use. This model fits over the bubbler stem of the undergravel filter. A common filefish swims over to inspect it.*

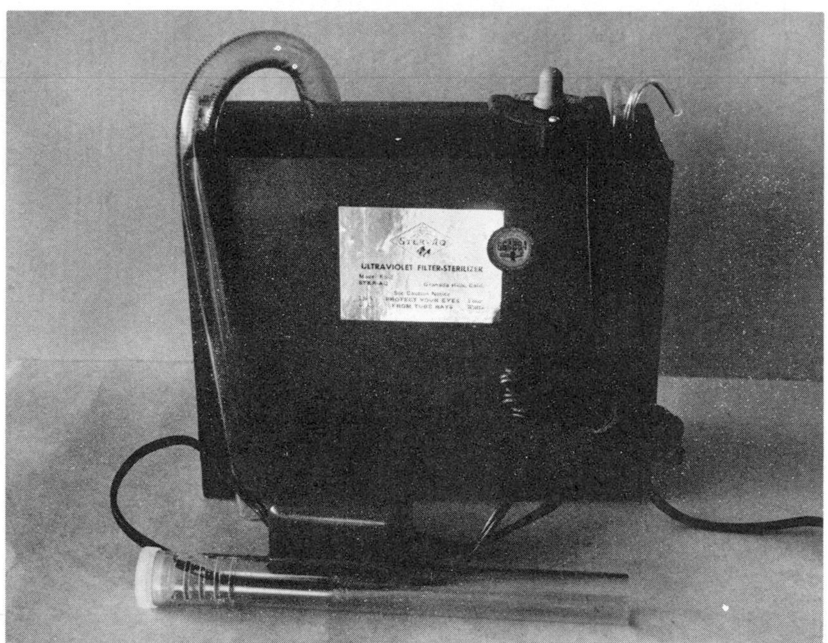

Fig. 43. *The Ultraviolet Filter Sterilizer Unit combines the ultraviolet light with a special filter. It shows good promise for the self-contained aquarium and may be especially useful in the eventual breeding of salt-water fish where absolute cleanliness is an extreme necessity.*

ultraviolet bulb and is constructed so that neither the fish nor the aquarist will see the ultraviolet right that would be harmful to both. It is especially useful in combating bacteria and its continued use on the aquarium should certainly be helpful. It should prove especially useful in live coral or invertebrate tanks which also contain fish. It will help control minute organisms without the necessity of adding copper or drugs to the water which of course would kill or harm the invertebrates. Nothing of course can solve all the problems in the aquarium but this unit looks very promising.

The hobbyist who is in doubt as to which piece of equipment he should or should not purchase would do well to ask the advice of his local aquarium store. A reputable dealer would not sell him something just to make a sale and could advise him as to which filter or combination of filters would be best suited to his particular need.

The Eheim Power Filter

This is one of the finest, most versatile filters made and the craftmanship and engineering of this filter is unsurpassed in fine quality.

The Rock Beauty (Holocanthus tricolor) *from Florida and Caribbean reefs, is among the most colorful fish in the world. The best aquarium size is two to four inches, although the fish is very beautiful regardless of size.*

The Townsend Angelfish (Angelichthys townsendi) *is the most colorful and exotic fish from the Caribbean area. Whether it is an inch long or a foot long it is extremely colorful. Large specimens in particular are brilliant orange and blue, especially when seen on the reef. The fish can subdue the colors at will and often a photo does not capture the real beauty of the fish. Note the small, spotted reef trunk-fish at top of photo.*

The French Angelfish (Pomacanthus paru) *is another highly colored angelfish from Florida and the Caribbean. As the fish matures, the yellow bands gradually fade out until the scales become flecked with gold as may be seen on this half grown specimen. The sea fans are not in the aquarium. They are up against the glass on the outside.*

A living cowrie crawls about a dense bed of green algae in one of the author's tanks. Keeping live sea shells is becoming a world wide hobby. It's a hobby where you can't lose for even if the animal dies, you can still keep the handsome shell.

Eheim filters are made in Germany and both large and small models are available to fit most any aquarium. The filters are generally sealed at the top so that they may be placed in back or even under the aquarium which has many advantages over the conventional filter. In addition, the aquarium doesn't have to be filled in order for the filter to operate which is a very favorable factor.

The filter is quiet and simple to operate. It is cleaned by simply opening the top of the filter and removing the carbon or nylon floss. It has an ingenious aerating device in which the water is sprayed down into the aquarium on a long, slender pipe perforated so that the water spurts out in numerous, fine streams which agitates the surface of the water remarkably well. The structure and arrangement of the filter intake and outlet is such that it can be arranged to function in several different ways not mentioned in the instructions but which appear to benefit the aquarium. For instance the outlet pipe may easily be pushed to the very bottom of the tank where it will force strong jets of water across the sand, thereby literally washing the sand clean. This loosens up dirt and debris which will then be picked up by the filter material. When the sand is sufficiently cleaned, the outlet pipe may then be returned to the surface as originally prescribed. Also, it is possible to switch the intake and outlet pipes around so that the water will be drawn through the long, perforated pipe with its many holes, and may be placed directly on the bottom of the tank. Both inlet and outlet stems are held securely in place with plastic suction cups, another very desirable and important feature. Indeed, this is the finest filter the author has tested to date. It is now being sold in the U.S. and should be very popular.

Temperatures

The colorful tropical fish from the Florida and Bahama Reefs as well as those from the warm Pacific areas should be kept at an aquarium temperature of 70 to 80 degrees or as close to that as possible. If the temperature drops much below this, it will be necessary to purchase an aquarium heater. Obtain a thermostat heater combination that has a plastic control panel so that it won't rust in the salt water. There are many fine heaters available and your fish dealer will be able to suggest the proper wattage for your aquarium. The single tube thermostat heater combinations are the most practical and these should be suspended into the aquarium far enough to cover most of the glass tube. Do not submerge them or allow salt water to get into the control knob at the top. Most northern aquarists will find it necessary to obtain a heater unless their house is thermostatically heated during the cold months.

During excessively hot weather, if the water in the aquarium should get much above 90 degrees it will be necessary to cool the aquarium a little. This is simply accomplished by floating a jar of ice cubes in the aquarium until the desired cooling is obtained. Most tropical marine fish can withstand temperature extremes of slightly above 90 degrees to slightly below 60 degrees if the change is not sudden and if it is not prolonged more than six or eight hours. Aeration should always be increased during high temperatures.

Cold-water fishes from the tide pools or bay areas along the northern coast of the country must be kept in cool water to survive. Most of them will require a temperature of between 50 to 60 degrees so instead of a heater, the aquarist may need a cooling system for his tank unless he raids the ice cubes daily during the warm weather. For a small aquarium this would not be a herculean task for a daily change of cubes morning and night would keep the temperature well below the danger level.

Cover Glass

The aquarium should be covered with a sheet of glass to keep the fish from jumping out, to retard evaporation, and to keep out dust and other debris. The glass should be suspended inside the aquarium one quarter to a half inch so condensation and water which has collected on the underside of the cover glass will not drip down the outside of the aquarium. The glass may be suspended with plastic cover glass holders which may be easily made by cementing three strips of plastic together with acetate.

A more permanent cover glass may be made by simply welding a set of glass handles to the cover which has been cut so that it will fit down into the aquarium. Silicone rubber is used as the welding agent and it is quite simple to use. First, the cover glass is cut to the proper size. Next, two strips of glass approximately three inches wide by six inches long are cut to be used as handles. Lay the cover glass on a flat surface and apply some of the silicone rubber sealer to the glass strips and press them down on top of the cover glass so they are half on the glass and half protruding over the edge. Allow the glue to harden overnight and you will have a permanent cover glass. It is best to use at least quarter inch glass for the cover and the edges should be smoothed with a carborundum stone so you won't cut yourself when handling it.

The glass should be tight fitting but should have one corner cut off to a depth of about two inches so at feeding time, you won't have to remove the whole cover. The opening may be covered with a small piece of glass when not in use and in winter it can be used for the insertion of the aquarium heater.

Of course the cover glass doesn't have to be made this way. It can simply be placed on top of the aquarium and if it is removed twice a week and washed with fresh water, it will still serve the purpose.

Protection of Stand

Many marine aquarists will desire to place their aquarium on a stand made especially for this purpose. These stands are usually made of angle iron which is painted black or other colors. Since they have been made primarily for fresh water, they will rust badly with salt water unless given special care. The best procedure is to spray the entire stand with two coats of clear plastic spray. Or, the aquarium may be separated from the stand by a sheet of exterior plywood which is cut to the same size as the top of the stand. This will eliminate rusting between the bottom of the aquarium and the stand where the corrosive salt water is likely to spill over the top. The plywood can be painted the same color as the stand so it will hardly be noticed.

Fig. 44. *Realistic background effect may be obtained by placing a large box, painted flat black, in back of the aquarium. Objects such as sea fans, drift wood, etc., appear to be inside the aquarium when placed in the box.*

Backgrounds

The marine hobbyist often wishes to decorate his aquarium with driftwood, colored sea fans, sponges, etc. and although these items are certainly a part of the sea, with few exceptions, they cannot be kept inside the aquarium with the fish. However, a simple background effect can be produced that will make them appear to be inside the aquarium, even to the most observing eye.

Simply construct a box the same size as the aquarium and attach it to the stand as shown in the illustration. Then paint the inside of the box flat black. After it has dried, sand, coral, sponge, sea fans, or anything your heart desires may be placed in this outside container. If the back aquarium glass is kept sparkling clean and the shadow box properly lighted, it will be extremely difficult to tell that the objects are not in the aquarium. The flat black color creates this illusion. The box should be painted no other color. The sand in this outside box may be piled into small dunes and hills gradually working it away from the aquarium glass and the sea fans and decorations should be placed to conform to those in the aquarium itself so it looks like a continuation of the general scene.

Aquariums without stands may be decorated in a similar fashion either with the shadow box or by merely hanging a black cloth in back of the tank. Objects placed between the cloth and the aquarium will appear to be inside the aquarium.*

Fig. 45. *Sand should be piled into little dunes in an irregular pattern simulating the sea floor and should meet evenly with the sand in the aquarium. Sea fans, large uncured corals, sponges, etc., which would normally pollute the aquarium, may be placed in the background, yet they will appear to be inside the aquarium.*

* See June, 1954 issue of *Aquarium magazine.*

Fig. 46. *Finished aquarium shows startling underwater effect.*

Extra Sea Water

Always keep in mind that the most important item for the marine aquarium is pure, fresh, sea water. Unless you live right on the seashore and can get fresh sea water whenever you need it, it is best to keep a complete change on hand for emergencies. If the water is obtained fresh and stored in glass containers, it will keep for a long while so you will have it when you need it most.

Artificial Lighting

Unless the aquarium is in a brightly lighted room, it will be of distinct advantage to obtain a light for your aquarium. The lights are generally made to fit the aquarium and are placed on top, where they illuminate the aquarium to the best advantage. The fluorescent light should be used in preference to the incandescent type as it is much cooler and consequently may be left on without worry of overheating. Although fluorescent lights cost more, they use much less current and pay for themselves in a short while.

The light should be placed on top of the cover glass so it will not come in contact with the corrosive salt water. Care must be taken that should it break the glass, it will not fall into the aquarium. A heavy cover glass will usually withstand the small amount of heat

Fig. 47. *In 1954, the author established Coral Reef Exhibits and opened the nation's first exclusive salt-water aquarium store featuring all kinds of marine fish, live salt water plants and both live and cured corals. It was a milestone in the marine hobby. Note extreme clarity of water in the aquariums.*

created by this type of lighting fixture. The unit may be further protected by spraying it with a clear plastic before use.

Most marine specimens will enjoy six to eight hours of light daily in their aquarium, providing they are given a place to hide, when they desire to get away from the light. This is important as many marine fish are easily blinded. Fish with large eyes, which indicates they may be nocturnal, should be protected against strong light by protective coral ledges or large tridacna shells that will afford them a completely dark area in which they may retreat. Such specimens as Porcupine fish, Squirrel fish, Lion fish, Big-Eyes, Moray eels, Rock Beauties, etc. are easily blinded by too much light. Bay fishes like the Spiny Boxfish, Sea Horses, etc. should also be watched as they can also be blinded by excessive lighting. On the other hand, marine plants and certain Demoiselles require a considerable amount of light every day so that six or eight hours of light will in no way harm them and they may require even more.

Beautiful and perhaps healthful lighting effects may be obtained by using either a blue or a green fluorescent bulb in your lighting fixture. The blue bulb would be for reef specimens and the green for the bay specimens as these colors are more apparent in these areas. It seems to have a psychological effect upon the specimens when their water assumes a natural hue.

Crowding Specimens

Although the author does not recommend crowding of marine fish, there may be times when it is necessary. It is entirely possible to safely keep dozens of colorful marine beauties in rather small aquariums for periods of three to six months and longer.

This is accomplished with the use of the sub-sand filter and sufficient cover so that the specimens will not fight. Of course the aeration must be strong enough so that the fish will breathe properly and feeding must be done carefully so that the water will not become foul. Fish excretions which accumulate rapidly in a crowded aquarium, must be constantly removed. An inside bottom filter, filled with nylon floss will prove useful here.

The author has successfully kept in one fifty gallon aquarium the following:

two 4-inch Cubbyu
one 4-inch Spanish Hogfish
one 3-inch Cardinal fish
six 1½ to 2½ Porkfish
one 3-inch Coral shrimp
six 1½ inch Neon Gobies
eight 1½ inch Beau Gregories
one 1-inch Sharp Nosed Puffer
ten 1 to 3 inch Black Angelfish
five 1½ to 4 inch Queen Angelfish
two 2-inch Parrot fish
three 2-inch Unicorn Blennies
one 1½ inch Orange Demoiselle
one 1½ inch Glass Goby
one 3-inch Lima scallop
one 2-inch Pistol shrimp
one 1-inch Hermit crab
one 1-inch Convict Goby
three 3-inch Four Eye Butterflyfish
55 Fish Total

Although the aquarium was extremely crowded, there was no serious fighting and the fish were not breathing heavily. The aquarium could easily have withstood another dozen or more fish. A larger aquarium, three feet square by twelve inches high contained nearly a hundred fish with no ill effects, and for certain small specimens such as the Dwarf Sea Horses or Neon Gobies it is entirely feasible to keep as many as a thousand in a single fifty gallon aquarium with proper aeration and care. In addition to the sub-sand filter bubbler stems, it may be necessary to add an air stone or two to provide sufficient air in extreme cases. Of course no crowding of costly marine specimens should be attempted by anyone unless he has much experience with salt-water fish. A single mishap could cause a total loss.

Which System to Use

The author has outlined all the various methods in which salt water fish may be successfully kept in a self-contained aquarium. There are those who would advocate the use of an outside filter only, with no sand in the aquarium. There are those who would use only an undergravel filter. Some aquarists use the natural system, simply inserting an air stone in their tank of living rocks and corals (Lee Chin Eng of Indonesia). Many aquarists use only a large power filter with activated carbon for their salt water aquarium. At this point, the aquarist may be confused as to which procedure is the best or most practical for a salt water aquarium.

It should be pointed out that salt water fish can be kept by any of the various methods presented. You can keep them successfully in a large aquarium with only a power filter and a fine layer of sand in the bottom of the tank. Or you can keep them with just an undergravel filter, and no other type of filtration. You can use an inside filter or an outside filter, whichever you prefer or whichever is more practical for you. You can use a power filter or a regular outside filter in conjunction with an undergravel filter. The author of course stresses the sub-sand filter. His experiences are based on not just one or two aquariums which is often the case of some book writers in the marine field, but on hundreds, perhaps thousands, of his own aquariums set up in nearly two decades of work in the marine aquarium field. It is almost unbelievable how much marine life can be maintained in a single aquarium set up with the undergravel filter and a good outside filter. The new magnetic drive motor filters simplify the marine tank even more by making a good exchange of water and picking up suspended matter from the tank, keeping the aquarium in a healthy condition. At this writing, having tried all combinations of systems and methods for keeping marine fish, the author still recommends the sub-sand, or undergravel filter and a good outside filter or motor-driven filter with aged activated carbon as the simplest and most practical way of keeping salt water fish in the self-contained aquarium.

3

Maintenance of the Marine Tank

The salt-water aquarium cannot be left alone and unattended for very long. At least until it has been operating for a period of six months or more and has assumed a routine in behavior.

The first week that the aquarium is set up, will be the most important. Constant watching will be necessary to guard against foul water and tank failure. Dead fish, uneaten food, etc. should be promptly removed and a special close watch should be kept on the coral. If any signs of fungus or slime appear on the surface of the coral, it should be removed immediately and washed thoroughly before returning to the aquarium. Food should be fed sparingly and what food is not consumed should be siphoned from the aquarium. A diptube and aquarium scraper will prove valuable here and will often eliminate the need of placing the hands in the aquarium. This is important, for if the hands or arms contain any soap, it may mean the ruination of the entire display for soap is deadly to the marine aquarium.

Always wash and rinse hands thoroughly before placing in the aquarium. Use clean aquarium gadgets, nets, diptubes, etc. to work in your aquarium, and put your hands in the tank as little as possible.

First two weeks are the most important. Most failures with marine fish occur during this time. It is of utmost importance that the aquarium be given considerable care during this critical period. After that you may relax a little and just give your display a monthly check-up.

Things to Watch For

1. Count fish every day. If all are not present, look for them. They may be dead and lying under the coral.
2. Watch coral closely. If it gives off a milky smoke, remove it immediately. Also examine it closely for scum or fungus.

3. Observe the clearness of the water when aquarium is first set up. If it suddenly becomes cloudy, either the coral is bad or you have put too much food in the aquarium.
4. Watch the action of your marine fish. If they are swimming contentedly about the aquarium, then conditions are alright. However, if they are resting on the bottom and are breathing rapidly and don't take any interest in food or the other fish, then something is drastically wrong and immediate action must be taken to save your pets. Perhaps a good increase of aeration may remedy the situation, or a fresh filter change. If neither have any effect on the fish, they should be removed from the aquarium and placed in fresh sea water until they return back to normal. Meanwhile the aquarium should be checked thoroughly. The filter cleaned, the coral washed, and any uneaten food removed.
5. Check the fish for any signs of disease. Keep a close watch for tail rot, skin fungus, and especially for salt water "Ick." This is probably one of the chief causes of sudden death in a well managed aquarium. The fish will act uncomfortable and tiny white dots will appear on the transparent parts of the fins. These will rapidly spread and cover the entire fish if left unchecked. (See Chapter 5 for treatment.)
6. Notice the compatibility of your marine specimens. Practically all marine fish will make a "pass" at other fish if it comes too

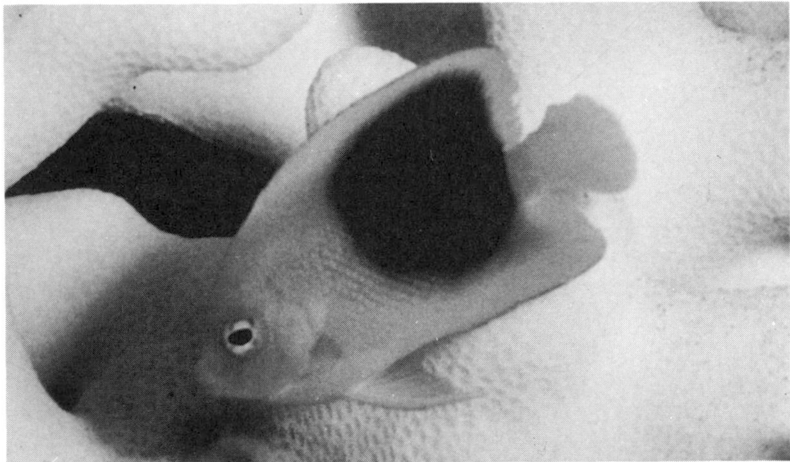

Fig. 48. *A young Rock Beauty's tail with a chunk missing. Fin nipping is characteristic of many marine fishes. If it becomes serious, the offender should be removed from the aquarium or isolated with a sheet of glass.*

Fig. 49. *The Cubbyu or High Hat* (Eques acuminatus) *with badly nipped dorsal fin. This delicate fish is often attacked by Demoiselle's or other aggressive fishes. The fine tail and fin structure is eaten by the other fish so that eventually the defenseless creature can no longer swim away from its tormentors. Unless promptly removed, it cannot survive.*

near them. This is not serious, but if a fish pursues another continuously and allows it no rest in the aquarium, the offended victim may starve. One of them should be removed from the aquarium, or separated with a sheet of glass. If a fish acts extremely aggressive and attacks other fish on sight, it should be removed immediately or it may kill the other specimens in a matter of minutes.

If all goes well, and the above observations are made, you may not have to do anything to your aquarium except feed the fish and make sure they have plenty of aeration for the first ten days. After that, the aquarium should have a safety clean-up. This is done as follows:

A. Remove all coral and wash thoroughly.
B. Siphon out the uneaten food and debris from under the coral.
C. Clean outside filter if one is used.
D. Return coral to aquarium if it smells clean and is free from odor.

This simple clean-up is done as a precaution because most coral will leach a harmful white scum during the first week or two of immersion in the aquarium. Also, it gives you a chance to check the coral for large uneaten chunks of food and possible dead fish.

If everything goes well, the aquarium will not need attention for another month. After that it should be given a good quarterly cleaning which can be done in a systematic fashion so that it will not take very long.

Quarterly Cleaning Schedule
(With Sub-Sand Filter and Outside Filter)

1. Remove all coral from aquarium.
2. Siphon out uneaten food and debris from under the coral, straining the water through several layers of filter material, and then return the water to the aquarium so that the outside filter will continue to operate.
3. Stir up the sand thoroughly and increase the air on the outside filter so that it will run fast.
4. Wash the coral and let it dry, preferably out in the sun. Meanwhile, stir the sand occasionally so that outside filter will pick up the suspended matter. Do not frighten the fish unnecessarily. They will usually enjoy the dirty water condition, as it helps them to rid their gills of internal parasites. This is a natural condition which occurs in the ocean every time there are strong winds. However, if the fish are very frightened, put one piece of coral back so they will have at least some cover.
5. Wipe the entire inside glass area with a clean handkerchief. This handkerchief should be rinsed several times in fresh water to remove all traces of soap before use. It should be contributed to your marine exhibit as it will be needed every month. After you have wiped the inside glass, wipe the scum off the plastic tubing and filter stems that are used inside the aquarium. Then rinse the handkerchief in fresh water and go over the top metal surface of the aquarium frame, wiping off the salt residue. If done properly, this will keep the top of the tank from rusting.
6. After aquarium is reasonably clear, slow down outside filter and increase air on bottom filter and airstones if you are using them. Then when most of the debris has settled, return the coral and regulate air back to normal.
7. At this time, a little fresh sea water may be added if any is on hand. Also, the salinity should be checked, and fresh water added if necessary.
8. Outside filter should now be cleaned. Carbon should be washed in a pail and all debris removed. Filter floss should be washed or replaced. Then attach filter to aquarium again and the display should require little attention for another month.
9. Sorry to bring up Number 9, but if the sand is very dirty after the first month, it would be wise to remove it completely from the aquarium and wash it or replace it with fresh sand. It can easily be removed, without disturbing the fish, by siphoning it from the aquarium into a wide-mouthed five gallon jar. The water may be promptly returned to the aquarium. A four-foot

piece of half-inch siphon hose may be purchased at any five and dime store and is excellent for this purpose. Sand may also be scooped up with a fish net, if aquarium is at an easy level to work with.

Washing the Sand

The necessity of washing the sand will depend entirely upon how crowded the aquarium is, and how careful you were in feeding and cleaning up uneaten food. It may not be necessary except once every three months; or, if you are really careful, you may let this go to twice a year. At any rate, it should not be neglected longer than this.

Sometimes it is only necessary to remove the top layer of sand as this will contain most of the dirt. This may be siphoned out, re-washed, and carefully replaced on top of the remaining sand. Or you may clean one half of the tank at a time if your undergravel filter is in two parts, which is usually the case. Just remove the sand from one filter, and by moving the corals to the other side of the tank you can clean one side completely without disturbing the fish or the aquarium to any extent. At a later date, after the tank has settled down, you may then do the other side. If the sand is polluted as in the case of a live coral tank where numerous decay has taken place; or if the tank has been victimized with numerous parasites and bacterial infestations; or if the tank contains a multitude of chemical medications DO NOT stir up the sand in hopes of having the outside filter pick up all the dirt and debris. This could kill your fish because you will release a tremendous cloud of bacteria, dirt, chemicals and harmful debris, which will poison the water, and rob it of oxygen, creating a potentially dangerous condition. In this instance, the best thing to do is to remove a few gallons of water from the top and place the fish in a bucket with some coral and an air stone. Then shut off all filters and let the water in the tank settle for a couple of hours. Next, carefully siphon out all the water into clean containers disturbing the sand as little as possible. Take it down to about an inch or two of the sand. You will now have the water in clean, excellent condition and practically all the bacteria, chemicals, etc. will be lodged in the sand. Scoop out and discard the sand with a net and remove the undergravel filters and clean the bottom of the tank thoroughly. Then you can return the water to the tank and set it up with clean, freshly-washed sand. After you've washed it a few times and it looks good and clean, wash it a few more times to make certain it is as clean as you can get it. Let the filters run for a few hours before replacing the fish. It will also be necessary to replace a few gallons of the salt water at this time as some of it will be lost in the cleaning process.

Quarterly Cleaning Schedule
(With Bottom Filter Only)

1. Remove all coral from aquarium. Wash thoroughly and dry.
2. Siphon all the sand into a five gallon jar; return water to aquarium. Here again, a little discretion will be needed to decide how often the sand must be washed. This may vary from once every month, to perhaps once every two or three months, depending on many factors.
3. Wash sand thoroughly and return it to aquarium.
4. Increase air to bubbler system so that it will clear up the water.
5. Wash coral thoroughly; let it dry in the sun, if possible, and return it to the aquarium as soon as water is reasonably clear.
6. Wipe inside glass and tubing as described above. Check salinity, etc.

This may all sound like a great deal of work, but for a fifteen or twenty gallon aquarium, the entire cleaning procedure may be done in about two hours or less, once a good system is devised. A small two gallon aquarium can be completely cleaned in about fifteen minutes, with the exception of drying the coral.

Quarterly Cleaning Schedule
(With Outside Filter and No Bottom Filter)

1. Remove all coral from aquarium.
2. Siphon bottom of aquarium, removing all sand, uneaten food, etc.
3. Replace sand with a fine layer scattered evenly on the bottom.
4. Wash outside filter thoroughly, replacing spun floss, if necessary.
5. Wipe inside glass and filter stem, tubing, etc. with clean handkerchief, as explained before. Also wipe top metal rim and rinse it with fresh water to prevent rust.
6. Check salinity, adding fresh water if necessary.

There are two reasons for wiping the inside glass of the aquarium with a handkerchief. First, it removes a semi-transparent scum which forms on the glass and which eventually gives the aquarium a dull appearance. Second, it removes algae which may start to grow there unless cleaned periodically. Of course, if the growth of algae is intentional, which it may be in some cases, then just the front glass should be cleaned. The top metal rim should always be cleaned with fresh water, because even though it may be stainless steel, it will usually rust if left unattended.

Outside Care. Salt water is highly corrosive and to keep your aquar-

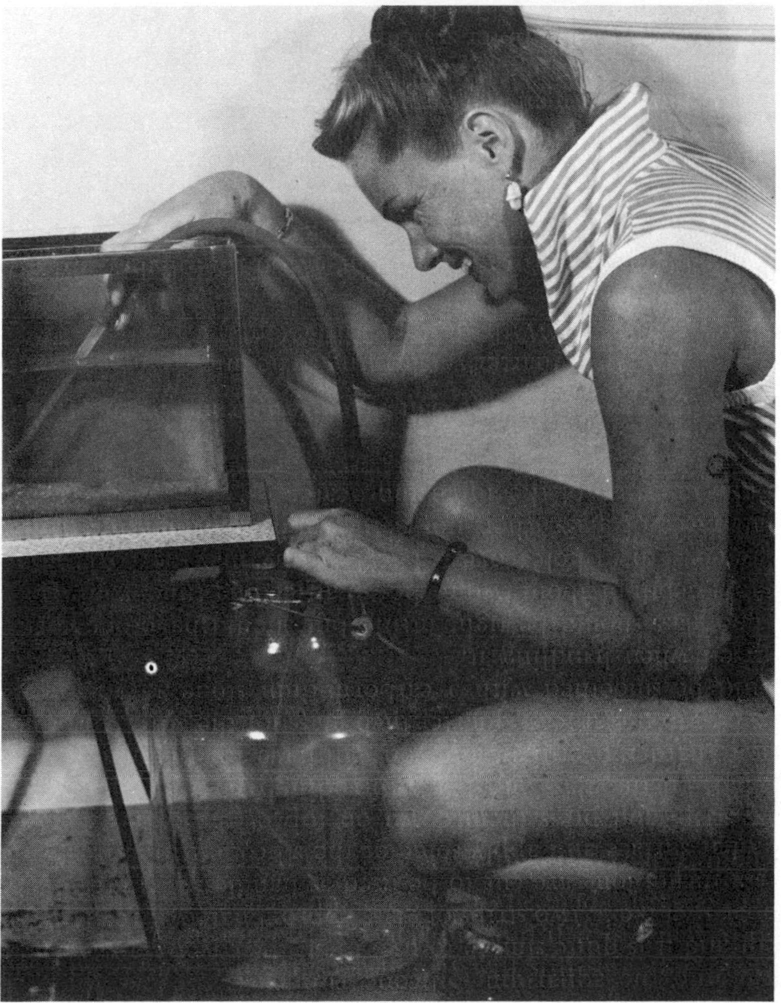

Fig. 50. *When sand becomes very dirty, it should be removed from the aquarium and washed thoroughly or replaced with clean, new sand. The sand may be removed two ways. It may be siphoned from the aquarium into jugs or buckets along with the water as shown here. It should then be allowed to stand until the sand has settled in the jugs, after which the water may be returned to the aquarium. However, if the sand is extremely dirty as in the case of a live coral tank; or if the tank has been repeatedly treated with chemicals; or the sand is suspected of housing numerous bacteria and parasites, it is best to siphon out the water only, disturbing the sand as little as possible. Then the sand may be scooped up with a net and the bottom of the tank thoroughly cleaned. This way you will have crystal clear water to return to the tank after you have washed the undergravel filters and sand.*

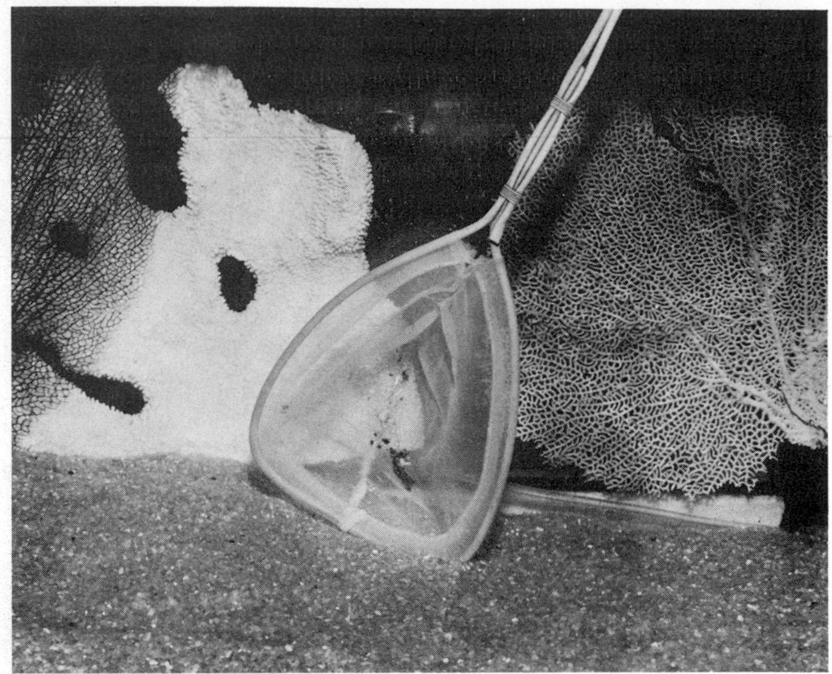

Fig. 51. *The FILTER NET, is a very fine nylon mesh net that is useful in cleaning the bottom of the tank. Simply sweep it back and forth along the bottom in a figure eight motion, so the bag stays open, and it will pick up a great deal of dirt and debris. This will aid both the outside and sub sand filters, and reduce the overall maintenance of the tank. It should be done once or twice a week.*

ium in a new and beautiful condition, care should be taken that it is not splashed on the outside of your aquarium or stand. Since this is nearly impossible, especially when you are working in the aquarium, the outside of your tank should be given a cleaning at least once a month. Rinse all metal surfaces with a sponge soaked in fresh water and dry thoroughly with a cloth. Wash the cover glass of the aquarium, and also check the light. Very often salt spray will get into it and unless this is removed, the light will rust badly. Rust or salt deposit on the stainless steel may be easily removed with an emery aquarium scraper, which has been moistened in fresh water. This useful gadget is simply a small square of rubber with an abrasive surface. It is also very useful inside the aquarium for removing stubborn algae.

Cleaning Glass. Many times a beautiful marine aquarium looks unkempt simply because the outside glass is dirty. This can often ruin an otherwise beautiful display. When salt water has spilled on the front glass of the aquarium, it must be removed with fresh water or the glass cannot be cleaned properly. It will smear and give the aquarium a very untidy appearance. To give your marine display the beauty it deserves, keep the front glass sparkling clean. It will brighten up the whole display.

First, rinse the glass lightly with fresh water. Then dry with paper towel, newspaper, or lint free cloth. Ordinary newspaper is actually the best cleaner. It is always available and you can use it profusely. It will amaze you how clean you can get the glass with a little effort and with sparkling clean water, it will look as though the fish are suspended in space and you will have a breath-taking display.

Cleaning Schedule With Live Coral

If the aquarium contains live coral, either with fish or by itself, it should be closely watched, especially during the first week or two. If the water in the aquarium does not become crystal clear within a few days or a week after coral has been placed in the tank, then some part or all of the coral is polluting the water and it should be removed from the aquarium if any signs of decay or lack of life are present. Sometimes a piece of sponge or a large mollusc attached to the coral may die, and this will quickly foul the water unless promptly removed. If the basic piece of coral appears healthy, quite often it may be left in the aquarium simply by removing the offending section, which may be a sponge, mollusc, or Gorgonia. These can be pruned from the main stem of coral and discarded.

Uneaten food and bits of decay or debris should be siphoned from around the base of the coral as well as from the corners of the aquarium. It usually is not necessary to move the coral if it appears healthy and the water is clear, as it is best left undisturbed. Once or twice a year or as needed, the end of the coral may be tipped up a few inches from the bottom so you can peer beneath it, and if there is considerable debris it should be carefully siphoned from the tank. The coral should be replaced in the same spot, as tiny marine creatures may be living in the sand beneath it. Live coral has the ability to clean the water and removes much suspended matter from the water in its natural process of feeding. Even on the reefs, this is very apparent, for on days when the water is extremely turbid it is usually clear directly on the reefs. In the aquarium, if the proper corals are chosen, the maintenance of the tank can be vastly reduced, for in addition to keeping the water clear and in a healthy condition, the coral polyps tend to eat much of the tiny pieces of food or decayed material which otherwise would settle in the sand and would need to be eventually removed from the tank. For this reason, unless the sand is very dirty or black from sulphide reaction, it will not be necessary to clean it for as long as six months to a year or more. A partial cleaning of the sand may be done by simply siphoning off the sand, particularly in the corners or along the edges of the tank where contamination of the sand may occur from contact with the aquarium cement. In this way, a little of the sand may be removed periodically without disturbing live plants or coral. Fresh sea water should be added to replace that which was drawn off with the sand. (Read Chapter 8 for additional information on live coral.)

Cloudy or Milky Water

The water in the aquarium may become cloudy or milky because of several different reasons. If you are using artificial water, it may sometimes become very cloudy shortly after the tank has been set up. This startles the aquarist at first but it is nothing to become alarmed about; all is not lost. It is a phenomenon of artificial water and is not uncommon. When first mixed, the water will become crystal clear, and after the tank is set up it will sparkle for a few days. Then suddenly it will become extremely dirty and cloudy. This is due to a chemical reaction of the salts with your local water supply. Some chemical in the fresh water causes the cloudiness. If this happens, turn up your filter or attach a power filter with activated carbon to the tank. The water will gradually clear and soon it will be crystal clear again. Sometimes it takes as long as two weeks to become really clear, depending upon the type of filtration and the size of the aquarium, but the clouding of the water does not seem to be harmful to the fish in any way. The condition seems to occur only when tap water is used for making artificial sea water and a change in temperature or atmospheric conditions seems to bring it on. The author has never seen it occur when the salts were mixed with well water or distilled water.

Another cause of cloudiness is from overfeeding, especially with fresh shrimp or scallop. These foods must be fed with the utmost care and should be shredded or chopped to the proper size so that the fish can swallow them without having to tear them apart. The foods should also be well washed and rinsed. If the water in the tank is milky due to overfeeding, the quickest way to clear it up is to remove all the coral, except perhaps for one or two pieces so the fish will have a place to hide, and then clean up the uneaten food with a fine mesh filter-net. This is a very fine mesh, nylon net, usually having a plastic frame. It can be a valuable aid in keeping your tank in good condition. Just sweep it back and forth along the bottom of the aquarium an inch or two above the sand, and you will see it lifting up particles of uneaten food and debris which will collect in the rear part of the net. Move the net slowly back and forth in a figure eight movement so that the bag stays open and you will be able to pick up a large portion of the uneaten food and dirt. Your aquarium will look cleaner almost at once. Replace the corals and clean under the two which you had left in the tank for hiding places. Then clean the carbon in your outside filter, and run the filter at maximum output. You may add a little copper solution to the tank as a safeguard against bacterial buildup. (See chapter 5)

Milky or cloudy water may also be caused from bacteria or parasites. The tank may become a living soup of minute organisms which may prove disastrous to the fish unless promptly treated. Copper sulfate solution seems to be the best, all around medication for this at the present time. Keep a bottle of the medication on hand and if your water becomes cloudy due to excess parasites or bacterial infestations, add the copper immediately. You can examine the water in the aquarium with a magnifying glass or low power lens, especially at night when the minute organisms will be seen swarming at the top near the light. Also, the fish will be breathing hard or scratching against the sand or coral. (See chapter 5 for complete instructions on parasite control)

The best defense against bacterial clouded water is to keep your tank as clean as possible at all times with good filtration and aeration. A weekly cleaning of the bottom of the tank with the filter-net, as mentioned above, should keep the tank sparkling clean when used in conjunction with the sub-sand filter and a good outside filter with activated carbon. It takes only a few minutes to thoroughly go over the bottom of the tank with the net and it will greatly prolong the length of time when the bottom sand will have to be washed. In fact, if the bottom of the tank is cleaned meticulously in this manner, the sand would need to be washed rarely, if ever.

Frequency of Water Change

This is a rather difficult question to answer as it depends on many factors: Such as:

A. Size of Aquariums. Small stainless steel aquariums under two gallons may need a complete change of water every three to six months depending how much life was sustained in them, whether or not the tank was sealed off with silicone rubber, how clean the aquarium was kept, and various other factors. If the tank was tightly covered and feeding and cleaning were tended to carefully, then the tank could probably go a year or more without a water change. Larger aquariums of ten to fifty gallons can often be maintained for at least a year without a complete water change if the tank is not too crowded. Sometimes a "Complete" change of water may do more harm than good because the fish will be accustomed to the old water and may not do as well in the new water. For this reason, rather than change all the water at one time, it is usually best to siphon out a small amount of water each month when you are cleaning the tank. This can serve a two-fold purpose. You can siphon out all the dirt and debris around the coral and along the edge of the aquarium, while you are removing the water. It is difficult to determine exactly how much water should be replaced each month as it depends on so many factors, but a rough estimate would be a tenth or twelfth of the total volume of water in the aquarium.

You could take this down to inches so that for a twelve-inch high aquarium, you would replace about one inch of water per month. The water should be replaced with aged artificial sea water or aged natural sea water which should be stored in glass jugs in a dark place before use. Replacing a small portion of water in the aquarium on a regular basis will keep the water from becoming excessively hard and should enable the aquarium to go on indefinitely. Of course it is possible to use the same water over and over for a year or several years without any change when using activated carbon or in the case of a natural aquarium, but even under these conditions, a partial water change would be better than none at all, especially if one wishes to add new fish from time to time.

B. Type of Container. All glass containers, or plastic containers where there will be no metal contact or cement trouble, can go much longer without changing the water, but to be completely safe, the water should be changed at least once or twice a year.

C. Condition of Water. (How to tell if it needs changing) If all the fish in the aquarium suddenly stop eating, and show no interest in food, yet there is sufficient air, the water is clear, and the fish have no signs of disease, then it is a good indication that the water needs changing. In this instance, a partial change may help, but if it doesn't then all the water should be replaced.

D. Bad Coral, Dead Fish, Dead Anemones. Water which has gone bad and has a very foul odor should be replaced with a fresh solution. Improperly cured coral often quickly fouls the water. Also large dead fish or a sea anemone can foul the water, and if it is in bad shape it should be replaced rather than try to filter it clean. This may take a little experimenting on your part to determine just how bad the water can go before it is completely useless. If it is only slightly milky and the fish show no real discomfort, it can usually be filtered and saved, but if it is very dirty and some of the fish have already died, then it should be replaced at once.

The same rules apply to artificial or natural sea water, although there is a considerable edge on natural sea water since it contains more of the natural minerals and other substances. A very broad rule would be to change the water completely once a year whether using artificial or natural sea water.

Adding New Fish

If an aquarium has been set up longer than three or four months, it is sometimes difficult to add new fish to this same aquarium, even though all the fish in the aquarium are doing fine. Not only will new fish be attacked by the older residents of the aquarium, but besides, they will have trouble adjusting to the differences in the water and may not survive more than a few days.

In view of this, it is always best to set up the aquarium with a full complement of fish at the beginning and if more fish are desired, another aquarium should be set up for them. However, if this is not practical, new fish can be introduced to the old aquarium by gradually getting them accustomed to the old water over a period of six to twelve days. The newcomers should be placed in a separate bowl in the water they arrive in, and given a shell to hide under. Then, each day take a cupful of water from the aquarium and add it to the bowl and in return take a cupful of water from the bowl and add it to the aquarium. After a week or two, the new fish may be floated in a small jar and slowly transferred to the aquarium. Often it is necessary to separate new fish with a sheet of glass when they are first placed in the aquarium if the other fish attack them. The older fish should be fed at the time of the transfer so that they will be occupied with eating when you add the new residents. Of course, if there is serious fighting, the offenders should be removed or isolated with the sheet of glass.

My Fish All Died!

If this tragedy should occur, it is best to start all over again. Discard the water, wash and soak the coral thoroughly, clean out the aquarium, try to determine what went wrong, and start from scratch. Don't try to use the same water over again even if it looks clean. Chances are there is something wrong with it or the fish wouldn't have died. If you have had no aquarium experience, it is always best to start small with a five or ten gallon aquarium and just one or two fish. The Beau Bregory and the Spider crab, for example, are the two good starters. They are both interesting and colorful and will give you the experience and confidence you need. If possible, get a little fresh sea water from your dealer and start out with these two specimens. They will live fine and grow by leaps and bounds. The author has raised them from tiny one-fourth-inch babies to maturity and found them to be one of the very best of all marine aquarium fish! Also, of course, the Dwarf Sea Horses are highly recommended for a beginner, as they are very easy to keep.

Reasons for Failure with Marine Aquarium

Listed below are a number of important factors that could lead to failure with your salt-water aquarium. Check over the list carefully and if one applies to you you will know what went wrong.

1. Hands were placed in aquarium without rinsing. This could have introduced soap or hand oils to tank, with harmful results.
2. Fish were not introduced to the aquarium properly. If fish were not floated in a jar or plastic bag and introduced to the tank slowly they could have developed "Ick" or they could suffer from shock, especially if changed from natural to artificial water.
3. Coral was not well cured.
4. Insufficient aeration. If not enough air, fish will die, sometimes slowly. Always have strong aeration so the water circulates all over the aquarium.
5. Fish were in poor condition when purchased. This is sometimes a leading factor and if the fish are in very bad condition it may well be impossible to save them. Before you purchase a fish examine it closely and observe whether or not it is swimming contentedly about the aquarium. Also be certain it is eating. If the fish will not eat and if it stays at the bottom or top of the aquarium without swimming around, it most likely is in poor health. Also check the fine, transparent portions of the fins for signs of "Ick" or fin rot and fungus. Never buy fish if they are dashing about the aquarium erratically or are continuously rubbing themselves against the coral as they are diseased and will infect your fish, and soon die unless quickly cured. It is especially important that you observe the fish for ten or fifteen minutes at least, before you buy. Many marine fish are being treated with copper sulfate before shipment and often the solution is too strong. The fish becomes poisoned and although he may not die right away, he will usually refuse food and gradually waste away. That's why it's important to see him eat before you buy. Healthy fish have healthy appetites.
6. If you had your fish flown in from an out-of-town dealer there can be complications that could lead to failure. At the present time, many dealers are using artificial sea water to ship their fish, and this could be a source of trouble. The fish first are caught by the collector, who brings them in to his main base, where they are then shipped to jobbers or dealers. Quite often the jobbers are not near the ocean, so they must use artificial sea water. The fish in this case are taken from natural sea water and transferred to artificial water before they are shipped. This is all right if the fish have been gradually acclimated to the artificial water, but sometimes that is not the case. The fish are simply dumped into the man-made water and shipped on to the dealers. Then the dealers, who may have an entirely different brand of artificial water, will put the fish into their mixture.

When the customer purchases the fish he may transfer them into still another brand of artificial water. The constant change from one type of water to another, each having a different *p*H and mineral structure can easily result in the death of the fish. Not only are synthetic sea water mixtures quite different in structure, but the fresh water this salt is mixed with to make sea water can vary tremendously from one state to another. Therefore, if it is possible, hobbyists or dealers should request that their fish be shipped in pure sea water so that they won't have to go through so many changes of salt solution. I suspect this one factor alone results in heavy losses of salt-water fish, both to dealer and hobbyist. If a fish is caught fresh from the sea and then shipped directly to the customer in pure sea water, the customer can float the fish in this same water and add the water to his aquarium. This will lessen the shock to the fish in the transition from natural water to man-made water and also add trace elements to the aquarium water.

Algae: Brown Spots on Coral

Many people ask what makes brown spots on the coral or glass. This is caused from algae and is nothing with which to be concerned. In fact a little algae, particularly green algae, can be highly beneficial to the aquarium as it tends to condition the water and helps to oxygenate it. Many of the fish also nibble on it and consume it as food. Very often when an aquarium has been set up for a few weeks dark patches will appear on the coral or on the sand. This is the first stage of algae. If it appears on the glass, it may easily be removed with an aquarium scraper or sponge. It is always caused by light so that if it becomes annoying and it is not wanted, it may be controlled by cutting down on the light in the aquarium. If the aquarium receives natural light from a window, then the tank should be shaded with cardboard or moved to another location where it gets less light. If the aquarium light itself has been left on a great deal, simply regulating the amount of time the light is left on will control the algae. However, if you want the algae to grow then of course you should leave the light on. Sometimes it will grow profusely in just a few weeks; other times it will hardly grow at all. Apparently it depends upon the condition of the aquarium water, the intensity of the light, and numerous other factors. But at any rate, the dark spots that appear on your corals and glass are nothing to worry about. Simply cut down on the light and they will usually disappear or add copper solution to the aquarium if reducing the light doesn't bring the desired results. Ordinary plastic window screen is excellent for removing stubborn algae from the glass. Use a six-inch square of screen and fold it into a pad. It will remove the most stubborn algae from either glass or plastic aquariums with little or no danger of scratching the surface. (See Chapter 4 for more on algae.)

Deadly Plant and Lacquer

If you have just finished painting or spraying furniture in your home, and a marine aquarium which was doing well suddenly goes completely bad, then undoubtedly the fumes have reached your display. Nothing is more disheartening than to lose a beautiful tankful of fish through your own carelessness. Yet, each year many expensive aquariums are subjected to the dangers of paint and lacquer, usually with fatal results. The best procedure, if painting is to be done in the fish room, is to empty the aquarium down about half way and move it to another room where it will be out of danger. This will be far better than taking a chance with the expensive marine fish.

Covering the aquarium tightly is seldom effective for protection against paint fumes, as the air pump picks up the vapors and distributes them to the aquarium under the glass. Quite often a fish will not die for several days after exposure depending on how severe the fumes were. So rather than go through useless apprehension, in the long run it will be to your advantage to move the aquarium if painting must be done in the room. The aquarium should be moved very carefully so that it won't leak. If it is fairly large, the job will take two people and the stand and all should be carried intact rather than move the aquarium separately.

Fly spray and other insecticides are also harmful to the aquarium fish and these should not be sprayed near the tank. However, if spray or other dangerous fumes are suspected of having come in contact with the aquarium, the water surface of the aquarium should be cleaned. This is accomplished by laying a sheet of newspaper on the water and drawing it slowly across the surface and out of the aquarium. Oil or scum will adhere to the paper and after several applications, most of the surface film will be removed. Do not allow the newspaper to soak in the aquarium as the ink could also do harm. Just lie it flat briefly on the water, and then drag it slowly over the rim of the tank. Paper towels also do an excellent job and are a little safer than newspaper and should be used if they are available.

The Hydrometer

Hydrometers come in two general sizes; large and small, and although both may give a fairly accurate reading, the larger size is recommended for the fish dealer and the marine aquarist who in-

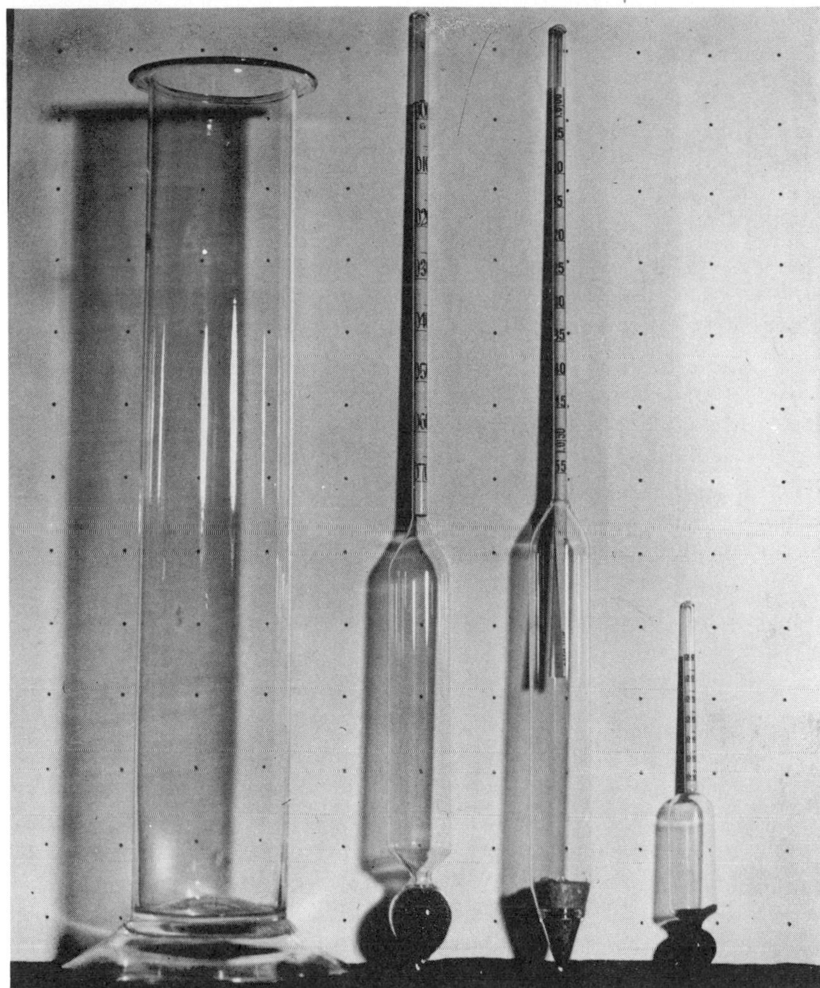

Fig. 52. *The hydrometer is indispensable for the serious marine aquarist. The larger models are more accurate and easier to read than the smaller types. Hydrometer may be floated in aquarium or, if aquarium is not deep enough, it may be placed in vial which has been filled with sea water (left). Reading is taken directly at the water line when hydrometer settles.*

tends to do serious work. Also, since the larger type is easier to read, and gives a much more accurate reading, it should be used when mixing artificial sea water so that the correct salinity or specific gravity may be determined as accurately as possible. The smaller hydrometer is much less expensive and may still be used quite successfully by the hobbyist, for although it is not as accurate as the larger type, it is still sufficiently accurate, as the specific gravity or density of the water is not too critical as long as it is maintained at a reasonable level. Small hydrometers have the advantage, in that they can be inserted in shallow aquariums to take a reading; while with the larger instrument, a quantity of the water must be placed in a vial or other deep container before a reading can be taken.

Taking the Reading

Place hydrometer in aquarium slowly so that no bubbles form along the stem and allow it to float in the aquarium. After it has completely settled, and lies motionless in the water, the reading is taken directly at the surface of the water. This should be around 1.025 or slightly less. Some aquarists keep it at 1.022 and this slight variation makes little difference. If the hydrometer rises high in the water up to around 1.030 or more, then it is time to add fresh water and bring it back down to 1.025 or less, if you are keeping it that way. The most accurate reading is made with the large hydrometer and vial. Water is taken from the aquarium and the vial is filled to about an inch from the top and the hydrometer inserted slowly. When it comes to rest, the reading may be taken. Technically, the hydrometer is not the most accurate way of checking the salt content of the aquarium water, but it is accurate enough for salt-water fish keeping.

It is not recommended to keep the hydrometer floating in the aquarium when not in use as it will pick up surface scum and oil and will give a false reading. It should be carefully wiped with a clean cloth before each reading and stored in its vial, or a glass jar if it is the smaller type, when not in use.

In warm climates of 90 degree temperatures and over, salinity should be checked once a week and fresh water added weekly, if necessary. In most temperate climates, it may be checked twice a month, or monthly if there is little evaporation. If the aquarium is filled to about an inch from the top, or so it is just even with the bottom edge of the stainless steel frame, fresh water may be added whenever it drops below this mark, and then it would usually be necessary to check with a hydrometer just once a month.

4

Feeding Marine Tropicals

Many salt-water fish in home aquariums die of starvation. So much emphasis has been placed on the danger of overfeeding for fear of pollution, the general public has gone to the other extreme and many unwittingly allowed their pets to slowly wither away and die.

Since marine fish are usually very active, they must be fed often and in sufficient quantity so that their vivacious appetites are fully satisfied. Unlike their fresh-water relatives, who may nibble on plants when the aquarist neglects their meals, the marine fish is solely dependent upon food placed in his artificial home by you. In this barren, hospital-clean atmosphere, the marine fish hopelessly nibbles on long dead coral that contains not a trace of food. There are no plants to appease his appetite and the thoughtful aquarist, trying to do right, has removed every last trace of food that was not instantly eaten, so that the unfortunate fish is in a constant state of hunger.

But each year, we are learning more and more about marine fish. Even now there are beautiful plants and algae that will help alleviate this situation. Not only do they decorate the marine aquarium, giving that much-needed touch of green, but more important, they act as a supplement in the diet of the fish.

Furthermore, with the addition of the sub-sand filter, there is much less chance of an aquarium going bad because of excess food left in the aquarium. A few scraps of fresh shrimp left on the bottom will provide something for hungry fish to nibble on in between meals.

The author has spent endless hours beneath the sea observing the feeding habits of the coral fish. It was found that the Angelfish, Demoiselles, Jewel fish, and other small-mouthed beauties, fed chiefly on algae and that it constitutes much of their main diet. Therefore, it seems logical that in the aquarium some form of algae must be present to insure that the marine fish will keep its health and color over a long period of time. This is still in the experimental state,

Fig. 53. *Black Angelfish nibbles at marine plants in the aquarium. This vegetation undoubtedly provides food between meals.*

however, and although there are some advantages in growing algae in the aquarium, there is also the disadvantage that it requires much more cleaning and maintenance of the tank.

How to Grow Marine Algae
(Location of the aquarium is important!)

Choose a location that is comparatively draft free and will receive a small amount of sunlight in one corner of the tank at some time of the day. Avoid too much light for it will cause such rapid growth of algae that maintenance will be difficult.

Some forms of marine algae will grow merely by the introduction of light. Strong natural light from a window often induces algae to grow on the coral facing the source of light. This process may be hastened by using a fluorescent light over the aquarium. Keep the light on continuously for several days or longer and the algae will usually start forming in small patches at the greatest concentration of light. If the algae forms on the glass, wipe it off with a clean handkerchief, so that it will only grow on the coral. It usually starts in very tiny patches gradually spreading in all directions as it grows. After a good growth of algae has formed, turn the unexposed areas

Fig. 54. *Green algae grows on most of the coral in this aquarium. It was cultivated by giving the aquarium excess light. The young Queen Angelfish feeds upon the algae which is very similar to its natural food.*

of the coral toward the light so that the growth will be even and attractive.

It is possible by using this method, to have a beautiful green mantle of algae that will completely cover all the coral in the aquarium and even grow on the sand. The fish will continuously feed and nibble on this healthful food in much the same way that they do on the reef and it will give the water a healthy condition which may prolong the lives of the marine fish over an indefinite period of time.

Some aquarists like to grow algae on the back and side glass of the aquarium, leaving only the front glass clear for observation. This is a healthful procedure and if the aquarium is properly maintained, with new sea water added occasionally to revitalize the whole condition, it could develop into perhaps a suitable spawning medium for marine fish.

The meticulous aquarist who doesn't want green algae to grow on his beautiful coral, may still add this important food element to his exhibit. First, he should locate his aquarium where it will receive little or no natural light. Under these conditions, any algae growth can be completely controlled by the light above the aquarium. Next, he should place a small piece of coral in a two-gallon bowl partly filled with fresh sea water, and place in it a window where it will receive strong sunlight. After several days or more, a fine growth of green algae will form on the coral. The coral may then be placed in the aquarium and another small chunk placed in the bowl for greening. Usually after two or three greening processes, the water in the bowl will need replacing with fresh sea water, and the whole process repeated as often as needed. This controlled greening process is especially useful for the display aquarist who must maintain aquariums outside his own home where daily inspection is not possible.

Brown algae often forms where there is insufficient light to maintain the green growth. It often grows first in the aquarium and as the water becomes aged, it gradually turns into the more desirable green color. Sometimes the green algae will start, but lacking sufficient light, it will die and turn brown.

If the whole aquarium turns green it is because there is too much light. In this case, the situation may be remedied by covering the aquarium completely for a week or more and then if the water is clear, the first covering may be removed. If the water continues to get green, it is best that the aquarium be moved to a new location where there is not so much light.

Marine Plants

Most marine plants are classified scientifically as algae. This includes many of the decorative leafy varieties seen by the underwater adventurer and includes practically everything except the grasses which are the true plants.

No attempts should be made to grow marine vegetation in the aquarium unless the sub-sand filter is used, for without it you will have little success. Poisonous gases will soon form beneath the sand with disastrous results. The plants should be planted in an inch or two of coure silica sand. They should be planted the same as any other plant, piling the sand carefully around the roots and part way up the base, so that the plant is well anchored. The fluorescent light over the aquarium should be left on for several days until the plant takes on a rich green color and then the light need only be turned on when looking at the exhibit. A fluorescent light is recommended instead of the incandescent type because it may be left on for long periods of time without creating excessive heat at the top of the aquarium. Also, it gives more light and although the initial cost of this type of unit is somewhat higher than the other, its operating cost is much less and the bulb itself has a very long life span.

Very often during transportation, some marine plants will lose all traces of color. They may appear to be dead but if in a firm, healthy condition, they will get back their natural green appearance after several days in the aquarium—provided there is plenty of light.

Properly-collected marine plants should contain a small clump of the actual sea bottom and this should be left intact when transplanted in the aquarium. Not only does this protect the roots, but it also contains important natural food and nourishment which will insure the life and growth of the plant in the aquarium. It requires much care and research to determine the proper vegetation for a salt water tank. An aquarist who fills his display aquarium with a multitude of various types of algaes, without first testing them, may be in for trouble. He may awake some morning to find that a penetrating odor is asphyxiating the household. Upon further examination, he may find that by following his nose he will soon be in front of his marine tank and that the asphyxiating odor is coming from same. Most plants just won't live in the aquarium and to avoid complete ruin of a beautiful display, the marine underwater horticulturist should proceed with caution. Try marine plants in a small experimental tank first, then if they are successful, you may introduce them to your main aquarium. Most forms of kelp, seaweed, etc., will not live in the aquarium, but there is a tremendous field of exploration and experimentation to be done in selecting and trying new types of marine vegetation for the salt water aquarium. (See Chapter 8 for further information.)

Fig. 55. *Mushroom or rose coral is readily eaten by the dainty Four Eye Butterfly fish who shuns most foods. The coral may be placed in the tank while it is alive or it may be frozen and used as needed. Sometimes the Butterfly fish will eat scallop which has been pressed into a piece of the rose coral to simulate the live polyp.*

Live Coral as Food

The addition of one or two pieces of live coral which is partly overgrown with live algae will furnish food for many marine fish, particularly the Angelfish and Butterfly fish. This will supplement their aquarium diet and often the fish will retain their spectacular colors much longer than in an aquarium without this special food. Young fish a half-inch to an inch will usually mature faster and have better color when live coral is introduced to the aquarium. They will be seen constantly nibbling on the coral in much the same fashion as they do out in the ocean, and since baby fish must eat a great deal, the success of raising them to maturity will be increased with live coral. Of course, as pointed out earlier, live corals will usually require fresh sea water, and if the aquarist is using an artificial mix he should mix a portion of fresh sea water to his tank if he wishes to add live coral. In this instance, it would be best to use a very small piece first to determine whether it is going to live. Then if it is successful, larger pieces may be added. Algae-covered rocks are also excellent as a source of food for the Tangs, Angelfish, and small Parrot fish. These should be placed in the tank where they will get good light and should be removed when all the algae is eaten and replaced with a new rock. Some aquarists cultivate algae on clean rocks by placing the rocks in a fish bowl in sea water and putting them in a window where they get strong sunlight. When the algae is quite dense, the stone is placed in the aquarium as food. Algae-covered rocks from the sea are especially good, as they contain a fine assortment of algaes which afford a superb diet for the fish. These may be collected near shore or shipped to inland aquarists by collectors.

One type of mushroom or rose coral is especially suitable as food for the Four Eye Butterfly fish. It will eagerly devour the polyp of this coral and will thrive on it. Dr. Marshall Bishop, a well-known marine aquarist of long standing, demonstrated this to the author and it was an amazing sight. Dr. Bishop had a dozen or more Four Eye Butterfly fish so tame that they would all swim to the top of the tank and actually eat from his fingers! This particular fish is normally rather shy and a finicky eater, but it will eat the mushroom coral ravenously. The coral may be fed in the live state or it can be frozen and thawed before feeding. Dr. Bishop deserves much credit for his discovery, which will help other aquarists keep the delicate Butterfly fish.

When to Feed . . . What to Feed . . . How to Feed

Marine fish should be fed three or four times a day. If this is not

he Deep Bigeye (Pseudopriacanthus altus) *is a prized aquarium fish d relatively rare in comparison to the common bigeye. The Deep geye has a very short, rounded body while the common bigeye is more ɔngated.*

he Emperor Angelfish (Pomacanthus imperator) *is one of the most lorful of angelfish from the Indo-Pacific area. It is among the most ghly prized of Pacific marine fish for the aquarium.*

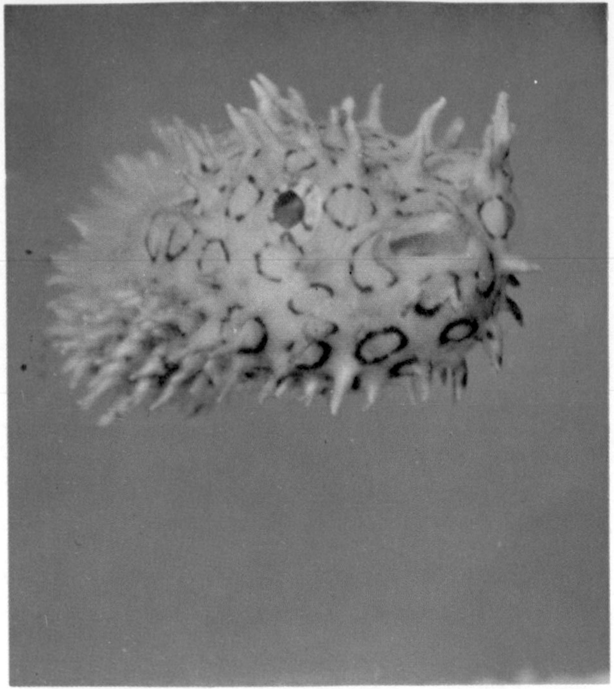

The Sausage Fish or Clown Boxfish (Chilomycterus sp.) *is a most unusual fish that hardly looks like a fish at all. This specimen comes from Florida and Bahama water, but similar species are found in all tropical oceans.*

The spectacular deepwater Jacknife or Ribbon Fish (Eques) *is a rare gem from the deep reefs. It differs from the shallow water, inshore species in that it is more spectacular, having a wider dorsal which it unfurls like a flag. It becomes spotted along the soft dorsal and anal fins as it matures making it even more exotic in appearance.*

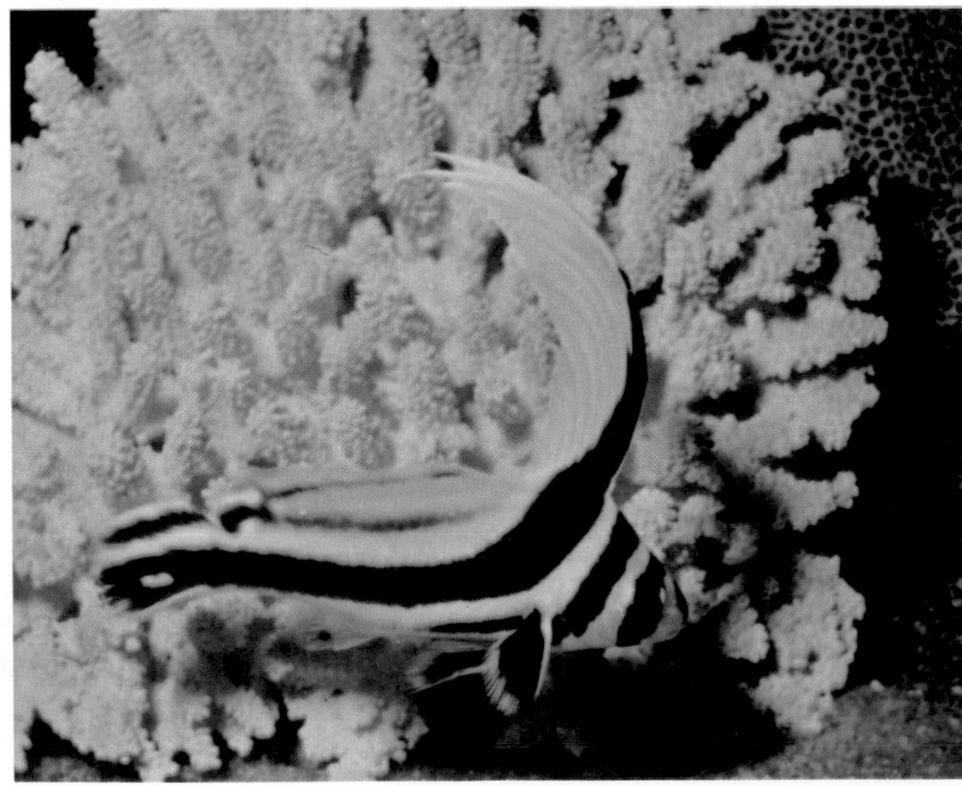

Fig. 56. *Common salad grater is ideal for shredding small amounts of chopped shrimp or scallop. First, peel the fresh shrimp and scallop and freeze it a day or two in the freezer. Then, shred it on the widest holes as shown here. It comes out a perfect size for most small aquarium fish. The shredded shrimp should be rinsed well with fresh water to remove milky juice. The author uses a mixture of three-quarters shrimp to one-quarter scallop and freezes it in one clump.*

possible, morning and night feeding will suffice if done properly. Importance of the green algae can be realized here, for with this extra source of food in the aquarium, the often-hungry marine fish will have something to nibble on between meals; whereas in an aquarium with no extra source of food, the fish will soon be nibbling on each other. Baby fish, tiny Angels, etc. should be fed much more often than the larger fish, and a continuous supply of live brine shrimp will insure them sufficient food.

What to feed. Marine fish should be fed a variety of foods which may include fresh shrimp, dry food, lean beef, beef heart, white-worm, tubiflex worms, brine shrimp, live or frozen, daphnae, green algae, baby guppies, small minnows, etc. Although all of these foods are good, for practical purposes, a good main diet would be fresh shrimp, dry food, lean beef, and green algae if possible. About twice a week a good feeding of live brine shrimp will be appreciated by most of the smaller fish.

How to feed dry food. Most of the marine tropicals will eat and enjoy dry food. Some will eat it immediately, others must be trained to this type of food by other fish. Sergeant Majors, Beau Gregories, Orange Demoiselles, Filefish, Jewell fish, etc., will all eat dry food readily. It is best to start the aquarium with a few Sergeant Majors or one or two of these active feeders as they will encourage the more timid fish to eat.

Select a coarse grade of tropical fish food and choose a known brand that is enriched with vitamins and minerals. Do not feed new specimens for a couple of days until they have become accustomed to their new home. Then sprinkle a small amount of food on the surface and remain perfectly still. Until the fish become accustomed to you, any sudden movement outside the aquarium will interrupt their feeding and send them scurrying to the safety of the coral. Then feeding will have to be delayed until they have overcome their fright. Usually the active feeders like the Sergeant Majors and others mentioned above, will take the dry food immediately, but if they

Fig. 57. *A beautiful Pacific Long Nosed Butterflyfish eating tiny shreds of scallop. Because of its extremely specialized mouth, the fish could not eat chunks of shrimp as it could not tear the shrimp apart. In fact if it tried to swallow a piece of shrimp that was too large it could easily choke on it as the food would become lodged in its narrow throat. Fish with tiny mouths should be fed live brine shrimp, white worms, tubifex worms, or very finely chopped shrimp or scallop.*

are a little shy and don't come to the surface, tap the food slightly and it will sink to the bottom. If aquarium conditions are right, the fish will usually intercept the food before it reaches the bottom and you will have been successful in getting them to eat. Soon you will find them eagerly swimming about the aquarium when you approach their home with the familiar food can. Always watch all specimens at feeding time to be sure that each receives food at meal time. Sometimes a shy individual will starve to death unless removed to another aquarium where there is less competition.

Feed just enough of the dry food so that it is all eaten in five or ten minutes. Should a larger amount be accidentally spilled, remove it with a fine dipnet; otherwise it may foul the water. Certain large-mouthed fish, like the Cardinal, Squirrel fish, Sargassum fish, etc. will seldom eat dry food. You may still give them the benefits of this food by making a food ball of fresh shrimp mixed with dry food. Squeeze it into a tight ball and feed it to them along with their regular food. It will give them added vitamins and may prolong their lives considerably.

How to feed fresh shrimp. Fresh shrimp has long been recognized by aquarists as an excellent food for adding growth and vitality to their aquarium fish. It is rich in vitamins, highly nutritious, and practically every salt-water fish will eat it if it is introduced to them properly. It should be chopped into small, bite-sized pieces, rinsed slightly under running water to remove excess juices, and then generously fed to the fish, so that each will have plenty to eat. If a few small pieces fall to the bottom, they need not be removed right away when the fish are eating well for they will usually consume these stray pieces during the day. However, if this uneaten food is not consumed by nightfall, it is best to remove it with a small net or diptube rather than take a chance of it fouling the water. A small piece of plywood four or five inches long makes an excellent chopping board for cutting the shrimp into bite-sized chunks. Bite-sized chunks refers to the fish rather than the aquarist. Don't put huge chunks of shrimp in the aquarium and expect your little pets to swallow them. If they have small mouths, cut the food into tiny pieces so that it may be easily swallowed. Large mouthed fish like the Cardinal and Squirrel fish can take a fairly large-sized chunk of food. Porcupine fish, six inches or more, will often eat the entire tail section of the shrimp and the shell should be left on the shrimp when feeding to these interesting fellows. Spiny Boxfish also like their shrimp with the shell left on for they like to crush their food with their powerful jaws. Some of the larger fish, who just won't associate chopped shrimp with their natural food, can be taught to eat this food by obtaining one or two live shrimp from a bait store and

Fig. 58. *Fresh shrimp is a good basic food for most marine fish. Large quantities of ordinary eating shrimp, table variety, may be chopped at one time and stored for future use. Equipment needed will be fish net or strainer, jar, shrimp, Osterizer and wax paper.* Do not *use a regular blender. Use only the Osterizer with the chopping blades which require no liquid.*

feeding these to the hungry fish. Then as the lucky fellow chops his food into small enough pieces to swallow, you may drop a few chunks of the shrimp nearby and he will usually consume this added food along with his meal. This method is quite effective with large Porcupines, Scorpion fish, Sea Robins and other large-mouthed fish who are accustomed to eating living food in their natural environment.

Fresh shrimp may be purchased in the local fish market or grocery store. If it is bought in the frozen condition, thaw out one or two tails or whatever amount you will need at one feeding. A toothpick will come in handy for placing the shrimp in the aquarium. It should be fed once or twice daily, preferably in the morning so that all the stray pieces will be cleaned up by nightfall.

Live brine shrimp. This is an excellent tidbit and a healthy food for the marine tropical. It should be fed several times a week if possible, especially to the smaller fish. Care should be taken to feed only the live shrimp and not the eggs to your pets. Usually if you

Fig. 59. *The fresh shrimp should be washed, peeled and then frozen solid in freezer before chopping. Next, start Osterizer motor and drop several tails onto the blades, replacing the cover of machine quickly so that pieces will not fly out. After ten or fifteen seconds, if the shrimp is completely chopped, remove lid and add several more chunks of shrimp until chopped shrimp piles up to the cutting blades. Then shut off motor, fill glass container with water and pour through net as shown above. Do not put any water in machine while grinding shrimp or it will become a sticky, useless mess. The food chops best when frozen dry and solid.*

Fig. 60. *After the shrimp has been washed, chopped and drained, divide it into daily rations. Then cover with wax paper and keep in the freezer until needed. This method takes care of a month's supply of chopped shrimp.*

will allow the brine shrimp container to settle for a half hour or so, the brine shrimp will all congregate in one section and may be siphoned through a handkerchief, leaving most of the eggs in the container. The handkerchief may then be dipped into the aquarium until the shrimp have been rinsed off. Be sure that you use a clean handkerchief that has been thoroughly rinsed in fresh water to remove all traces of soap!

Hatching instructions for the shrimp are supplied with the eggs. Also, your local pet shop or tropical fish store will be happy to help you with suggestions for rearing sufficient brine shrimp to supply your needs. Some stores carry the live shrimp already hatched and will sell a good portion at a reasonable price.

Butterfly fish, dwarf Sea Horses, Neon Gobies and very small marine fish should be fed live brine shrimp daily and in good quantities. The outside filter should be turned off during the first half hour of feeding so that the main portion of shrimp will be consumed by the fish rather than be drawn into the filter. The filter may then be turned on slowly until nightfall when it should be run at its normal speed. However, if you are at all forgetful, it is best not to turn off the filter just for the sake of a few brine shrimp, especially if the filter is aerating the aquarium.

Fig. 61. *The Lion fish may be fed by placing food on the end of a toothpick fastened to a wooden dowel. This enables the food to be placed directly in the fish's mouth without hands coming in contact with the poisonous spines.*

Fig. 62. *A Batfish eating a small minnow offered to it on the end of a slender stick. Many shy aquarium feeders such as the anglerfish, batfish, lionfish, stonefish, and other fish who normally eat live foods, may be tempted to eat by impaling a minnow on a slender rod and moving the food temptingly in front of them.*

Live earthworms. This is a superb food for most of the larger marine fish. It is readily obtainable and inexpensive and various sizes can be obtained to suit the specimens being fed. The worms are best consumed if broken in halves or smaller pieces depending upon the size of the fish eating them. Sargassum fish, Spiny Boxfish, Porcupine fish, Cowfish, large Angelfish, Cardinal fish, to mention a few, are especially fond of them and they can constitute a main part of the diet of these fish.

Fish roe. A healthy, rich food which may be fed to baby fish or larger specimens. It is often sold in a canned condition or frozen, and can be obtained fresh from fishermen. Most fish eat it readily, but it should be fed cautiously as it gives off milky juice which can foul the water. The author finds it beneficial as a treat rather than the main food and gives it to the fish once or twice a month. Baby fish are fed this food more often, usually weekly, as they must eat more often than the larger specimens.

Adult brine shrimp. Large Sea Horses, and a few of the more delicate marine specimens like the Butterfly fish, Pearl fish, etc., will eat only living food as a general rule. The brine shrimp may be reared to adult size with a little patience and practice. Place a five gallon jar or old aquarium in a window where it will receive strong sunlight. Fill with fresh sea water or salt brine solution and let it age for a week or two. Then add a good hatch of live brine shrimp from your regular hatching jar and if conditions are right, you will be a full fledged adult brine shrimp grower. In a few weeks, the shrimp will mature and even reproduce in the container. By siphoning off just a portion at a time, you will have a continued supply of this superb food. Green algae will form along the sides of the container and will furnish food for the growing shrimp so that all you will have to do is check the salinity occasionally and add a little fresh water when necessary. About every three or four months, replace about one fourth of the solution with fresh sea water and if all goes well, the growing process will go on indefinitely. If the container is left outside, cover it partially with a piece of glass so that just a little rain will enter the container during storms. Aeration is helpful where a large quantity is desired, but it is not necessary if clean water is used and the container is not too crowded. Evidently the growing algae give off oxygen for the author has raised large quantities in the method described above and used neither aeration nor food.

Other foods. Mosquito larvae, daphnia, tubiflex worms, white

Fig. 63. *Sharp-toothed specimens like this Queen Triggerfish, should be fed by impaling food on toothpick. This protects fingers from over-anxious eaters.*

worms, chopped earthworms, etc. all make tempting food for your marine tropicals. They should be fed if the fish will eat them right away, as they die quickly in salt water. Feed a few at a time so that the fish will clean them up before more are added.

Frozen brine shrimp. This is a fair food and should be fed cautiously. Place a small chunk in a fish net and rinse under running water. This will thaw it out and remove the milky juices that will otherwise cloud up the aquarium. It should not be used as a main diet for it does not seem to contain sufficient food value and hence should be used as a treat rather than the basic food. The adult frozen brine shrimp only should be used in marine aquariums, unless you are attempting to raise baby marine tropicals.

Lean beef or beef heart. Many successful marine aquarists report this to be an excellent food. It should be chopped or scraped into very small bite-sized chunks and then rinsed under running water to remove excess juices. Very small shredded pieces of raw beef will often tempt the delicate eaters and is a highly nutritious food. Very often, when a fish stops eating, it may be tempted with this choice delicacy.

Fig. 64. *Sea anemones should be fed half-inch chunks of fresh shrimp, with the shell removed. Food must be dropped on their tentacles, or placed directly in their grasp as shown here.*

Fig. 65. *Live minnows intended as food for the Lion fish, should be floated in the aquarium and introduced gradually so that the minnows will not develop "Ick" and infect the entire aquarium if they are not eaten. Note the interest this fellow shows in his prospective meal. This is a healthy sign.*

Live plankton. This is no doubt one of nature's most perfect foods for all marine tropicals. It may be gathered in the ocean with fine plankton nets and frozen for future use. When marine tropicals are raised in captivity, this will be probably the only food that the young fry will eat. Certain marine research laboratories have raised baby salt-water fish from the larvae stage to a length of several inches by feeding this superb food. Actually, plankton is the basis of all the fish in the sea and no more perfect food exists. The author has planned for many years to process and freeze this choice food so that it may be shipped to the marine aquarist throughout the nation, but there are still numerous problems to be worked out. When it does prove practical, it may solve the feeding problem for practically all the salt-water aquarium specimens.

Live foods. Occasional specimens will eat nothing but live foods. The large Sea Horse in particular must have living food in one form or another and if you live near the seashore, his feeding problem will be somewhat easier. Small, half-inch shrimp, which is the Sea Horses' natural food, may be collected from the floating seaweed, or may be gathered from the grasses that grow close to shore. Simply run a fine net through the grass and you will collect many small shrimp suitable as food for the pet horses. Even in fresh water, little shrimp may be collected in the same manner.

Large-mouthed specimens like the Sargassum fish, Cardinal, Scorpion, Batfish, etc., will demand an occasional minnow of fair size. Usually a minnow one-fourth the body length of your pet will be accepted as a good meal. Very often you can start your pet eating by feeding live food and then gradually change him over to fresh shrimp. The author has discovered that even the Sargassum fish, which formerly was believed to eat nothing but live food, could be trained to eat chunks of fresh shrimp by teasing it with the food. In this case, the food is held on a toothpick and touched slightly against the "Fishing Rod" on the Sargassum's nose. He will make a vicious grab and the food will be gone in one mad gulp. Many other fish may be tempted to eat in this manner. A good procedure is to drop several chunks of food directly in front of the specimen, remain perfectly still, and if the pet doesn't eat the food right away, remove it promptly and try again later on.

Most fresh-water fish will not live more than a day in salt water, so if they are placed in the aquarium as food, be sure to take them out when they die. Mollies, however, can often live in salt water indefinitely and make a fine food for marine fish. Their babies are especially suitable for large Sea Horses.

My Fish Won't Eat! Why?

Check the salinity. The salt-water aquarium should be maintained at a specific gravity reading of 1.025 or slightly less. As the solution evaporates, most of the salts stay in the aquarium, making the solution denser and less livable for your pets. Fresh water must be added to bring the water back to normal and either rain water or distilled water should be used. Tap water often contains an excess of minerals and should not be used. It takes so little water to replace that which has evaporated that this hardly presents a problem for you can catch enough rain water during a storm to last you a year. If the salinity is off too much, your pets will not eat until the situation is corrected.

Improper aquarium conditions. This is the main reason why fish refuse food and often it can be detected at a glance. If the water is slightly milky, or has a bad odor, something is wrong and immediate steps should be taken to protect the lives of your fish. Very often, the coral was not sufficiently cleaned and should be checked first as a possible source of trouble. If it is blackish on the bottom and has a foul odor, remove it promptly and replace with a clean piece. As a precaution, it is always best ot remove the coral from the aquarium once a week during the first month, wash it thoroughly and replace it. This is usually only necessary for about a month or so, or until you are certain that the coral is free from any decomposing elements within. The nose test is one of the most accurate ways for testing coral. If the coral smells bad, it is bad!

Toxic aquarium cement. Some aquarium cements are poisonous to marine fish. All new aquariums should be soaked in brine solution for several days before use. Put three or four tablespoons of salt to the gallon of water, mix thoroughly, and leave this solution in the aquarium until you are ready to set up the exhibit. Questionable tanks should have the seams sealed with fiberglass rosin or plastic sealant.

Overcrowding. Too many fish in an aquarium will create a dangerous condition. If just one dies during the night, it could start a chain reaction and kill every fish in the aquarium. Crowding too many fish together in a small space will make them uncomfortable, even though they have enough aeration and they may refuse to eat. Only certain marine fish can be kept together and if an aggressive specimen is placed in the aquarium, the other fish will be fearing for their lives and certainly won't be interested in eating. Observe each fish in the aquarium very carefully. If you see a bully, take him out or he may kill the other fish. If you see an especially shy specimen who is afraid to come out in the open during feeding time, take him out also for otherwise he will starve to death. In this case, however, it is best to first load the aquarium with live brine shrimp as this free-swimming food will reach every section of the tank and the bashful one will be able to eat without exposing himself to the slightest danger.

Improper aeration or filtration. Marine Jewell fish, Blue Reef fish, Rock Beauties, etc. need plenty of aeration and will show little interest in food if denied this necessity. They may even give up the ghost if there isn't enough oxygen in the water. Use a rapid-flow filter rather than air stones as the latter tend to evaporate the water too fast. The sub-sand filter should be used in every marine aquarium as it gives circulation of the water and eliminates the harmful gases usually present in the bottom of the aquarium. If an outside filter is used, clean it periodically, so that it will not be a source of contamination. Often the very source of trouble can be traced to the filter which has been neglected.

Temperature. Keep the temperature between 70 and 80 degrees at all times. If the temperature rises above that, be sure to increase the aeration as the warm water loses its oxygen content. Improper

Fig. 66. *The author feeds a pet French Angelfish by hand in one of his aquariums. These beautiful fish quickly become tame and can recognize the aquarist from several feet away.*

temperatures will affect the general health of the fish and they will not eat, especially if the water is cold. If you don't have a heater, you may leave the aquarium light on during cold snaps and this will help a great deal.

Sea lice. Large Sea Horses are usually infested with sea lice. These flat, quarter-inch-long parasites, will multiply rapidly in the aquarium and soon rob the Sea Horse of bodily nourishment. He will refuse to eat any food until they are removed. Inspect the Sea Horse before placing him in the aquarium and remove all lice with a pair of tweezers. The lice are free swimming and once they have settled in an aquarium, it is difficult to control them. A few fish collectors will painstakingly remove all lice from the Sea Horses before they are shipped, but these collectors are in the minority so you must do the job yourself. Also, there are often eggs on the horse which hatch after the specimen has been in the aquarium for some time.

Other forms of sea lice and parasites will live on the fish and their control is still a matter of experimentation. Methylene Blue, if used fresh, can be used as a germicide for parasite control. Make a stock solution of one level teaspoon of Methylene Blue to twelves ounces of fresh water. Use one teaspoon of this solution to each gallon of aquarium water for treatment of diseases. Methylene Blue must be used right after it is mixed for maximum results.

5

Disease in the Marine Aquarium

Salt-water fish were formerly thought to be practically free of diseases in comparison to their fresh-water relatives. Now we have found that they have many similar diseases. It is reasonable to presume many are yet undiscovered due to the complexity of salt water. It will take years to identify even a portion of the diseases which may affect the salt-water aquarium fish but at present considerable progress has been made so that at least some of the ailments can be cured.

External Parasites and Bacterial Infestations

The salt water hobby has increased in such magnitude that we now have disease and bacterial infestations on a world-wide scale with which to contend. To go into an actual diagnosis of specific diseases would be impractical at this time, for little is known as to the exact identity of few, if any, salt water aquarium diseases. Unfortunately, many of the disease symptoms are identical so far as fish behavior is concerned, yet the minute organism causing them may be startlingly different. A marine micro-biologist has informed the author that to positively identify a specific organism that caused the death of a fish in the marine aquarium would be a gigantic project, entailing several years of painstaking work by a trained scientist with assistants who would have to cultivate every living organism in the water, determine which organisms were harmful, and finally, which organisms had actually caused the death of the fish. The results would take years, and even then they may not be absolutely certain.

For this reason, we can only treat general conditions in the aquarium. We can treat the water to make it toxic enough to kill off many of the harmful marine organisms, yet not toxic enough to kill the fish. Copper sulfate solution seems to be the most practical medication for general use, and when used properly, it will not kill the fish. As aquarist Michael Martin of Hawaii pointed out to the author, most people kill their fish by NOT *adding enough* copper to their tank rather than adding too much. Very often, a single, proper dose of copper added to a tank of gasping fish will bring almost immediate relief, especially if the tank is carefully cleaned of all uneaten foods with a fine net at the same time the medication is added.

Copper Sulfate Solution for General Use

Unless one collects all his own fish in a clean, unpolluted area (which is becoming increasingly difficult to find) the addition of copper sulfate solution to the aquarium at periodic intervals will keep parasites and minute life to a safe minimum. The author has been experimenting with the chemical in self-contained aquariums for many years and has found that it may be added to an aquarium periodically when needed without changing the water at all, as had been first suggested when using the chemical. If the aquarium is carbon filtered, the copper solution may be added whenever the fish show signs of excess parasitic infestation. Of course this doesn't mean you can add copper indiscriminately for it would be lethal to the fish if too strong a concentration is added to the aquarium at one time or too strong a dosage is accumulated in the aquarium by repeated doses without sufficient filtration.

To be safe, it is best to either buy a commercially prepared copper solution that is manufactured by a reputable firm and known to be effective, or you can make your own copper solution. To do this, you would need an accurate gram scale, as it is important that precise measurement of the chemicals is observed so that you can administer the chemical accurately. The author uses a mixture of one gram of cupric sulfate to one quart of water, to which is added one-eighth gram of citric acid. Shake well until completely dissolved and seal with a plastic lid. The solution should be crystal clear with a slight, bluish tinge. This is a stock, copper solution. It should be stored in a glass bottle, preferably brown, and will keep for many months, perhaps years. It should be added to the aquarium at the first sign of itching, scratching, or excessive rapid breathing. Also it should be added if the aquarium is very cloudy due to excess bacteria. Do not confuse the cloudiness that appears when using artificial sea water, because of chemical changes in the water, with bacterial clouding. In bacteria clouded water you can actually see many tiny free swimming organisms in the water by observing the aquarium at night with only the tank light turned on. Turn off the air pump for a few minutes so the water will be quiet and then observe the water near the surface close to the light. If there is a bac-

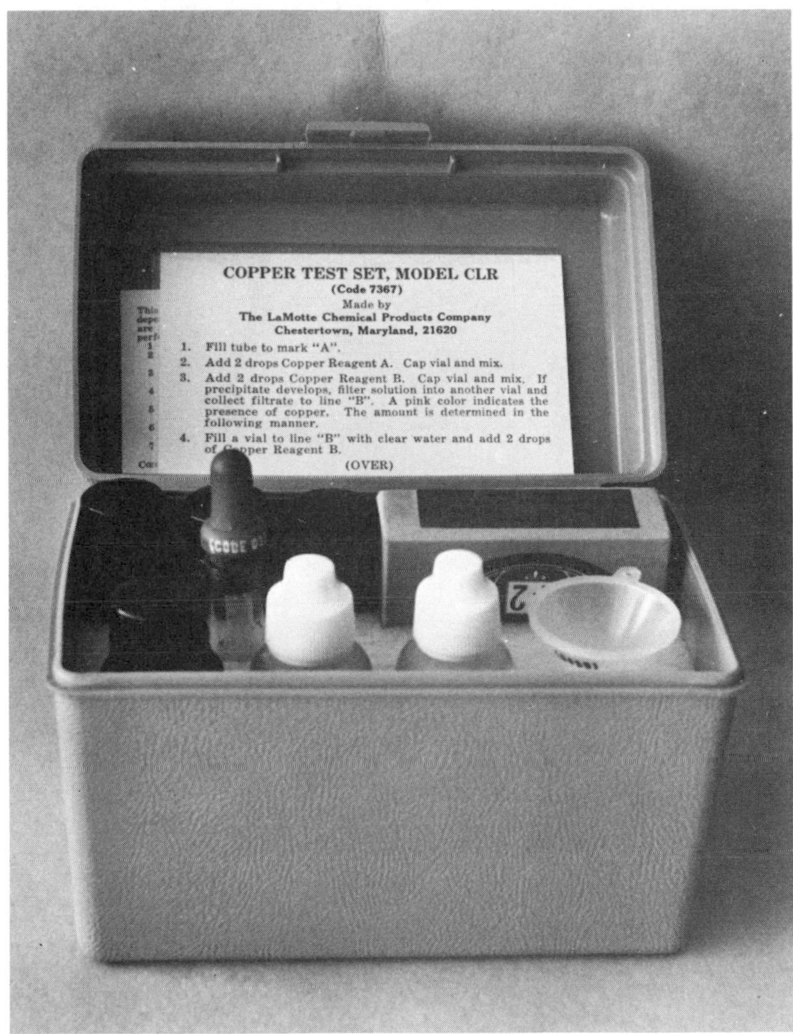

Fig. 67. *A copper test kit manufactured by La Motte Chemical Co. is simple to use and is a valuable aid in the continued experimentation of using copper sulfate for parasite control in the self-contained aquarium.*

Fig. 68. *A dangerous isopod that may sometimes be carried into the aquarium on a fish or in a piece of live coral. They attach themselves to the fish eating away at their flesh, and unless promptly removed will kill or injure the fish. If one is seen holding on to a fish, dip up the fish with a net and usually the isopod will drop off into the bottom of the net where it may be destroyed. If it doesn't let go it can be crushed with tweezers and carefully removed.*

terial infestation, the water will be swarming with minute life. A low power lens will prove helpful for examining the water more closely. If copper is used on a continual basis in the aquarium, it may be best to eliminate the citric acid entirely from your stock solution to avoid buildup in the water.

Proper Dosage for Copper Solution

The proper dosage from your stock solution is one tablespoonful for each three gallons of water in the aquarium. If the tank contains delicate fish such as baby butterflys or very small fish, you can add a half dosage in the morning and the other half in the late afternoon if the fish do not show signs of discomfort from the copper. Of course no invertebrates of any kind should be left in the tank if copper is to be added. Anemones in particular will die quickly from copper. If the tank has many invertebrates, simply take out the fish and treat them separately, meanwhile clean up the tank removing all uneaten food and debris. The undergravel filter should be left running but if the tank has an outside filter with carbon, it should be turned off for the first five days when copper is added. However if the fish appear better after a couple days, the filter may be turned on again so that the aquarium is properly filtered. There are so many types of parasites and minute organisms in the ocean that could prove harmful in the aquarium, especially when they increase to epidemic proportions, that there is no ONE solution that will keep them in check or kill them. Neither is there an exact dosage of copper or any chemical that will rid the aquarium of all minute life, without also killing the fish. The above dosage of copper will keep many parasites in check without being lethal to the fish. It will kill most of the external parasites, many of which attach themselves to the fins and outer surfaces of the fish. A simple examination of the fish with a magnifying glass will show that the parasites are gone. If parasites are still present on the fins three days after copper treatment, then an additional half-dose of copper should be added. This should be repeated in three more days if parasites still persist. However, no additional copper should be added after this for at least two weeks unless the fish are heavily infested, in which case a full dose of copper should be added. A small emergency tank of clean sea water should be on hand in case the copper solution proves too much for the fish. If the fish begin to lie down or act in distress because of the copper, remove them immediately and place them in the clean water. Let their aquarium sterilize in the copper for a couple days and then turn on the carbon filter full and clear up the water, introducing the fish to it with caution.

A copper testing kit would prove invaluable for determining the amount of copper in the tank as it would take out the guess work. How much copper stays in the aquarium and how much precipitates out is difficult to determine because the coral, sand, and carbon, as well as the water itself all vary from area to area, but we do not remove all the coral and sand when treating with copper as has been recommended in the past, nor do we change any of the water unless there is a definite need for it. Just add the copper directly to the aquarium, turning off the outside filter as mentioned above, or the inside filter if using one. Increase the aeration if needed when you cut off the filters so the fish will have sufficient air. The copper solution is also effective against salt water ick and itch which the author formerly had recommended sulfathiozole sodium for treatment. Many salt water ailments appear as ick in that the minute parasites or organisms all appear the same to the naked eye so that many of them look like "ick" when in reality they are just one of the many countless marine infestations that appear in the aquarium from time to time. Fortunately, the copper solution will keep most of them in check.

Of course it is not a cure-all for if all disease problems could be solved with a simple chemical, then there would be no problems whatsoever to keeping marine fish. The sea is a living soup of countless minute organisms that number in the thousands, perhaps millions of varieties and species. Many look very much the same, yet are completely different species. Many are of such small size that they can't even be seen with an electron microscope. Which are harmful and which are beneficial to the fish in an aquarium is an unsolved factor in the present time. We know a very little about them but we have a great deal to learn.

Those that cannot be controlled with copper might be effected with ultraviolet light or with ozone. The author suspects that the minute bacteria and viruses fall in this category and often these are much more difficult to cope with in the aquarium than the external parasites that show up as tiny white specks on the clear portions of the fish. Fish affected with virus or bacterial disease usually hover in the corner of a tank breathing heavily as a person would with a bad fever. Very often copper will have little or no effect on the condition and other remedies must be used if the fish is to be saved.

An ultraviolet sterilizer might solve the problem as would an ozonizer depending on the specific organism causing the problem. Sometimes a minute dose of clorox or formalin on the basis of one drop per each ten gallons of water in the tank will help, increasing the dosage to one drop for each five gallons if the fish show no signs of distress. Malachite Green solution helps in certain ick-like infestations and it may be purchased in most pet shops where it is sold for fresh water ick cure. Also the drugs Acriflavine, Tetracycline, Quinehydrochloride, and Trypaflavine all have proven useful in treatment of bacterial diseases when other remedies failed. The exact dosage on the above is experimental but safe, and effective dosages are available in commercial concentrations of the drugs sold specifically for treatment of fish diseases. The aquarists would do better to buy them in prepared solution rather than experiment on his own unless he has a ready supply of specimens and wishes to experiment with the hopes of developing a proven cure that would benefit other aquarists. In the field of diseases, we all have a great deal to learn. This includes all of the leading aquariums and marine institutions throughout the entire world, for none are completely free of fish problems when it comes to keeping salt-water fish alive for a reasonable length of time. There is no magic potion that will cure all diseases in the aquarium. Fortunately, there are many fine medications available to the hobbyist today, many made exclusively for salt water use. Your local dealer will be able to inform you whether or not the product is useful for your specific needs. Many of the fresh water remedies in particular have taken advantage of the latest and highest quality drugs in combating disease in the aquarium. Generally, if they work in fresh water, they will also work in salt water. If the medication is in dry powder form, it is best to dissolve it in fresh water before adding to the tank. As with all products, some medications are far better than others. Check to see what your local dealer uses in his aquariums. If it works for him, it should work for you.

Salt-Water Ick

This disease is a killer and accounts for many unexplained total losses in the marine aquarium. Like its fresh water counterpart, Ichthyophthirius, it is a fatal disease if left unchecked and soon multiplies to a fantastic proportion quickly killing the aquarium fish. It is usually started as a result of chill, either to the fish while in transit, or by a sudden change in temperature in the aquarium. An open door with a strong cold breeze that strikes the aquarium, is usually the cause in the home. The water in the aquarium may be crystal clear and in perfect condition, but if "Ick" strikes, the aquarium is doomed unless immediate action is taken. First signs of this disease will be a general restlessness of the fish. They will dash parts of their body against the sand or coral, as though relieving an itch, and will repeat this procedure over and over for they are fighting for their lives. Most marine fish will occasionally scrape themselves against the sand or coral to remove an irritating parasite, but they will usually keep this up for just a few minutes, so if a healthy fish does this occasionally, it does not necessarily mean the tank is infected. It is when the scratching attempt is done repeatedly that the disease may be present and then extremely close observation should be made.

First examine the fine transparent portions of the tail and fins. If tiny white spots are present, and the fish is dashing against the sand in a plain attempt to scratch itself, then the aquarium is infected with "Ick" and should be treated immediately. The tiny white spots are smaller in size from those of the fresh-water disease but they are clearly visible to the naked eye. They should not be confused with natural white spots which appear as part of the coloration of many fish. These natural spots will appear in uniform clusters whereas the white disease spots will be all over the body. They usually are first observed on the clear parts of the fins, but a closer look will show that they are on the darker parts of the fish and if in the advanced stages, the entire body will be covered with them.

Since this disease is still in the discovery stage in relation to salt water, its treatment can only be described in brief and no doubt, as more people become familiar with it, a wide variety of cures will be offered. The author first became aware of this killer disease when most "Marine Experts" were boldly stating that marine fish had no aquarium diseases. Several books even published this ridiculous fact and attributed losses in the salt-water aquarium to water breakdown and mysteries of the sea.

Treatment of Ick. Fortunately, if recognized in time, "Ick" can be cured. The most successful method is the heat treatment in which the water in the aquarium is raised to 85 to 90 degrees in temperature with an aquarium heater. The aeration should be increased and the temperature allowed to drop down slightly at night. This treatment should be kept up for several days until all symptoms of the disease have disappeared and the fish are back to normal. If the disease persists, add one level teaspoon of Sulfathiazole Sodium for each five gallons of water in the aquarium. Dissolve the drug in a glass of fresh water before adding to the aquarium. The Sulfathiazole drug should be obtained in the water-soluble form and may be obtained at any drug store. It is sold on prescription only but usually if you tell the druggist that you are using it to treat your aquarium fish, he will sell you a small amount. It is by far the best drug for salt water and leaves no harmful after effects.

Mild cases of "Ick" if caught in time, may be cured by adding the drug in the recommended dosage without the heat treatment, but if the disease is not checked immediately, the heat should be applied.

Marine "Ick" is highly contagious and can be easily transferred from one aquarium to another by a careless aquarist. Always make it a practice to rinse hands in fresh water after working in an aquarium so that when you go to the next tank, you will not transfer any germs.

People often ask why marine fish don't get "Ick" out in the ocean when they swim from warm water to cold water, a condition often present in the sea. Undoubtedly the fish do get the disease and probably many die from it. The author has observed diseased fish on the reefs and as these fish become weaker, they are probably consumed as food by larger fish.

Marine "Ick" is quite often transferred to a healthy aquarium by the introduction of new specimens. Since the disease is nearly always started as a result of chill, quite often marine fish have the disease when they are shipped. Because of their high cost, they are always shipped by air and if they arrive in a cold climate or if the plane flies at a high altitude the fish may be sufficiently chilled so that the disease will start. Due to the rapid turnover of salt-water fish, many hobbyists pick up their fish at the pet shop as soon as they come in so that symptoms of the disease will not have had time to show up. This often accounts for many heavy unexplained losses. When an aquarist reports that his fish died in three days after he got them home, they probably died of "Ick." Healthy fish would last several weeks in an aquarium even without food.

To prevent such wholesale tragedy, always keep new fish for a week in a separate aquarium so that you can be fairly certain they are in good health when you transfer them to your aquarium. Then transfer them slowly. Also, keep the aquarium out of drafts and never add either fresh or salt water to the aquarium unless it has been allowed to set by the aquarium for twenty-four hours so that it will be the same temperature when added to the aquarium.

Salt-Water Itch

This cannot actually be called a disease for it is usually caused from too many micro-organisms in the aquarium. The water may become slightly cloudy, a condition caused from over feeding, and close examination will reveal that it is alive with small swimming parasites. The fish will be very uncomfortable and will rub their bodies against the sand or coral in much the same way when "Ick" is present, except that in this case, no white spots will appear. One organism in particular will usually appear on the glass and can be easily seen with the naked eye. It will look like tiny white threads an eighth of an inch long and will crawl about on the glass in caterpillar fashion. No doubt it causes the fish much misery for even baby sharks and moray eels were very uncomfortable in the author's aquariums when large numbers of this organism were present.

When the water becomes infested, the fish will "twitch," rub their bodies against the sand, and, in the final stages, dash madly about the aquarium, finally dying of exhaustion and suffocation. Some of the parasites are extremely small and are almost invisible to the naked eye. They may appear as fine "dust" or tiny white spots on the fish similar to "Ick." There are a great variety of minute marine organisms and no treatment can kill them all without also killing the fish, so that the aquarist must be content merely with keeping them under control.

Copper sulfate is probably the best chemical for controlling them. Add copper sulfate solution promptly as mentioned at the beginning of this chapter at first signs of twitching. Don't be afraid to use the copper, for if you don't use enough your fish may die should the parasites get out of control. Use the proper dosage of copper and if the fish still act in distress after several days, add another dose. If fish act sluggish or uncomfortable during the copper treatment, turn on carbon filter immediately, which will remove much of the copper and repeat treatment more cautiously.

Some types of copepods can cause havoc in an aquarium and grow as large or larger than brine shrimp. Copper treatment is not always successful in treating them as they may require such a strong dosage that it proves harmful to the fish. If this is the case, the fish should be placed in repeated changes of fresh sea water, and if this is not available, artificial sea water of the same temperature and density can be used. Copper Sulfate should not be added to aquariums containing live coral, algae, or invertebrates. If fish in such aquariums become infected, they should be removed and treated in separate containers. The author is indebted to Mr. Bill Kelly of the Cleveland Aquarium, who suggested that Citric Acid be used with the Sulfate to prolong its usefulness in the salt water. Without the acid, the copper precipitates out rapidly before it can be of much benefit.

External Parasites

Many form of external parasites exist in the sea water. The larger sizes occasionally may be seen clinging to the sides of a fish and they should be removed when sighted. Simply catch the fish in a net, hold him firmly, and remove the pest with a pair of tweezers. If there is a wound under the parasite, be certain to treat it with a swab of Mercurochrome or Merthiolate. Most external parasites are leeches and care must be used in extracting them lest the fish be severely damaged. Parasites attached directly to the gill tissue must be removed with great caution. Sometimes these may be removed with some success by placing the fish in a weaker salt solution of 1.015 for a few hours. Be sure temperatures are the same when you place infected fish in this solution. If this fails, try swabbing the parasite with an antiseptic, and if parasite still refuses to let go, as a last resort, crush it with tweezers and remove small portions of it at a time.

Sea Horse Parasites

The large Sea Horses are frequently infected with external parasites which must be removed. They are small flat creatures and assume the same coloring as their host but they can be easily distinguished by careful observation. Their favorite resting place is usually around the head of the Sea Horse, especially in the nape of the neck.

They will appear as small semi-transparent bumps varying in size from one quarter of an inch to as small as a sixteenth of an inch and smaller, and will reproduce and grow if left unchecked in the aquarium. Frequently they may be seen swimming about the aquarium and may swim from one horse to another. They are easily removed with a pair of tweezers, by holding the Sea Horse with one hand. If there are quite a few parasites, the horse may be lifted out of the aquarium for fifteen or twenty seconds at a time while you extract the unwelcome guests. Usually if all the parasites are removed, they will not reappear in the aquarium so that a little effort in the beginning is well worth while. Not all horses are infested with parasites and the number of pests varies with the individual. A large horse may contain just one or two parasites which may be easily removed, or it may have as many as several dozen varying in size from pin-point-sized babies to the adults. Since it would be rather difficult to remove these tiny babies with a pair of tweezers, it is usually best to remove them when they are large enough to be easily seen. In this manner, since there will be no adults to reproduce, the entire colony will soon be eradicated.

It is the author's opinion that these parasites are kept in check out in the ocean by small cowfish and trunkfish which live in close association with the Sea Horses. These small interesting fish will gently nibble at the Sea Horse and are undoubtedly eating the small pests. The same action may be observed in the aquarium. Small File fish and Puffers occasionally behave in a similar fashion, but sometimes they will eat the Sea Horse's delicate fins as well as parasites and these two fish should be closely watched if kept in the same aquarium with the slower moving Horses. Large Puffers and File fish should not be kept in with Sea Horses as they will nearly always attack the slower moving fish, eating away the tiny fins and often large patches of skin as well.

Fungus

This ailment is nearly always associated with cold weather or chill. Apparently the fish's resistance is lowered in cold water and this disease breaks out. Usually the best treatment is to raise the temperature to 85 to 90 degrees for most of the day and repeat the treatment for several days at a time. Always increase aeration when raising temperature. It will also be helpful to add a teaspoon of Sulfathiazole Sodium for each five gallons of water to the aquarium. Clownfish, large Sea Horses, and Rock Beauties are especially susceptible to this disease.

Local fungus which may result from a wound in the body, may be cured by swabbing the area with a strong germicide such as Salacylic

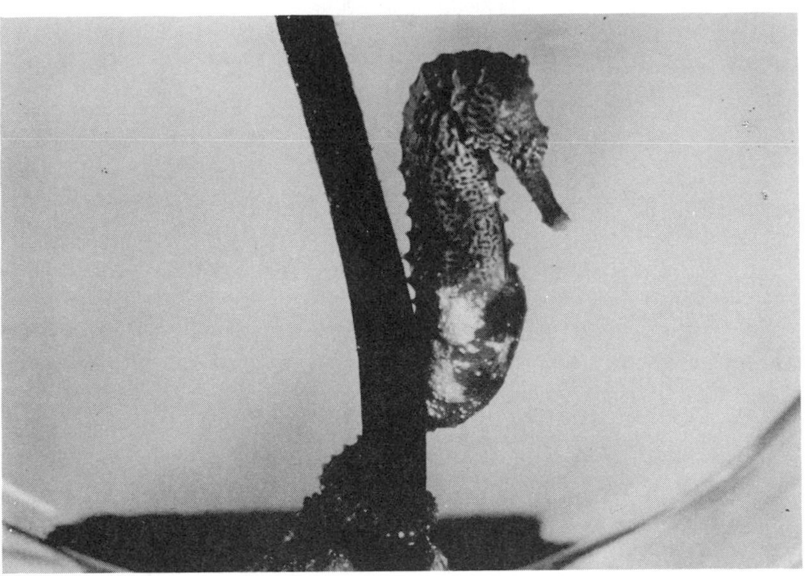

Fig. 69. *Diseased Sea Horse with large fungus area on pouch. Horses should not be collected or purchased in this condition as the disease is difficult to control.*

acid. Aureomycin or sulfa drugs may be used and several should be tried since there is no way of telling the exact nature of the infection. Sulfathiazole Sodium may be made into a paste by mixing it with castor oil and this will adhere to the wounded area with good results depending on the nature of the infection.

During the cold weather, large Sea Horses are frequently collected with badly fungused areas on their bodies. Rather than attempt curing this malady, they are usually returned to the ocean where the disease may disappear in warmer weather. Aquarists should not purchase Sea Horses offered for sale in this condition, for many times fungus diseases are highly contagious and the disease may be spread to other fishes if introduced to the aquarium.

Body Rot

A peculiar disease in which large portions of the fish usually waste away and drops off. The author has seen Dwarf Sea Horses affected with this disease in which the entire snout was completely gone making it impossible for the fish to feed. Large Sea Horses have been oberved in a similar condition and it is a pitiful situation. It is usually, though not always, associated with high salinity and probably caused by small harmful bacteria. Suggested treatment is to bring the salinity down to 1.018, increase the temperature and aeration.

Also add one half teaspoon of Sulfathiazole Sodium to each five gallons of water in the aquarium. Hydrogen Peroxide, Neo-Silvol, Argyrol, Aureomycin, and other germicides may be helpful, if applied directly to infected area.

Fin and Tail Rot

This is similar to the above-mentioned disease though not as fatal. The fine transparent parts of the fins will appear to rot away and if left unchecked, the fish will soon die as it will no longer be able to swim properly. It is usually though not always associated with a high salinity so that for treatment the water should be brought down to about 1.020. Fish suffering from this disease should be fed live brine shrimp so that they will not have to chase their food and can let it swim to them. They should be placed in a shallow container so that they will not have to swim as much, and the fins may be swabbed with Peroxide of Hydrogen solution or other germicide. Valuable specimens should be hand fed if necessary to be sure they are getting plenty of food which is important for their recovery.

Blindness

When a fish suddenly shows no interest in food, it may have gone blind. Excess light is usually the cause, especially when the fish was not given a dark hiding place in the aquarium where it could retreat once in a while. The fish may bump into coral or snap wildly at food which it can feel but cannot see, and prompt action must be taken to save your pet. You can usually see if the fish is blind by moving your hand quickly in front of the glass. If he shows no response even though you attempt to frighten him from the outside, and if he swims to the end of the aquarium and bumps into the glass or coral, then he is most likely blind. This does not necessarily have to be a permanent condition and it can usually be cured, with time and patience.

First remove the victim to a separate aquarium, and cover the sides and top of the tank with cardboard to keep out most of the light. Since the fish is blind, it will have to be hand fed and this may be accomplished by holding the fish gently with one hand and forcing chunks of chopped shrimp into its mouth with the other. Usually, if the fish is tame, it will accept food eagerly in this fashion and if it does, it is well on the road to recovery. Usually when hand feeding a blind fish, it is best to handle the fish very gently so that it will not become excited, then release it equally as gentle after the food has been placed well in its mouth. It will usually swallow the food and the whole procedure may be repeated until the fish has eaten his full.

If, after a week or so, the fish responds to light, remove one side of the cardboard so that the aquarium will be partly lighted. The fish may be returned to the regular aquarium after its sight has returned, but this time, it should be given a good coral hiding place so that it can get completely out of the light when it desires. This is a perfectly natural situation as anyone who has observed marine life on the reef can testify. The fish will swim out into the bright sunlight of the reef for brief periods of time and then periodically retreat to the dark seclusion of a coral ledge or other protection.

Large Porcupine fish, Rock Beauties, and Angelfish, are especially susceptible to blindness from too much light, and can be blinded in a matter of hours if left in direct sunlight with no cover or protection. Also the Lion fish, Clownfish, and any other fish which tend to stay out in the open, can be blinded if subjected to intense aquarium light. This condition is often brought on, when fish are placed on public display. The lights are left on for long periods of time, and the fish are given no place to hide so that usually in a week or so, the fish are blinded.

Other causes of blindness in the aquarium may be due to a disease called Pop-eye, in which the eyes become enormously swollen and protrude from their sockets. The exact cause of this disease is not known but it is believed to be caused from a gas condition in the eye itself, and also believed in some cases to be caused from a parasite. It usually starts with one eye at first and then later affects both eyes. Although no definite treatment can be given that will positively produce results, the eyes can sometimes be saved by coating them every three days with Neoprontosil, a red sulfa-based drug. It coats the eye with an opaque red covering and is sometimes beneficial. The fish is usually blinded in advanced stages of Pop-eye and must be hand fed. Ordinary castor oil or boric acid is also beneficial for eye treatment. In all cases of blindness, the fish should be placed in a darkened aquarium as described above.

Injury to the eye of a fish is usually not serious and often goes away by itself. The eye may appear very discolored and swollen and if the fish eats well and shows no apparent discomfort, it may be left in the aquarium with the others as this is an injury which is best left alone.

Paralytic Shock

Paralytic shock is usually caused from a combination of overexcitement and rapid change in salinity or pH. The fish will stiffen and fall motionless in the water and may die shortly if left unattended. This condition is usually brought on when the fish is transferred to the aquarium. It is especially prevalent in Demoiselles, Butterfly fish, and other highly excitable fish, but can occur with Sea Horses and nearly all other fish.

Fig. 70. *A rare Anglerfish* (Antenarrius) *and its food, consisting of live Grunts, are floated in the aquarium before being placed in their new home.*

Density of ocean water varies from one location to another. In some localities it may vary from 1.015 to 1.040 within a radius of ten miles. Also, it will vary considerably in mineral content as well so that great care must be taken at all times when transferring fish to the aquarium. Even aquariums that have been set up for some time may vary greatly from one another in salinity, mineral content and pH, as well as other factors, so that care must be taken even when transferring a fish from one tank to another, even though both aquariums were set up at the same time with the same water! Artificial sea water also varies since the fresh water it is mixed with varies greatly in different parts of the country.

In view of all this, if you take a fish from a shipping container, and after checking the temperature, drop him promptly into an aquarium, he may die within a few minutes unless you are very fortunate and the water he was in, was very similar to the water in your aquarium. Just imagine how you would feel if you were suddenly dropped into a hundred feet of water with an aqua lung. You might be able to breathe, but the sudden change in pressure would probably paralyze you. Whereas, if you had been gently placed on the surface and allowed to swim down slowly, so that you could gradually get used to the pressure, you would suffer no ill effects. The same is true with a fish. They cannot stand sudden changes and must be introduced to the aquarium very slowly.

If transfer is done too quickly, the fish may go into paralytic shock. Its body will stiffen and it may quiver slightly or swim spasmodically about the aquarium. When this happens the fish must be removed from the aquarium immediately and placed back in its original container. If it does not come out of the shock immediately, it should be placed in a small net in an upright position and moved back and forth through the water in such a way that water will be forced through its gills. This must be done in the water that the fish arrived in and usually the fish will return to normal in a few minutes. Then it may be introduced much more slowly to the aquarium.

Paralytic Fright

This is a condition that also may be fatal if neglected. In this case, the fish is actually frightened to death and probably dies of heart failure. It is especially common among small Demoiselles. These colorful little fish are so accustomed to hiding in holes and crevices that to be left out in the open with no place to hide, is a devastating horror to them and they often pass out from sheer fright. They should be handled very carefully when transferring them to an aquarium so that they are not unduly excited. If the fish arrive in a shipping box, it is usually a great strain on the fish when the box is first opened. Usually, with the box closed, the fish are in a semi-sleep condition and it can easily be understood how badly they could.be frightened if they are suddenly subjected to bright light and chased by a huge monster with a net (You). Even Sea Horses which are normally rather quiet, can occasionally be frightened to death with rough handling. If a fish shows signs of extreme wariness and exhaustion and its gills are working fast, it should be placed in a darkened container until it quiets down.

Toxic Poisoning

This is usually caused from an accumulation of harmful solvents in the aquarium. It may be from the contact of the salt water with the metal at the top of the aquarium, or a reaction of the cement in the aquarium, or a combination of both. Sometimes plastic tubing or other plastics or accessories will contribute to this but at any rate, it may eventually build up to a toxic condition. Quite often, this build up is so gradual that the fish becomes used to it and if the water is kept at the proper salinity and feeding is sufficient the fish will live quite happily. But, depending upon the toxicity of the cement and other factors, this condition may be bad enough to kill the fish unless the situation is remedied.

If your fish suddenly stops eating and shows no interest in food, and if your coral is clean, the fish have no signs of disease, and the water is clear, then most likely your fish are suffering from toxic poisoning.

There is only one cure, and that is to completely replace all the water in the aquarium with fresh sea water. The coral should be cleaned, and new sand should be used and the fish must be introduced to this new water by floating them in a jar of their old water. At this time, the aquarium should be checked. If there are large areas of seepage or pockets where the aquarium cement holds the glass in place, then a new aquarium should be used as the old aquarium will undoubtedly contaminate the new sea water in a short while. All plastic aquariums or all-glass containers have this one definite advantage over the regular aquarium for sea water as they have no metal or cement that can cause trouble.

Hermit crabs, Sea Spiders, Coral shrimp, and other invertebrates are highly susceptible to toxic poisoning and the slightest trace can quickly kill them. Even the Toadfish, which can live in the foulest water, will die from toxic poisoning in the aquarium.

Oodinium Disease

This is a gill disease and has been studied quite extensively by salt-water aquarists in public aquariums. It is caused from a tiny miscroscopic parasite that makes its home in the gill chambers of the fish and which eventually multiplies to such proportions that the fish cannot breathe properly and dies.

Symptoms of the disease are usually a lack of interest in food at first, and in the advanced stages, the fish will gather near the surface of the water as though gasping for breath. Even a change of water will be of no value, if the fish have this disease as the infection is in the fish but the disease can be cured with Copper Sulfate if used properly. But first, before any treatment is used, all aquarium conditions should be checked to be certain that this is the trouble. Fish will swim to the surface for other reasons. Check the coral, the air supply, and the condition of the water. If all of these things appear alright, then a complete change of water is recommended because perhaps the fish are suffering from toxic poisoning. But, if the fish still congregate at the surface gasping for breath, even after a complete change of water, then they probably have Oodinium disease. Treatment should be started right away.

Robert P. Dempster of the Steinhart Aquarium, gives a complete account of this disease in the May, 1956 issue of *Aquarium Journal* in which he states:

"Steinhart Aquarium has been receiving fish from Hawaii for many years and until 1951 the fish collected there and introduced into the aquarium tanks seemed to be relatively free from disease, at least from any that could be considered epidemic. In that year, however, about ten days after an exceptionally large shipment arrived from Honolulu, a gill disease broke out in the tanks. At first the fish were not suspected of having any specific disease. Many of them congregated near the surface and were observed to be respiring very rapidly, obviously in great distress. It was apparent that either the water was deficient in oxygen or the fish for some reason were not able to utilize the oxygen that was present. On the assumption that the tanks had become contaminated, they were drained and refilled with fresh sea water and the circulation of water was substantially increased, but the fish were not relieved of their respiratory trouble. As time went on more individuals congregated near the surface, gasping for air and it was not long before some of them died.

"Microscopic examination revealed innumerable minute, oval, parasitic organisms clinging to the gill filaments of the dead fish, so thickly planted that they were obviously interfering with the respiratory function of the gills. They were determined to be a species of Oodinium, possibly ocellatum. Left overnight in a dish of water, they were re-examined the next morning and it was found that some had divided once and many twice, so that all had passed into the two or four-cell state of development within the period of about twenty-four hours. Nigrelli (1936) found that each Oodinium organism after becoming detached from the gills of a fish, settled to the substratum, where it gave rise to palmella states of 2, 4, 8, 16, 32, 64, and 128 cells. One more palmella division took place to form 256 flagellated free-swimming dinospores. Later the dinospores settled to the bottom where they developed into typical peridinian dinoflagellates, the infective form. These dinoflagellates, which are also free swimming, apparently invade the bronchial chamber of the fish, become attached to the gill filaments and metamorphose into the parasite form."

According to Jacobs (1946), Oodinium ocellatum is the first dinoflagellate known to parasitize marine vertebrates.

Treatment. "The immediate problem," Mr. Dempster continued, "was to determine how to relieve the fish of this very prolific parasite and how to eradicate it from the aquarium's water system. Several methods of treatment were tried: the most effective entailed the use of Copper Sulfate. This chemical is highly toxic to fish, so of course it must be used with extreme caution. After making a considerable number of tests with tropical marine fish, we found that 0.5 ppm of copper (this is approximately two ppm copper sulfate) is a safe concentration and is lethal to Oodinium. Copper induces the fish to secrete a copius amount of mucus which causes the parasites to become detached.

"After they are sloughed from the body and settle to the bottom, cell division takes place and development proceeds normally to the free-swimming dinoflagellate stage and at this point the copper sulfate apparently becomes lethal to them. Since it takes about seven days for the Oodinium organisms to develop into free-swimming dinoflagellates it is necessary to maintain the copper concentration in the tank for at least that long. A ten-day treatment with copper sulfate is recommended."

Adding copper to the water. "Because it takes such a minute amount of copper sulfate to treat a small tank such as the fish hobbyist usually has, it is essential to make up a very dilute stock solution of this chemical and add a carefully calculated amount of it rather than add the Copper Sulfate crystals directly to the treatment tank. This stock solution may be made up in the following way:

"Add 1 gram of Copper Sulfate chemically pure, very carefully weighed, to 1 liter of distilled water and stir with a glass rod until it is completely dissolved. This solution will contain 1 milligram of Copper Sulfate in each milliliter. From your carefully-prepared stock solution, add 7.43 ml. to each gallon of water in the tank. If you have a ten gallon tank, you would of course add 74.3 ml. of stock solution to obtain the correct concentration.

"When your marine fish are seen to congregate at the surface and gasp for air you may suspect them of having the gill disease but of course a positive diagnosis cannot be made without a microscope. If, however, you do not have a microscope and there is doubt as to whether the fish actually have the disease, it is advisable to change the water in the tank and if after a few minutes the fish act the same as they did before, treatment should be given at once. Never add copper sulfate to a tank containing sand, gravel, coral, shells, etc. It should be devoid of all such material. If another clean tank is available, preferably an all-glass container, it is advisable to use it as the treatment tank. After you have carefully measured the capacity of this tank and filled it with clean sea water, Copper Sulfate, from your stock solution may be added to it. Be very sure that you know the exact number of gallons of water in the tank before the Copper Sulfate is added. It is all right to aerate the water in this tank, but do not filter it, as the filter tends to gradually remove the copper from the water. The fish should be allowed to remain in this water for a week or ten days, as it takes that long to completely cure them of this disease. If there are many specimens in the tank it is advisable to transfer them after the third or fourth day to another freshly treated tank for the remainder of the treatment period. Never add Copper Sulfate to an already-treated tank unless you have the laboratory equipment and chemicals necessary to make a copper test of the water."

Harmful Micro-organisms in the Water

This condition is usually present in the aquarium after it has been set up for a few months, especially if chopped shrimp or fish have been fed too profusely. The water will suddenly become alive with tiny free-swimming bacteria and in sufficient quantity they will use up enough oxygen so that the fish may suffocate unless the situation is remedied. The first symptom of this condition is a slight cloudiness in the aquarium and an accelerated rate of breathing in the fish. They will appear to be panting hard and that is usually a danger sign. The first thing to do when this condition occurs is to increase the aeration. Next, lift up the coral and remove any uneaten food, being especially watchful for dead fish. Often times, the death of a single fish if it is proportionately large, can bring about this condition in the aquarium, especially if there is a surplus of uneaten food left in the tank. Then, empty the outside filter, wash carbon thoroughly and replace it, turning it on full force. If the condition was caught in time, and if feeding is done sparingly, the water may clear up and everything will be alright. However, if after a few days, the water remains slightly cloudy, and there is presence of a large number of free swimming micro-organisms, add one tablespoon of copper solution for each three gallons of water in the tank. This should kill most of the bacteria in a few days.

Clorox Treatment of Water

This is an interesting field for experiment in treating large aquariums of sea water in which a multitude of parasites and untold varieties of small swimming organisms have taken over the aquarium. Sometimes an aquarium will become infested with millions of micro-organisms, copepods, flukes, and various minute crustacea, many as yet unidentified. If there is a large volume of water, one hesitates to run it down the drain so that an effort to reclaim it should be made. The author has been experimenting with ordinary household clorox for a number of years, and would use it and recommend it to other aquarists for parasite and bacteria control when nothing else including copper seemed to be effective.

Clorox seems to kill everything. To completely sterilize a large aquarium, remove the fish to a smaller tank and pour in a cupful of clorox for each fifty gallons of water in the tank. Leave filters in operation but remove all coral and decorations. After two days, the tank should be quite sterile and microscopic life may be checked with a low power lens along the edge of the glass if desired. The clorox may now be driven out of the tank by adding a small amount of sodium thiosulfate (quarter teaspoon to 50 gallons) to the aquarium, or by adding any of the prepared chlorine eradicators on the market. You can test the water for chlorine with a common swimming pool test kit which also will give the pH of the water. The water should then be well aerated. The filter carbon should be removed and replaced with fresh carbon and the tank should be operated for a week or two before fish are returned to it. It may be necessary to adjust the pH and it may be helpful to replace a portion of the water with freshly mixed water before adding the fish. This treatment is still experimental but the author has tried it on numerous occasions with good success. In fact clorox treated water was used in the tank in which the first squid eggs were hatched out. Also at this writing lionfish are living in a tank that was treated in the above manner. Some aquarists have been adding clorox to their newly collected sea water before setting up their aquarium at the rate of a teaspoon to each five gallons and report excellent results. Chlorine eliminators are sold in most pet shops and are very inexpensive and would be more practical for the hobbyist in the removal of chlorine than the sodium thiosulfate, except for very large aquariums. Warren Zeiller of Miami Seaquarium has been experimenting with a chlorine-type medication called Microcide which has been reported to be very effective for killing microorganisms unaffected by other treatments.

Cotton Fungus, Boils, Infections

Occasionally a white, cotton-like fungus will appear on the fin or tail of a fish. Rather than medicate the water, it is best to remove the fish from the tank in a net and brush off the fungus with a cue-tip swab dipped in Merthiolate. Usually it will go away with one treatment. Boils, lumps or infected areas can be cured by probing them with a sterile needle to open them. Remove the pus and swab the area with Merthiolate or Bactine. This is also useful in treating deep punctures, wounds or sores. Badly infected fins may be cured by brushing away the infected area with the cue-tip swab dipped in Merthiolate or similar medication. Don't keep the fish out of the water longer than a half minute. If operation takes longer, hold the net in the aquarium so the fish can recuperate for a few minutes before working on him further. Sometimes it is better to treat a bad area a little at a time rather than all at once for the safety of the fish.

Heat Treatment of Infected Water

If a large aquarium becomes heavily infested with parasites, copepods, and other organisms, they can be killed by raising the temperature of the water to about 125 degrees and maintaining this temperature for several hours. Of course the fish must be removed and placed in a separate container during the treatment. Large aquariums of fifty or one hundred gallons may be heated by placing several "instant" water heaters slightly beneath the surface. The water should be slowly stirred so that the warm water reaches the bottom; otherwise the water can be hot at the surface and almost cool at the bottom. If under-gravel filter is in use it should bubble slowly to help circulate the water. Be careful not to get the salt water into the wiring of the heaters, as it may shock you. Smaller aquariums can be heated with an aquarium heater designed for a large tank. When turned up high it will heat a small tank sufficiently to kill the parasites. The purpose of heat treatment in this fashion is twofold. First, if a tank is heavily infested and the fish are removed from the tank for treatment, the fish will quickly become infested again unless the tank water is sterilized. It makes little sense to rid a fish of parasites only to place him in a tank that is still infested. Second, a large aquarium of sea water might be very difficult to replace, especially for an inland aquarist, so that ridding it of parasites without adding chemicals could save a lot of hauling and expense. Heat treatment of sea water is still experimental but shows promising results. After treatment, the salinity of the water should be checked and fresh water added to bring it back to normal. The water also should be heavily aerated to reoxygenate it.

Dr. Earl Herald of Steinhart Aquarium has been experimenting with ultraviolet sterilization of sea water for control of parasites, and reports it to be very successful. Control of parasites without chemicals is the best method in salt-water aquariums, as it does not alter the composition of the sea water and there is no doubt that eventually a sound and foolproof system will come into general use for the marine hobbyist. There are also reports that ozone has been used in treatment of salt water with good results.

Discoloration From Sulfathiazole Sodium

There have been conflicting reports about the drug Sulfathiazole Sodium in the past decade and the author has investigated them carefully. Some hobbyists are reluctant to use the drug because it discolors the water in their aquarium. This does not always happen and apparently depends upon the grade of the drug used, whether or not the drug is exposed to light before use, and the general condition of the aquarium itself. Like all drugs, there are superior and inferior products. Sulfathiazole Sodium comes in a fine snow-white powder that is highly refined or in a coarse yellow powder; and no doubt the inferior products are mixed with fillers to increase their weight and reduce their cost. The high-quality drug is used for medicinal purposes and often cannot be purchased without a prescription, but usually a druggist will sell it to an aquarist if he knows it is to be used for treating fish diseases. However, even the best-quality drug could discolor the water; so, to avoid this, the aquarist can simply treat his sick fish in a small container and when they are cured return them to the main tank. If the disease occurs in the main tank, then a very mild dose of the drug may be added to the aquarium itself. The discoloration of the water may be completely removed by placing a small amount of well-aged Carbon in the filter. If an outside or inside filter is not being used, the Carbon may be placed in a piece of silk stocking and buried under the sand, preferably near the filter bubbler stem. It will clear up the water and may easily be removed for cleaning.

General Pollution

Although this was the number one failure for marine aquarists in the past few years, it is now becoming a thing of the past, especially to the experienced aquarist. The main causes of pollution are improperly cured coral, over-feeding, failure to remove dead specimens,

Fig. 71. *At the present time there is no known cure for all marine diseases. If there was we would have no problems. An experimental system for treating diseased fish or newly arrived specimens can be made by use of the Douglass Tank Bucketts which hang on the side of the tank. Place a few drops of clorox in first container, copper solution in the second, and sulfathiazole sodium or other medication in the third. Fish is moved from one to the other after being in each solution for ten to twenty minutes or until it shows signs of distress. Sea water or artificial water is used.*

insufficient aeration, and dead Sea Anemones. A badly polluted aquarium can easily be detected some distance away by its smell. It will have a very bad odor! The water will be milky in color with poor visibility and the fish if they are not already dead, will be gasping for their lives. Only immediate action can save them. They should be removed and placed in fresh sea water if any is available and the whole aquarium will need a general clean-up. First, the aeration should be increased, and the outside filter removed and cleaned. Next, the coral and sand should be removed from the aquarium and washed thoroughly. If the water does not smell too bad, and it is fairly clean, it can usually be brought back to normal after a few days, especially if the sub-sand filter is used. This clever device removes much of the suspended matter from the water, and can clear up a cloudy aquarium faster than any outside filter.

Water which has become badly contaminated, with a dead sea anemone, or large fish, is best discarded and a fresh solution used. In view of the expense and extra effort required in setting up your marine tank, it would be well worth while to keep ten or twenty gallons of fresh sea water on hand for emergencies. Then when this is used, it should be replaced with another batch so that you will always have extra sea water on hand for emergencies.

Fig. 72. *Young French Angelfish suffering from "Skin Blotch" disease. In extreme cases the entire fish will turn white. Note mottled effect, especially near top edge of center strip. Disease can be cured with Sulfathiozole Sodium treatment.*

Drugged Fish

Although this cannot be called a disease, the author feels that drugged fish are responsible for many unexplained deaths in the aquarium. If a fish has been subjected to an overdose of drugs either when collected or while being shipped, it will die NO MATTER WHAT THE HOBBYIST DOES OR HOW SKILLFUL HE IS! The following article written by the author is reprinted from *Salt Water Aquarium Magazine.*

Tragedy of Drugged Fish

"The drugging of fish adds an unknown, uncertain factor to the keeping of salt water fish. It's a fact that a drugged fish usually will not live as long in the aquarium as an undrugged specimen. The degree of longevity regarding drugged fish versus undrugged fish depends upon many factors. First, the type of drug used. Second how much of a dose the fish received and third how long the fish were exposed to the drug.

Advocates of drugs (and there are many) usually state that the drugs are completely harmless and give no lasting effects to the fish. They may say that laboratory tests under precise conditions have proven that the fish can be drugged and will recover with absolutely no harm to the fish whatsoever. I have heard this over and over again from numerous users of the drugs and in all probability it is quite correct. But, the phrase "Under Precise Conditions," is the catch! If all the fish that were drugged were placed in laboratories and the drug was administered by a skilled technician under the most exacting standards, there would be little problem with drugs for as we all know even with humans, the proper administration of a drug by a skilled physician usually is quite safe and beneficial to the patient. But an overdose of drugs is another matter and can easily prove fatal. The same is true of fish. Too much drug or too much exposure to a drug and the fish will die, either right away or a week, month or several months later depending on numerous factors and conditions.

The drugging of fish is done in two ways so far as our hobby is concerned. The fish are drugged by collectors to make it easier for them to bring in a huge harvest without having to work as much and the drugs are used in the transportation of the fish either in handling them or shipping them. Either way the fish are drugged and a wide variety of drugs are used. The mortality of the fish drugged in any way, outside of the controlled laboratory experiment or the controlled environment of an aquarium in which a skilled technician administers the drug, is bound to be higher than fish which were not drugged at all. Percentage wise, the mortality of drugged fish may vary from five percent to one hundred percent despite ANYTHING the receiver of drugged fish can do. This is the tragedy of drugged fish. All the effort of collecting and shipping the fish, picking it up at the airport, acclimating it to the aquarium is wasted. If the fish has absorbed too much drug it will die.

Why use drugs at all? This is a good question and to date, I have not found any satisfactory answer. So far as collecting is concerned, a good collector can catch all the fish he could ever use or sell WITHOUT the use of drugs. This is not a statement without fact for as many of you readers probably know, I have been a professional marine collector for sixteen years with over 25,000 hours experience under the sea. I have caught practically every kind of fish that swim, from moray eels to sharks, royal grammas, pearly jawfish, pigmy angels and all the Atlantic reef fish without the use of drugs. I have caught so many fish at one time that even a large public aquarium could not carry them all on their boat. So who needs drugs to collect! I use hand nets, seines and traps. With these I could catch a hundred fish or a thousand if I needed them without damaging the reef or harming the fish. Others have done the same. But collecting with drugs is a shameful waste of our natural resources. The drug collector doesn't need any skill. He doesn't have to learn how to outwit a fish in its natural environment nor does he experience the thrill of capture. He spreads his drug around and scoops up poor lifeless bodies of the fish he has knocked senseless. Those he can't reach or those that settle down into the coral may or may not recover. Some will be eaten by other fish. Baby fish probably will die. Of the fish that are collected, those that recover and swim around when placed in the collecting container are brought home, the rest are tossed unceremoniously overboard. It's a sad fate for a beautiful little fish that has done no one any harm. The vogue these days seems to be collecting with drugs. There are those who can not see it any other way and I have not been winning any popularity contests by taking the opposite view. But regardless, my own opinion on the drugs is that it was a sorry day that they were introduced into the field of collecting salt water fish. The drugs are probably not all bad and I can see where they could have a useful place in the field where a rare specimen could not be obtained any other way but the wanton use of drugs in collecting is detrimental to the salt water hobby. Not only is there a higher mortality of fish collected this way but drug collecting enables the collector to take fish from difficult areas which normally would be by-passed by the regular collector and would serve as reserves for the fish, insuring a supply of fish for years to come. Drug collecting on a large scale can deplete an area for years. I personally do not collect with drugs although I have tried the drugs in the field to see and evaluate their results. I did find that the fish caught with the drugs did not live as long as fish caught the same day without drugs. To be fair about the drug collecting situation, I would like to hear from the drug collectors for perhaps they have devised methods of drugging and handling the fish so that the mortality of the fish is not so great. Also of course, there are no doubt skilled collectors who use the drugs with caution, taking care that the fish do not get too much. We should hear from them so that the entire picture is presented.

The other use of drugs is in the transportation and handling of the fish. The drugs are used so that more fish can be carried in a given container at one time. This is done either in bringing the fish from the reefs to the staging area or when the fish are shipped. Either way it may not be good news to the final receiver of the fish. Again the quantity and quality of the drug, the number of fish in it, and the time and temperature from when the fish are drugged to the time they are placed in clean sea water enter into the picture. Fish shipped in drugs, particularly from out of the country have perhaps a sixty-forty chance of living longer than thirty days after they have been placed in the aquarium. Far East shipment may run higher than that and in some instances the losses from drugged fish may run as high as ninety percent or more!

This is a tragic, wasted effort on everyone's part. The collector does his job well and brings the fish to the shipper in perfect condition. The shipper keeps the fish in good shape until he has enough to make a shipment. Then the fish are handled by numerous airlines and finally after an incredible journey of sometimes more than ten thousand miles, the fish reach their destination and a dealer stays up half the night or all night bringing the fish to his store; meeting the plane so there won't be a moment's delay. Then finally, the fish are home, the boxes are opened and he joyfully finds that the fish weren't frozen and many of them are swimming around. He carefully places them in various aquariums especially prepared for them, sees that they are all swimming around comfortably and then goes to bed exhausted. The next day, most of the fish look fine and perhaps he even sells a few to his customers since they look so good. But, ten days later, the fish begin dying like flies. Or they never show any interest in food and slowly waste away sometimes living as long as a month or two. They may show an abnormal interest in food eating ravenously but if they were over drugged, they will die no matter what is done to keep them alive. This is the tragedy of drugged fish. All along the line the effort is wasted in trying to bring a beautiful little fish to some aquarist's home from a far away ocean. No matter what the aquarist does the fish will die. Recent tests on drugged fish indicate that the liver of the fish is damaged or destroyed by an overdose of drugs. No doubt the brain and other vital organs suffer damage too. As for myself, I would not want a drugged fish free, for I don't want to waste the time trying to find out whether it is going to live or not. There are enough unknown factors in keeping salt water fish from the oceans of the world without adding another over which we have no control. Fish can be shipped without drugs. We always request it on our overseas shipments stating in the letter that we do not want the fish shipped at all if they can't be shipped without drugs. We have shipped fish all over the world without drugs and they always got there. Just recently, I spent a week in the Virgin Islands on a scientific mission. It was not a collecting trip but I never go anywhere near the ocean without my nets so consequently I collected about fifty fish to bring back with me. There were no facilities for oxygen and I could only carry one box along with my luggage so I put the entire fifty fish in a single bag without oxygen, sealed the bag tightly with rubber bands and checked them through with my luggage from the Virgin Islands to Miami. The fish were packed at seven in the morning and layed in Puerto Rico for several hours where they changed airlines. I finally unpacked the fish in Miami at 6 p.m., with a loss or just *one* fish! Who needs drugs!"

What can the hobbyist do about purchasing drugged fish? The answer isn't easy because drugged fish often look BETTER than fish which have not been drugged. Fish that are drugged react in two ways. Either they show tremendous interest in food, madly gulping down any food thrown in the tank, or they don't eat at all and slowly waste away. Their eyes are not alert and they may swim about the tank bumping into things. Either way they will die, usually within the first two or three weeks. The fact that some eat ravenously is deceiving, for normally, healthy fish have healthy appetites, but the drugging of fish is not a normal condition. The fish are eating by instinct only. They are eating in desperation, trying to stay alive but their vital organs are destroyed and no matter how much they eat, their poor bodies cannot assimilate the food and soon they will be dead.

The only sure way a hobbyist or dealer can be certain that his fish are not drugged is to request both the collector and shipper that drugs should not be used in the shipping of the fish or in the collecting of them. Of the two evils, the shipping of the fish in the drugs seems to be by far the worst as the fish become thoroughly saturated with it. They usually arrive in fine condition but they die like flies a week or two later. This is how the hobbyist can at least be partially assured that his fish have not been drugged. He can wait a month after the dealer obtains the fish. If the fish look good and are eating well then chances are they are all right. Don't buy fish right out of the shipping box unless you want to gamble with them, or unless you know they were not shipped in drugs. It is not possible to tell positively that a fish was not drugged somewhere along the line, either in the collecting, shipping, or handling of the fish. The salt water hobby is relatively new and these things will all be worked out in time. But the hobbyist should be aware of drugged fish and learn to recognize some of the symptoms. Pacific fish, in particular, are often shipped in drugs and the fact that the fish sometimes must spend two days or more in the shipping box, makes it almost a certainty that the fish will be over drugged and doomed to certain death, even though they swim about the tank for a week or two. Nothing is more distressing than to have a rare and beautiful exotic fish swimming in your aquarium and never show an interest in food. His fins and body may be flawless when you get him but if he has been drugged, he will slowly waste away despite ALL efforts you make to save him. Always request undrugged fish from your dealer so that you will at least have a chance to keep the wondrous and spectacular marine beauties alive in your aquarium for a reasonable length of time.

6

Natural and Artificial Sea Water

We are living in changing times and, alas, our shorelines and coastal waters are becoming so polluted with pesticides, sewage, and industrial waste that it is becoming increasingly difficult to get clean, pure, sea water unless one goes out a long way from shore in a boat. Even then the water is becoming more polluted each year except out in the open sea. In the past, the author has always stressed pure, fresh sea water as the best medium for keeping salt-water fish.

Two things have made him change his mind, to a degree. One was a hurricane that devastated the Florida coast and made the water so dirty that it looked like coffee, even weeks after the storm had passed. The hurricane had washed clean across the shallow waters along both coasts mixing the shallow mangrove mud, inshore waters and coastal waters into a fine blend. Mosquito spray and pesticides which had lain in shallow water for years was pushed to sea in one fell sweep. Every type of bacteria from both coasts was swirled into the open sea. The result was bacteria and poisoned water so lethal that fish, if confined, wouldn't live in it for even a few hours. Aquarists from all over the state were caught in a deluge of parasitic infestations in their aquariums, and my phone rang constantly from aquarists seeking help. The fish plainly could not live in the natural sea water and we had to switch everything to artificial water to save them. The switch to artificial water saved many fish which would have died in the natural water, and it also taught me something else. It was far easier to mix up the artificial water than to haul the natural water from the ocean. This alone made me have some second thoughts about the artificial water. In the many years I have been keeping salt-water fish, I have found that on the average, the hobbyist would keep his fish just about as long in artificial water as he would natural seawater. In view of this, I now recommend that if an aquarist is near the sea and he can obtain good, clean sea water without too much work, then he should use the natural product. Or if he plans to keep experimental tanks of live corals and invertebrates, then the natural water would certainly be more practical, especially if he lives right on the ocean and the water is very clean nearby.

On the other hand, if he lives on a salt-water canal or inlet, his natural water may be slightly polluted or contain an over-abundance of harmful bacteria. He may find it more practical to use the artificial water. It depends whether he wants to keep local fish that he catches himself or wishes to purchase expensive fish. If the latter is the case, perhaps the ersatz solution would be best. Generally if sea water is handy, it is more practical to try it first and if it works out then there is no problem. If the sea water is questionable as to parasites, it can be sterilized by adding a tablespoon of copper sulfate solution to each three gallons of water and letting it stand for a couple days before use. If copper is not available, use a tablespoon of clorox to each five gallons of water. Then add anti-chlorine tablets or liquid to drive out the clorox before using the water in the aquarium. The ultraviolet sterilizer should also help although if the water has numerous small swimming organisms in it, usually the clorox or copper will be needed to kill them.

Extremely pure sea water can be obtained from the Gulf Stream off the Florida coast and it is so clear that it is practically colorless. It does not have to be boiled, settled, or aged and can be used right from the sea. It has a year round specific gravity of 1.025 and varies just slightly according to temperature changes and will support nearly all forms of marine life. Clear water may sometimes be obtained quite close to shore, especially if there has been little wind and the tide is high. But this will depend upon the area and it may take some experimenting to determine at which time of the tide the water will be cleanest.

In some areas the water is best at low tide, and in other areas, the water at low tide would be entirely unsuitable. Examples of this would be in large bay areas where at high tide the water would be cleanest if in a direct line with the sea so it is affected by the tides. In some bay areas if water is collected at low tides it is apt to be of high salinity and teeming with bacteria and parasites. It may also contain drainage from mangrove areas or pollution from sewerage. Only Sea Horses and the hardiest specimens could live in such water. If clean water cannot be obtained close to shore then it should be collected from a boat or it may be obtained from the deep channels under bridges and is usually best when the tide is high. In northern waters, clean water can often be collected in the large tide pools that are present after the tide goes out. The heavy debris usually settles in these pools and sometimes very clean water may be obtained. The water should be collected from the pools nearest to the ocean as it is less likely to be stale. Excellent pools of this type may be found on both coasts of the country, especially off the New England coast and the Northwestern part of the country. Tide pools which are quite far from the surf, with comparatively warm water, may contain an over abundance of harmful marine life. Also, water obtained in very shallow bay areas should be checked carefully. Unless obtaining water from the open sea, it is usually best to carry a hydrometer with you when gathering sea water. If there has been much rain in your area, the salinity may be quite low and in some extreme cases, it may be almost down to fresh water, depending on the tide. The author has found a variance of from 1.015 to 1.045 down in the Florida Keys in some areas where there was little change of water from the tides.

Sea water should be collected in clean glass jars. The five-gallon wide-mouth jar is the most popular container for this use as it can be filled quickly, is easy to clean, and in addition, it may also be used to carry specimens. The water should be collected and left in the sunlight during the trip so that it will become quite warm before you come in. This seems to kill most of the tiny micro-organisms that are present and at any rate can certainly do no harm. The author has found this simple procedure to be definitely beneficial and usually collects the water during the early part of the day unless due to the tide it is especially dirty. If water is collected near shore, particularly near a public beach, or commercial area, it is usually best at high tide and even then it may be full of suspended matter and quite cloudy. This water should be treated cautiously as it is already in a semi-polluted stage. It should not be left in the sun as recommended for clean sea water, but instead should be placed in a dark corner for several days to settle. If it is not too dirty, it may be placed right in the aquarium, if you are just setting up your tank but it should not be used until it is clear and free from odor. A good sub-sand filter will often clear up even the dirtiest water in one or two days, after which the sand should be removed and washed thoroughly, as it will contain all the debris which was in the water. An outside filter with glass wool only, will have little effect upon dirty water, especially if the water is slightly milky, and in this case, the sub-sand filter is highly recommended.

The chief advantage in obtaining clean, odorless sea water from a boat, is that in addition to its clarity, it is also much less likely to contain an over abundance of tiny living organisms which may sometimes prove harmful to your fish. Close examination of the water after it has cleared, will usually reveal their presence, especially near the top and around the light. If the water is swarming with "clouds" of these tiny organisms, they should be destroyed before the fish are introduced to the aquarium. An excellent method is to raise the water in the aquarium to about 95 to 100 degrees for a day or two and aerate the water very slightly, stirring occasionally so that all the warm water won't stay at the top. Again, the sub-sand filter will prove invaluable here for it will completely circulate the water. However, it should be run slowly at this time so that the water will not be aerated too much as this will prolong the lives of the organisms. After the water has heated for a day or two and the small swimming organisms have disappeared, the salinity should be checked and fresh water added to bring it back to normal if necessary.

The aquarist who lives far from the sea, and cannot collect his own sea water, can either have it shipped to him by a reliable collector, or he can use artificial sea water which he can mix in his own home. This man-made water is very successful and while the hobbyist should not expect the impossible of it, he can still keep most of the desired salt-water specimens alive in this solution, especially if it is mixed in part with fresh sea water, and the entire mixture completely changed every four to eight months.

Since salt water will be at a premium for the inland aquarist, he must be especially careful with his marine aquarium and follow all the rules rigidly. All glass aquariums and the newer plastic aquariums will prove invaluable to the aquarist who is a long way from the sea. These tanks will require fewer changes of water in comparison to the regular stainless steel aquariums. There will be no metal poisoning or toxic cement troubles to worry about and although these tanks are not usually available in large sizes, the fact that they are smaller will make the whole marine project less costly. As the demand for plastic and glass aquariums increases, they will gradually become available in greater variety of sizes. Already they may be obtained in five, ten and twenty gallon sizes and even a fifty gallon plastic tank can be made to order.

Many inland aquarists use the three gallon all-glass aquariums and request small marine fish. Thus when the shipment arrives, since the fish are usually shipped in two to four gallons of sea water, the aquarist will have his fish and water delivered all at one time and even have a little extra water for emergencies. The smaller fish are often much more colorful than the larger types and are quite easy to maintain, as feeding and the rest of the project is done on a small scale. Larger plastic tanks of five to ten gallons can be operated on a similar scale and the necessary amount of sea water should be requested when the fish are ordered. Since marine fish are nearly always sent by air, the additional weight may make the freight bill considerably higher but it is usually worth it if not carried to extremes. Consider that if a small amount of sea water, say five or ten gallons, was ordered separately by truck or rail. By the time you pay for the water, the containers, and the freight, the cost would not be too much different and the inconvenience and waiting would hardly be worth the trouble for this small amount.

Artificial sea water, a product which recently reappeared on the market as a substitute for natural sea water, has much merit. It works well, and although it does not live up to the claims of some manufacturers, it can be used with discretion and positively support the more colorful marine beauties for a period of four to six months. "Man-made" sea water is not new and has been placed on the market periodically over the last fifteen or twenty years. However, either the older products were not chemically balanced and could not support life, or not enough was known about marine aquariums and the fish died from a variety of causes. The author suspects the latter and even in present day aquariums, many failures are quickly blamed on the artificial solution or the fish. Seldom are they blamed on the marine aquarist where they usually belong.

The advantages of man-made sea water are many and competition will eventually bring the price down so low that it can be used profusely. The author has been in correspondence with nearly every marine aquarist in the country and most agreed that they had success with the artificial sea water. As stated before, it cannot be expected to do the impossible and should be changed every four to eight months depending upon its condition, how many fish have been kept in it, and various other factors.

The first successful synthetic marine salt placed on the market in the past decade was a product known as Neptune Salts and it has proven very satisfactory for general aquarium use. Other marine salts include Aqua Salts, Rila Salts, Marine Magic, and Reef Salts. There are also other excellent brands on the market. The aquarist should follow instructions supplied with the salts for best results. However, if the fresh water that is to be mixed with the salts is highly mineralized, as it is in some areas of the nation, the salts may be mixed with rain water, distilled water, soft well water, or fresh water that has been run through a water softener. This is recommended if the synthetic mixture was not successful when mixed with regular tap or faucet water. Although some manufacturers recommend that their salt should not be mixed with natural sea water, the author suspects that the reason for this is that some aquarists might mix polluted sea water with their product and then blame any failures on the man-made solution.

Another very promising natural sea water substitute is a liquid product from the west coast of the country which is reputed to be pure sea water in a highly concentrated form. It is sold in one gallon containers which makes ten gallons when mixed with fresh water, and is very successful for the marine aquarium.

Other brands of artificial sea water are sold under various names. One type is made with condensed sea water which is adjusted and concentrated and this brand may be mixed with regular sea water in any amounts after it has been brought back to the normal salinity.

As with all products, there are always some which are extremely inferior and these may be nothing but common table salt mixed with a little rock salt to give variety to the mixture. Since the marine hobby might be somewhat expensive, only the proven brands should be used. Don't experiment with some unknown brand of artificial sea water with costly marine fish. Let your local fish dealer do the experimenting at his expense as he is in business and he should not sell products that he has not tested himself.

Ordinary Kosher salt obtainable in most super markets can be mixed with fresh water until the salinity reaches 1.025 and if this is mixed with pure sea water, it can be used as an extender and will make the sea water go farther. The author recommends a mixture of two-thirds sea water and one part of the Kosher solution and if this has been mixed properly, it can support Sergeant Majors, Beau Gregories, Angelfish, and most of the hardier specimens. An expensive Lion fish was successfully kept in this mixture when there was not quite enough sea water on hand to fill his aquarium. This salt mixture was first brought to the attention of the author by Ed Fisher in his book *Marine Tropicals,* an *All Pets Publication,* but like other marine projects, it is still largely in the experimental stage. The author recommends Kosher salt above rock salt as it is very pure, and dissolves almost instantly. Greater savings in sea water may be obtained by mixing the solution with equal parts of sea water, and for some specimens that are extremely hardy, the solution may be made mostly artificial by mixing to proportions of one-third sea water to two-thirds Kosher solution. This is still strictly in the experimental stage and the author suggests it only as an emergency measure and cannot guarantee results. Those wishing to carry the experiment further should proceed with caution and should not risk valuable specimens until satisfactory results have been obtained.

Chief advantages of artificial sea water is that it can be easily mixed at the convenience of the aquarist as it is needed, and also it is free of small swimming organisms which are usually present in natural water. However, it has some drawbacks in that some of the most interesting creatures, like the Sea anemones, Coral shrimp, Spider crabs, and most crustacea usually will not live well in it, unless it is mixed with large portions of sea water. Inland aquarists, who desire to keep both, should maintain two aquariums one for their fish, and a small, all-glass one for the Coral shrimp, Spider crabs, etc. This smaller container can be filled with the natural sea water in which the fish arrive and the more hardy specimens can be kept in the larger aquarium in the man-made solution.

Small swimming organisms, although not present in the artificial solution at first, soon become established in the aquarium as they are often introduced with the fish. Unless they become too densely populated, they will seldom do any harm.

It is the author's opinion, that while present day artificial sea water is very satisfactory and certainly a boon to the inland marine hobbyist, it is still meant as a substitute. Here it serves its purpose well. To state that it is better than actual sea water is quite a broad statement and the author who has tried both under a wide variety of conditions still feels that it will be some time before man can duplicate the sea water to where it is better than the ocean itself. There is no known solution that will support marine life indefinitely, in which the water will never have to be changed or replenished and regardless of whether the hobbyist uses natural sea water, or artificial, he cannot possibly keep marine fish for any length of time, unless he knows something about them. Water is merely one factor. There is also the feeding, maintenance, and general aquarium procedure which must be followed closely, plus a çertain amount of experience. Only then, can the marine hobbyist hope to achieve success in this fascinating field.

Formulas for Artificial Sea Water

The salt-water hobby badly needs an inexpensive artificial or condensed sea-water solution that will keep marine fish alive and healthy, and that can be made so cheaply that a hobbyist would find no expense in setting up a fifty or hundred gallon marine aquarium. Artificial salts at present are quite costly and some of them actually rival sea water in price even though they are sold in a condensed form.

According to Ciampi and Ray, in the *Underwater Guide to Marine Life*, a superb, informative book on the sea, "the four most important biological elements in the sea are Nitrogen, Phosphorous, Calcium, and Silicon. Less important are Iron and Magnesium." However, in addition, the sea contains dissolved salts of practically every known element. Therefore, it will be up to the individuals who may tackle this problem, to decide which chemicals are most important to support marine life. Below is a good analysis of sea water listing the most important elements. (Furnished by the University of Miami Marine Laboratory.)

Analysis of Sea Water

Figures in parts per thousand by weights (grams per kilograms) *

Salinity	36.50
Chlorinity	20.21
Chloride	20.19
Sulphate	2.82
Bicarbonate	0.149
Bromide	0.068,7
Fluoride	0.001,42
Boric Acid	0.027,7
Sodium	11.23
Magnesium	1.353
Calcium	0.426,6
Potassium	0.404,2
Strontium	0.014,2
Phosphate	0.000,000
Nitrite	0.000,004,6
Oxygen (dissolved gas)	0.009,98
Silicon	0.000,03
Aluminum	0.000,5
Iodine	0.000,001,5
Uranium	0.000,000,3
Silver	0.000,000,006
Gold	0.000,000,006

The University of Miami also gives a simpler breakdown of sea water off the Florida coast which lists the composition as follows:

Element	*Per Cent in Sea Water*
Chlorine	1.8980
Sodium	1.0561
Magnesium	0.1272
Sulfur	0.0884
Calcium	0.0400
Potassium	0.0380
Bromine	0.0065
Carbon	0.0028
Strontium	0.0013
Boron	0.0005
Silicon	0.0004
Fluorine	0.0001

*Formula for Sea Water Used in Berlin Aquarium**

* Reprinted from *Aquarium Journal.*

* Reprinted from *1001 Questions Answered About Your Aquarium* by Mellen and Lanier.

(in 100 Cubic Meters of fresh water)

2 816 kg. Nacl (Natrium Chloride)
65 kg. KCL (Potassium chloride)
550 kg. $MgCl_2 + 6H_2O$ (Magnesium chloride crystallized)
692 kg. $MgSO_4 + 7H_2O$ (Magnesium sulphate crystallized)
25 kg. $NAHCO_3$ (Natrium bicarbonate)
122 kg. $CaCI_2$ (Calcium chloride dried)
100 g KJ (Iodide potassium crystallized)
100 g NaBr (Natrium bromide crystallized)

Summing up the above information, it would appear that the main ingredients for the man-made mixture should be Sodium Chloride (Kosher salt), Magnesium Sulfate (Epsom salts), Magnesium Chloride, Sodium Phosphate, and Calcium Phosphate with a trace of one or two other chemicals. Since most of these are quite inexpensive, the author feels that the main expense in present-day artificial salts is in the advertising of the product rather than in the ingredients.

Simple Formula for Five Gallons of Sea Water

2 level teaspoons Potassium Chloride
22.3 oz. Sodium Chloride (Kosher salt)
3½ oz. Magnesium Sulphate (Epsom salts)
¼ teaspoon Potassium Iodide
⅛ teaspoon Sodium Bicarbonate
¼ teaspoon Sodium Bromide
1 tablespoon Calcium Chloride

Mix with approximately five gallons of fresh water. Dissolve chemicals thoroughly and aerate about a week before use, for best results. Bring to a specific gravity of 1.025 and transfer fish slowly to the solution, adding some fresh sea water to the mixture if it is available.

7

Receiving Marine Shipments by Air

Many of the local pet shops and aquarium stores may not be stocking salt-water fish at present, and the hobbyist who desires to keep the spectacular marine beauties may order them from an out-of-state dealer or collector. This chapter is especially written for them and also for fish dealers who may be ordering salt-water specimens for the first time, or for dealers who may have received fish in the past and were not successful with them.

The most critical time in keeping the beautiful salt-water fish, is when you first pick them up at the airport. The next six hours will determine whether your fish will live happily for the coming months or whether they will die within hours or even minutes after they are transferred to their new home.

Here is where a little forethought and planning will pay off. First, you should have the aquariums all ready before you pick up your fish. Next, you should meet the plane if possible so that the fish will not have to stay in the shipping containers unnecessarily at the airport. Most collectors will send a telegram giving the hour and flight number of when the fish were shipped and then you may call your airport to see exactly when they will arrive.

Few experienced shippers will guarantee live delivery of their fish so you will have little to gain and everything to lose if you open the boxes at the airport. If properly packed, salt-water fish ship exceedingly well and can certainly stand the trip from the airport to your home or store. If you have more than one box, the best procedure is to open each box, and insert an airstone. Then close the lid so that the fish will not become frightened. Any dead fish should be promptly removed and the box they are in should be emptied first.

Most inland dealers and hobbyists will be using artificial sea water in their aquariums so I will emphasize the special care needed to transfer the fish to this man-made solution. First, check the salinity of the water in the shipping container. It may vary from 1.015 to

1.045 depending which part of the world it has come from. This is very important for a sudden change in salinity will kill the hardiest of fish. The aquarium water should read about 1.025 or slightly less. If the water in the shipping container is near to this, then transfer will be comparatively simple. However, if it varies more than ten points, use the utmost caution, and lengthen out the transfer period to at least six hours so that the fish can gradually become adjusted to the change in salinity.

The actual transfer is best done with one-gallon wide-mouthed jars. Fill the jar a third full with water from the shipping box, place several fish in it, and float it in the aquarium. Be careful at this point not to excite the fish unnecessarily. Marine fish will panic when removed from the safety of the dark shipping box and extreme caution must be used lest they be frightened to death! Next, tip the jar slightly and allow a little of the water in the aquarium to mix with the water in the jar. Repeat this procedure several times during the span of an hour or so depending on the salinity. Then if the temperature in the aquarium and the jar are the same, you may now drop the fish slowly into the aquarium. Several jars should be used at a time depending upon how many fish you have to transfer so that you can finish the job faster. (See Chapter 2)

Floating the fish in the aquarium is done not only to adjust them to possible differences in salinity, but equally important, it adjusts them to changes in temperature. This is another factor that can make or break your first marine exhibit. Place a thermometer into one of the shipping boxes while you are opening them and then after all have been opened, take a reading. If it is below 60 degrees then your fish have been chilled and prompt action will be needed to save them, depending how long they were subjected to this cold temperature. Transfer them to the aquarium with the usual method and then examine them closely for signs of chill, skin fungus, and salt-water "Ick." Chilled fish will usually look sick and will swim very little, often clamping their fins, suggestive of being cold. Skin fungus, a condition often brought about by chill, will appear as tiny white bumps or raised scales that will be covered with a fuzzy fungus like coating. Salt-water "Ick," a disease which is usually fatal, and yet one which is not even acknowledged by many marine aquarium experts is a disease not to be trifled with. If left unchecked, it will quickly kill all aquarium fish and render the marine aquarium useless, making a complete change of water necessary. Fortunately, it as well as the other diseases can be easily cured with an ordinary aquarium heater and a marvelous drug known as Sulfathiazole Sodium. (See chapter on disease.)

Feeding will be the next thing of importance after the fish have been established in their new home. Feed them a little live or frozen brine shrimp but don't expect them to eat until they have settled down and learned their way around the new aquarium. Then they may be fed a variety of foods which include dry foods, fresh shrimp, lean beef, chopped lettuce, earthworms, tubifex worms, whiteworms, etc. Feed plenty once fish begin to eat and siphon off uneaten food to avoid possible pollution.

If this is your first shipment of marine fish, follow the above procedure closely, but if you already have some salt-water fish on hand then observe the following rules.

If you are receiving a large shipment of fish, it is best to mix up a new batch of sea water and place the new specimens in separate aquariums from the old ones. This is recommended because oftentimes, the older fish would resent the newcomers and fight them seriously. Also, because of the rapidly changing pH in salt-water aquariums, older fish become adjusted to this change, whereas new fish might die if placed in this water too suddenly. Therefore, if practical, a new batch of sea water should be prepared for each new shipment of fish, unless the shipment is so small that this is not feasible. In this case, transfer the fish very slowly making the change gradual so that the fish will feel right at home when you place him in with the older specimens.

Occasionally when transferring marine fish to their aquarium, they may go into a state of shock, either due to fright or too rapid a change of pH or salinity. The fish will stiffen, usually with mouth open and gills extended, and must be returned immediately to the shipping box to save him. Place him in a net and move him gently back and forth in a motion that will circulate water through his gills, and often he will revive completely. Then after he has recuperated, he may be introduced to the aquarium more gradually than before.

When Fish Arrive in Near-Frozen Condition

During the winter months, a shipment of fish may arrive frozen or in a near-frozen condition. Fortunately this does not happen often as the air lines generally handle the fish exceedingly well; but occasionally a shipment of valuable fish will arrive in this condition. Open the box, dip your finger into the water to see if it is very cold, and quickly examine the fish for any signs of life. If the fish move, even slightly, it is possible to save some of them or even the majority of them, depending upon how long they were frozen and upon other conditions. However, quick action on your part is necessary. First, quickly toss out those that are known to be dead, which is readily apparent by their whitened eyes and stiffened body. Half-frozen fish usually have bright, shiny eyes and these can often be brought back to life from their near-dead condition. Next, insert an air stone and then heat the water as rapidly as possible to about 85 or even 90 degrees. Increase the aeration, and if the fish start to move about, prod them with your hands or a net so they will keep moving. This will force them to work their gills and help revive them. The water can be heated quickly by immersing the plastic fish bags in a dishpan or other large container of warm water.

If all of the fish have died in your aquarium, by all means do not put any more fish in it, even if the water is perfectly clear. Chances are that there must be something wrong with it or the fish wouldn't have died. Siphon out the old water and fill the aquarium with fresh water for a few days to be sure it is clean. Then mix a new batch of sea water and start fresh again. If fish repeatedly die in an aquarium, then undoubtedly it either contains bad coral, insufficient aeration, or has an aquarium cement that is toxic to marine fish. If the latter is the case, then the aquarium should be used for fresh water and another type of vessel selected for marine use. The two and three gallon all-glass aquariums sold in many stores are an ideal container for your salt water experiments if you suspect toxic poisoning. Certainly in this all glass container, there can be no toxic effect and you may find that the cement wasn't the source of your trouble after all. Perhaps you weren't feeding enough, or perhaps you didn't keep a close check on the salinity. Water evaporates quite fast during warm weather and if you don't add fresh water to your aquarium occasionally, the salinity will soon be too high and your fish will suffer.

Instant Success with Your Salt-Water Aquarium

If you have tried keeping salt-water fish with artificial sea water and were unsuccessful, it would be worth while to try a real sea-water aquarium, importing your sea water and fish all at one time. Purchase a clear plastic aquarium of about eight-gallon capacity, an under-gravel filter, light, and other equipment, and order several choice beauties from the Florida or Bahama reefs. Request healthy, fresh-caught specimens and ask the shipper to include seven gallons of pure, fresh sea water with the shipment. Also request that one small piece of live coral partly overgrown with live coral be included in the shipment. This should be a small head about five inches across that has been carefully selected. Ask your shipper to send a telegram on the day of the shipment and arrange to pick up the fish at the airport. When you get home, you can put the fresh sea water in the aquarium, set up the under-gravel filter, cover it with an inch and a half of silica sand, hook up the air pump, and add the fish. You won't have to check salinity, temperature, or *p*H as the fish will be in the same ocean water in which they were collected and won't need to be carefully adjusted to it. You can have your aquarium set up ready for viewing ten minutes after you open the shipping box. Don't forget to add two or three *Tridacna* shells, to afford hiding places for the fish.

Dealers who are unsuccessful with their marine aquariums would do well to try this method. A dealer could set up four eight-gallon plastic aquariums and then order a stunning assortment of highly colored fish. He could request twenty-eight gallons of sea water along with the fish and have enough to fill his four tanks with the real ocean water. He would have instant success with his salt-water aquariums. Those who try this method should make certain they use the proper grade of silica sand on their under-gravel filters. This is very important. Artificial sands, colored sands, pebbles, etc., are all right for decoration, and some beach sands and artificial sands are helpful in maintaining an alkaline *p*H in the aquarium, but unfortunately they do not filter properly with the under-gravel filter. If an aquarist desires to use them, they should be used in conjunction with the silica sand, which is the best filtering medium to date.

At any rate, there is no teacher like experience. The beauty of the salt-water fish will take your breath away and you will find yourself sitting in front of their tank watching the wonders of the sea. But always remember, they don't die for no reason at all. Something is killing them and it might be you. Watch them, feed them, baby them, and love them. All they ask is air, food, and the right water mixture. You can do that for them, can't you?

8

Salt-Water Plants and Live Coral

The salt-water aquarium, filled with choice, snowy white corals, may often be enhanced by the careful addition of a few carefully chosen salt water plants. It will often give the aquarium a "touch of green" and will make it look a little more natural as well as provide a choice tidbit for hungry fish to nibble upon. These should not be chosen at random but selected with caution as certain types are undesirable in the marine aquarium.

Actually, the marine plants are really algaes with some exceptions, and algaes are an important part of the diet in many salt water tropical fish. Therefore their addition to the aquarium is two fold and although still in the experimental stage, there are some that will do quite well if given proper care.

All of them should be planted in a half inch to an inch of sand, using a sub-sand filter to remove the gases which may form about the roots or "holdfasts" which they are called by marine botanists. They should be planted in shallow aquariums as they need a great deal of light and they should be handled and treated the same as fishes, for they are alive. They should be floated in the aquarium and introduced to the water slowly and after they have been planted they should be given forty-eight hours of continuous light to help them get started in the aquarium. After that, a normal eight hours of light will be sufficient.

Aside from their decorative quality and their value as surplus food for the fish, the plants should not be expected to sprout miraculously into beautiful towering vegetation like their fresh-water counter-parts. Most of them will be eaten by the fish and those which survive will seldom last more than a year. Those wishing to concentrate on the plants should devote a separate aquarium to this and keep in it only very small fishes. Sufficient cover should be given so that the fish can occasionally get out of the strong light needed to grow marine algaes and although this may be a little extra work, the author encourages the marine hobbyist to try his hand at growing marine plants. This is a good field for exploration as very little has been done with it at present.

The sub-sand filter is always recommended for the serious growth of salt-water plants as stated before, because it keeps the sand in a healthy condition. Some plants will do better with slow circulation under the sand so the hobbyist will have to experiment along these lines as this is important to the normal growth of the plants. Also, most plants do better in a slight current above the sand and they may obtain their food this way. The power filters recommended by many marine aquarists, are helpful in growing plants for the serious aquarist as they whirl the suspended matter throughout the aquarium so that it can be picked up by the plants. If just a few plants are to be kept, they should be placed near the opening of the sub-sand filter, or in that portion of the aquarium that has the strongest currents.

The hobbyist who visits the ocean to collect his own plants should proceed with caution. First, if he is to set up a tropical aquarium with fish from the warm water of our Southeastern coast, or Indo-Pacific area, he must obtain his plants from the warmer seas. Kelp, and other types of undersea vegetation from the cold northern waters should not be used as they are accustomed to cold water and will usually die quickly in a warm aquarium. However, small algae covered rocks will provide a tasty meal for most fish but again, these should be obtained from warm waters.

The marine plants should be placed in the aquarium as soon as possible after they have been picked and given strong light for at least the first two days so that they will have a chance to get started. If they turn a pale green to white color and show no signs of life after a week, then they should be removed from the aquarium as they are probably dead. This may take a little experience on your part to tell whether a plant is actually alive and growing for sometimes the plants will turn a brilliant green which is nothing more than a mantel of green algae induced by the strong light. Those plants which turn snow white and then brown, can usually be considered dead and should be promptly removed.

When collecting plants, it is best to select only those that are rich green in color and those should be gently lifted from the ocean bed, so that their roots or "holdfasts" are left intact. If the bottom is soft, it is usually easy to scoop up a portion of the bottom around the roots and this may be washed and trimmed so that just a little of the actual bottom still adheres to the roots when the plants are placed in the aquarium. Plants which have deeply imbedded roots should not be used as it would not be feasible to replant them in the aquarium. Also plants from shallow water of less than three feet should not be collected as they are accustomed to intense daylight and usually will not do well in an aquarium. The author has found that plants obtained from a depth of five to seven feet in water that is not too clear will usually live the best in the home tank. These should be obtained rather close to shore where the varying conditions make them a hardier species than those obtained on the reefs.

Penicillus Capitatus

One of the very first marine plants to be grown in the aquarium by the author. It looks like a miniature palm tree or a shaving brush and if obtained in a healthy condition, it will grow quite well. *Penicillus* should be planted in an inch to two inches of sand and given strong light for at least two days. It should be placed in an aquarium with a good current, as it is accustomed to this, and of course a sub-sand filter must be used in the aquarium, so there will be good circulation under the sand. The best size for the aquarium are specimens that are about one-half grown. These can be distinguished with a little practice and at this stage, although they are not at their maximum beauty, they will live the longest in the aquarium. The plant regenerates by sending up a shoot that looks a little like a young asparagus plant. It is rather smooth and has little color until the top starts branching out, and this starts branching out until

Fig. 73. Penicillus capitatus *or Merman's Shaving Brush, growing in an aquarium. Newly formed plants resemble asparagus shoots and are pale green, like this young specimen in the center.*

Fig. 74. Udotea flabellum *looks like tiny sea fan but is no relation to the sea fan or corals. These young specimens are about two inches high.*

Fig. 75. Udotea flabellum *when mature, grows to height of six inches or more.*

it starts to look like a small shaving brush. Full-sized specimens may reach a height of about eight inches and at this time they are fully mature and are not as attractive as the younger plants. This is an excellent plant to keep with large Sea Horses and it can be made into a beautiful display. They will wrap their tails about the plant and give the aquarium a natural look. Furthermore, there is little chance of this plant fouling the water if used with discretion and it will add much beauty to the marine aquarium.

Udotea Flabellum

This attractive little plant looks very much like a tiny green sea fan and when first observed by the author many years ago, that was his belief. Best aquarium size is about three inches tall which at this size, will have spread of about two inches. Plant it in about an inch of gravel or sand and give strong light for the first two days like the *Penicillus*. Several of these beautiful little plants will handsomely decorate the salt-water aquarium. They may be obtained very small for miniature displays and for this purpose, are especially suited for Dwarf Sea Horses, Angelfish, Jewell fish, and the Demoiselles who will love to nibble on this algae. Since it is a rather common plant, it will no doubt prove very popular.

Thalassia Testudinum

A grass-like plant quite similar to the *Sagittaria* in fresh water aquariums. It can usually be found or purchased in an early stage so that the bulb or seed pod is still present. Usually there will be a two- or three-inch blade of grass protruding from the bulb with one or two small roots growing out the other end. It should be planted in an inch of gravel or sand and given normal aquarium light (about eight hours a day). It grows well and is exceptionally hardy. Experimenting with this plant may lead to better strains that can be mass produced for the marine aquarium hobby.

Caulerpa Prolifera, Crassifolia, Etc.

One of the fastest growing algaes suitable for the marine tank. It grows on a stringer with little roots spaced periodically to hold it in place. Once established, it will send out new shoots and will grow quite well. It does best in fine sand without too much current either above or below the sand. Some sunlight each day will hasten its growth. It is one of the most beautiful of all the algaes and an aquarium profusely planted with *Caulerpa* of one species or another, will look like a true under-sea garden.

Fig. 76. *One of the most delicate but beautiful marine algae is* Acetabularia, *with its tiny, pale-green inverted cups. Although it does not live too well in the aquarium, it is interesting to observe and often contains a myriad of marine life. A beautiful Nudibranch is visible at the top.*

Other members of thc family are *Crassifolia and Caulerpa sertularoides* both finely textured members of the group. *Caulerpa ashmeadii* and *Caulerpa paspaloides* are larger, growing to a height of nearly a foot and a length of several feet. Like the others, they should be given strong light and occasional sunlight if possible. *Caulerpa prolifers* and *Caulerpa crassifolia* seem to be the hardiest of the group and the author knows of an aquarist named Rick Fried who has grown a small cluster of *Caulerpa prolifers* into a very spacious plant. It grew so well it soon crowded everything out of his aquarium which was a five-gallon glass bowl in this instance.

Marine plants must be kept in good clean aquarium water with proper filtration and aeration. In short, treat them the same as the fish with the exception that if you plan to specialize in the plants, give them more light.

No doubt the serious aquarist will want to try all aspects of the salt-water hobby so it may please him to know that in addition to plants, live coral may also be kept in the aquarium. This field has been explored very little and its limitations or discoveries cannot be accurately determined for many years. At any rate, the author has found, that contrary to popular belief, many forms of sea life can be successfully kept in the aquarium. While it is true that some will last only a few days, there is no doubt that when more is learned about them, even the most fragile will probably be kept alive for months or years. Common simple forms of life, like the ordinary barnacles familiar to most people, will become live animals of tremendous interest when seen through the glass sides of an aquarium. Furthermore, even those low forms of life will live for months in a properly maintained tank.

The author has found that many forms of coral can be kept for six months to a year and longer in the home aquarium if selected and cared for properly. Delicate finger coral complete with plume worms have been kept alive even with a full array of fish. Brain corals, Mushroom coral, and even occasionally small sponges, will live in the aquarium for varying lengths of time depending upon how much care is given them.

First, the corals should be obtained in a small size and they should be collected fairly close to shore in shallow water. This type is usually much hardier than the regular reef corals as it is accustomed

Fig. 77. *A rock of live barnacles becomes a thing of wonder when brought home from the seashore and placed in a salt-water aquarium.*

A rare Angler Fish (Antennarius sp.) *in one of the author's tanks. Angler fish are among the most interesting of all fishes for the aquarium. Not only do they angle or "fish" for their dinner but they can change color, inflate themselves with air, and also walk along the bottom of the tank on legs which have evolved from fins. This orange-spotted beauty was collected in Florida waters.*

World's rarest photo, a smiling Stonefish! (Synanceja sp.) *Not only is it the most ugly and repulsive looking fish in the world, it is also the most deadly. One step upon its camouflaged back by a bare foot could result in a most hideous, dementing death from the poison of the hollow spines. The author kept this specimen alive for study in one of his aquariums. Its tank mate was the Florida scorpionfish but before the author could photograph them together, the smiling stonefish ate the scorpionfish with one quick gulp.*

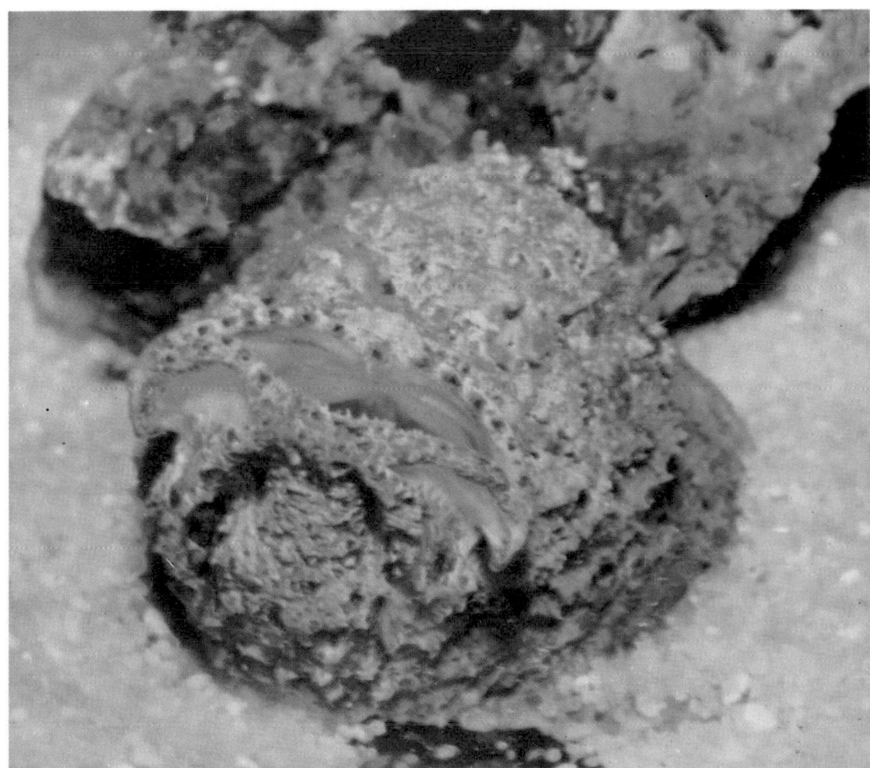

A hobby by itself is the keeping of live nudibranches in the aquarium. They may be kept in a small, two- to five-gallon tank with an algae-covered rock to provide food and a home for them. The colors on many species are fantastic and they are found in every color of the rainbow. This handsome specimen was collected in Florida waters.

A red-striped prawn or dancing shrimp, as the author calls them, lives an upside down existence both in the aquarium and under the sea. The specimen here, hovers under a head of live Moon Coral in one of the author's tanks.

Fig. 78. *"Undersea" scene is actually a photo of one of the author's live coral tanks in which the public was invited to come and see actual salt-water set-ups as outlined in this book. The author maintained as many as eighty marine aquariums at a time, from ten-gallon to six-foot tanks in his constant work of learning about the sea.*

to a wide salinity and temperature range. Coral must be treated the same as fish and should be introduced to the aquarium in the same manner. The Brain and Mushroom types are easier to keep than the more delicate finger coral, but the latter is by no means difficult if sufficient aeration and circulation are provided in the aquarium.

Beautiful multi-colored plume worms that look like Morning Glories may suddenly appear in your coral collection. Quite often they make their home inside the coral and won't come out until at rest in the aquarium. They are very amusing to watch for they will unfold into a flower right before your eyes, but the slightest movement will make them disappear so quickly that the eyes can scarcely follow.

Fig. 79. Caulerpa ashmeadii, *the tallest plant in above photograph, grows on runners of several feet or more and reaches a height of nearly one foot.*

Fig. 80. *A giant species of Caulerpa that is among the hardiest of all tropical marine algae is shown growing in one of the author's tanks. This plant has large, well-developed "Holdfasts" which appear to be true roots, for the plant does not do well unless they are planted in the sand. This plant will easily live past the year mark in the aquarium. The strange creature at the bottom is a sun jellyfish (cassiopeia). It lives surprisingly well.*

Live coral should not be placed indiscriminately in the aquarium, especially if it is well stocked with expensive marine beauties. The keeping of coral alive in the aquarium is strictly in the experimental stage, and those attempting to keep it should do so according to their experience. It is always best to perform these experiments with new creatures in a separate aquarium from your main exhibit unless you live by the sea shore and can change all your water if something goes wrong.

Some of the author's early experiments with living coral were done in an attempt to keep the delicate Four-Eyed Butterfly fish over a long period of time. Since these beautiful creatures lived around the finger coral and were often seen nibbling at it, the author assumed that this was their most essential food and live specimens of finger coral were carefully transferred to the aquarium. It was surprising how well the coral lived and it was especially interesting to see it at night when all the polyps come out of hiding. The entire coral tree takes on a fuzzy pussy-willow effect which is seldom seen during the day. This, as well as other surprises, will await the hobbyist with a scientific interest in the various forms of life in the sea. In addition to the many types of corals, there is also an endless variety of *gorgonia,* sea fans, sponges, and other forms of undersea growth that can be kept in the aquarium. Some types may not last overnight, but others will keep for months, even years. It will be interesting to find out which types can be kept the longest and only with the combined efforts of marine aquarists all over the world, can the secrets necessary to their keeping be learned.

Due to modern air transportation it is now possible to ship live coral to aquarists far inland, and this fascinating aspect of the hobby is likely to develop into a part of the marine hobby as important as the fish themselves, or perhaps even more so. Imagine a live coral reef in your living room! It sounds fantastic, but it actually can be done; and as more people experiment with it so much more will be learned about it that some day it may be a commonplace thing. Coral in itself is quite hardy, as are also the beautiful fan and tube worms that often accompany it. But it does best in pure sea water; so the hobbyist should take this into consideration before he sets his mind to acquiring it. We still have a great deal to learn about keeping coral in the aquarium but by following accepted aquarium procedures for salt-water fish keeping, most corals, as well as Gorgonias, will do surprisingly well in the self-contained tank, even for a beginner.

Give Live Coral Good Light and Strong Aeration

Proper filtration, good lighting, and strong aeration are the three main requisites for successfully keeping live coral in the home aquarium. An under-gravel filter should be used with silica sand as recommended throughout the book. In addition, an air stone should also be used. This should be turned on full force so that it furnishes sufficient aeration for the numerous coral polyps. It will also move the water about the aquarium, which will enable the coral to grasp tiny particles of food and suspended matter from the water. This is how coral feeds. Gorgonias also feed in this manner. The under-gravel filter should bubble rather slowly, in contrast to the rapid bubbling recommended for keeping the fish. Coral will eat live brine shrimp and at feeding time the under-gravel filter should be turned down very low so that it just gives out one or two bubbles per second. This will keep it from drawing the live shrimp down into the sand. Unlike fish, coral does not feed all the time. Usually the coral polyps come out at night, so it is best to place the live brine shrimp in the aquarium about an hour or so before dark. Early morning is also fine for feeding live brine shrimp, but if there are still live shrimp swimming in the aquarium from the night feeding it will

Fig. 81. *This rare, golden Sea Horse is perched on living coral. Sea Horses occur in other unusual colors, brilliant red, red and white, maroon, orange and purple.*

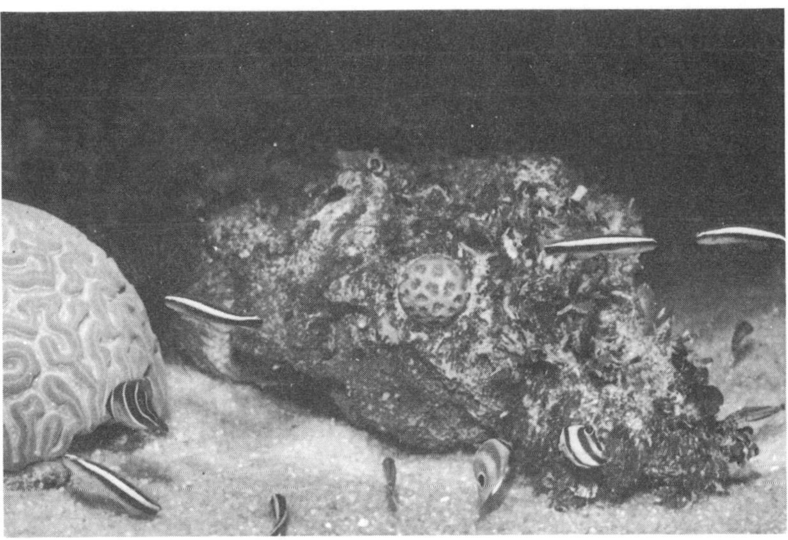

Fig. 82. *A beautiful group of coral fishes lives in harmony with live coral and includes Blue Neon Gobies, Convict Gobies, Angelfish and two species of Butterfly fish. Live Brain Coral* (Meandra) *is at the left.*

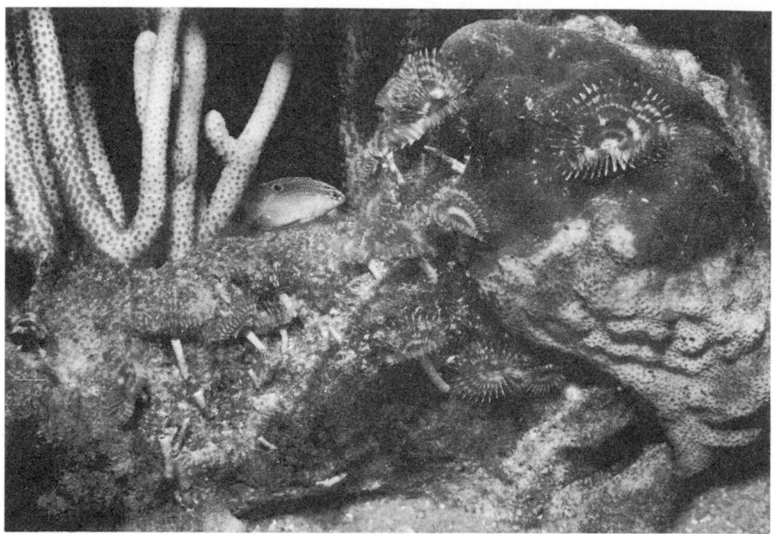

Fig. 83. *A piece of live coral complete with Tube Worms makes a fascinating addition to the salt-water aquarium. Live Gorgonias have been planted in the rear of the tank. A Beau Gregory* (Pomacentrus leucostictus) *pauses for a moment above the coral.*

not be necessary to feed in the morning. Too many brine shrimp can cause trouble as they may die in the aquarium before they are eaten.

Live Gorgonias come out in the daytime and several of them will make a fine addition to the marine aquarium. Very often they will "bloom," or extend their beautiful flowery polyps, right after a heavy batch of live brine shrimp have been introduced to the aquarium, so that it is possible to train them to open while you are awake to enjoy them. Aquarist Rich Fried reports that he has trained a Gorgonia to come out at a certain time each day. This could probably be done with coral as well. The author has noticed, while diving on the reefs, that on cloudy days, or when there is much turbidity in the water, the corals and Gorgonias extend their polyps to feed. Apparently the tips of the coral polyp can sense when the sky has darkened and a cloudy day or murky water probably gives the effect of the approach of darkness and the coral polyps come out to feed.

Live coral is carnivorous and in addition to brine shrimp will eat very fine shredded beef heart, shredded fish, clam meal, and other foods, which should be introduced in small amounts at night when the coral is feeding. Coral can even devour small fish an inch or so in length, and this is not unusual. But the author suspects that most of the fish caught by the coral are either weakened or sick and that the coral has caught them while they were dying or nearly dead. Baby fish are the usual victims of live coral in the aquarium. Larger fish can usually pull themselves from the grasp of the tiny polyps with little effort.

Fig. 84. *An aquarium containing both live coral, live Gorgonias, and fish. In addition to giving the aquarium a natural look, the live coral also furnishes food for the fish. Fire coral at extreme right contains several Feather worms. Swallow Tail Blue Reef Fish and Rock Beauty congregate about the fire coral. Tank holds approximately 20 gallons.*

Fig. 85. *Live Gorgonias live quite well in the aquarium and "blossom" during the daytime when they extend their polyps to feed. Small specimens six to ten inches are best for the home aquarium. The base should be firmly imbedded in the sand.*

There has been a tremendous increase in keeping live coral in the past few years and much of this has been brought about by articles in *Tropical Fish Hobbyist Magazine* by Mr. Lee Chin Eng of Indonesia. Mr. Eng has been corresponding with the author for a number of years and has been promoting interest in marine aquaria in his fabulous country. In recent years he has been promoting his own method of keeping salt-water fish without any filter whatsoever, even having several of his friends write directly to the author about his findings. I have found through careful testing and evaluation that an under-gravel filter works best with live coral, as it allows control of the aquarium and also allows the aquarist to keep a wide variety of marine organisms without fear of sudden contamination and pollution of the water. With the under-gravel filter, the hobbyist can regulate exactly how much filtration he wants simply by running the air through the bubbler stems, fast or slow, whichever he desires. If he is feeding live brine shrimp, he can cut down the filtration so the coral can feed as described above. On the other hand, if the aquarium starts to become cloudy, he can turn up the filters

Fig. 86. *A fine example of "Living Rock" and live coral. The living rock is the large portion to the left. It contains live tube worms, many mollusks, minute plant growth, etc. Much of its life is deep inside. To the right is live coral of the brain-type coral. It is not as easy to keep alive as the living rock.*

and clear the water. With no filter, the aquarist has little control over what might happen.

Nevertheless, Mr. Eng's system apparently is quite successful. He no doubt has chosen certain types of algae-covered rocks or dead coral rock with numerous molluscs, anemones, and some live coral polyps, all of which, he has learned over a period of time, will live in the aquarium, and has achieved a sort of "balanced" marine tank which is a wonderful thing. A full account of his system appears in the February, 1961 issue of *Tropical Fish Hobbyist* and is well worth reading.

People living by the sea, either in Florida, the Bahamas or along other tropical shores, can really bring the sea indoors and have an aquarium that looks just like the reef itself. Of course they must use some discretion; but by trial and error they can soon learn which types of coral and marine growth will live in their tank, and because they live by the sea everything is simplified. If the water goes bad, they can simply change it in a few minutes; or if their coral looks bad, it is an easy task to put it back into the sea and pick up a new piece. Aquarists who live in the Bahamas, in particular, can have spectacular aquariums with little effort, for here the reefs and coral

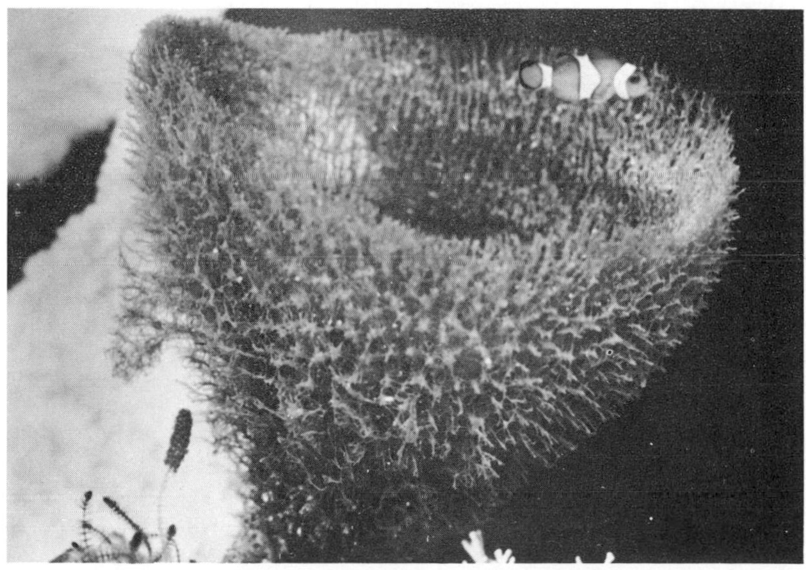

Fig. 87. *The beautiful basket sponge, when cured properly, makes an unusual decoration for the marine aquarium. If thoroughly cleaned until nearly transparent, it will last about a year in the aquarium, then deteriorates and must be removed. Unless one has an ample supply of them, it is recommended that they be kept in the background outside the aquarium.*

Fig. 88. *A head of moon coral measuring a foot across was kept alive by the author, in just a ten-gallon tank for over a year. The coral eventually died while the author was away on an extended trip but parts of the original head are still living after nearly three years! This included plume worms and mollusks which are exceptionally hardy.*

Fig. 89. *The hardiest and most spectacular of Caribbean corals is Moon Coral, a species of moderate depths which adapts well to the aquarium. It has huge polyps resembling small anemones. The author has kept this interesting coral past the year mark in the aquarium.*

Fig. 90. *A black angel, townsend angel, high hat, and butterflyfish all living in the same "Miniature Ocean" with the many plants and corals. The fish stayed in superb health, and even the tiny high hat was reared to marketable size. All were eventually shipped out except the tiny parrot fish which is still in the tank at this writing.*

grow practically to the shore in some areas and it is just a matter of wading out waist deep to secure specimens. Nothing makes the author feel worse than to visit someone living at the seashore and see their aquarium set up with guppies or goldfish! It's a pathetic situation. If they only knew how much more interesting a salt-water aquarium is they would be out skin diving from dawn to dark, catching fish for their tank. They would never be able to get enough of it. It is the world's most fascinating hobby.

The Double Tank System

Two is usually better than one in most instances and the same can apply to aquariums. One salt water tank is nice but two is even nicer. Besides, it gives you a safety tank as well as an experimental tank should something go wrong in your main tank.

With the rising interest in keeping live corals and invertebrates, the double tank system is a natural for with it you may keep both fish and corals, one tank complimenting the other. Here is how to do it.

Fig. 91. *This "miniature Ocean" astounded many visitors to the author's aquarium research store in Miami. Though the aquarium houses a fantastic variety of marine life from lowly sea cucumbers to gorgonians, live corals, live sea shells, anemones, starfish as well as fish, it is operated solely with a sub-sand filter. Once or twice a month a Dynaflo Motor Filter is operated on the tank using activated carbon for a few hours to clean up the bottom.*

Fig. 92. *A beautiful black and yellow Black Angelfish nibbles on a live Gorgonia in a salt-water aquarium. Sea flower at top is a snow-white Anemone. Coral growth at right is Pillar Coral named for its appearance. It lives in deep water in Florida and Bahama reefs.*

Set up one tank with live plants, live corals, anemones, anemone rocks or living rocks. Set it up with both the undergravel filter and the carbon filter as explained in earlier articles. This is your live tank and it can be set up with either natural or artificial water. It should have a good light. This tank may be used for both invertebrates or fish but is primarily an invertebrate tank. In addition to the corals and plants, it may also house sea cucumbers, starfish, hermit crabs, snails, and other live sea shells.

The other tank is a sterile tank set up with bleached corals and cured sea fans. It should also be set up with undergravel filter and carbon filter. This will be your main fish tank and it can be set up with either artificial or natural sea-water depending on your location. A good size for both the live tank and the sterile tank is ten to twenty gallons. Both tanks should be kept at the same specific gravity of 1.025 and of course the same temperature. They should be located side by side or one above the other, whichever is the most practical.

Fish may be kept in both tanks or they may be started out in the sterile tank and transferred to the live tank after a few weeks. The

Fig. 93. *Live Mushroom Coral in one of the author's tanks. The specimen at left has the polyps extended while the coral at the right has polyps completely retracted.*

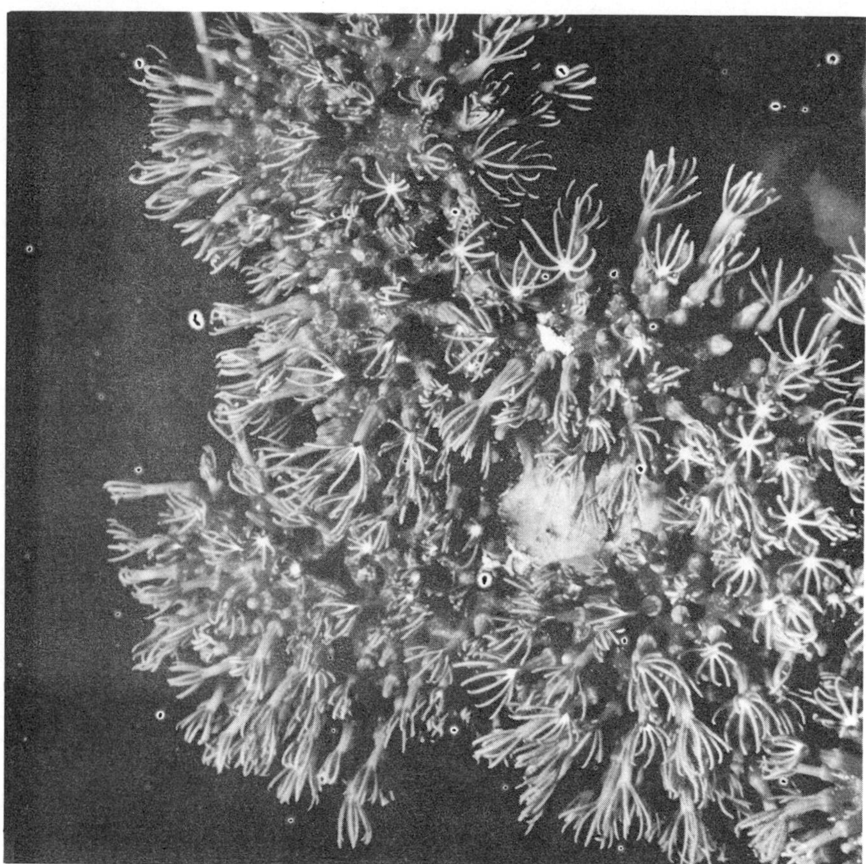

Fig. 94. *Closeup of the purple gorgonian, introduced to the salt water aquarium world by the author. It is the hardiest of gorgonians and does well in the aquarium.*

sterile tank may be medicated with copper sulfate if it is needed. No medication should ever be placed in the live tank. Invertebrates seldom need medication.

Not much is known about keeping live fish and corals together in the same tank and this is one of the purposes of the double-tank system. It gives you two completely different environments in which to keep the fish. Thus you have a double chance of keeping even the most delicate of salt-water fish. An aquarium with live corals and fish is a beautiful sight. The fish are often very healthy and in better color than in the sterile tank, but sometimes problems arise that could wipe out a collection of valuable fish unless they are promptly treated. The author has set up identical tanks of live corals and plants, and though he put in the same fish collected from the same area on the same day, the end results in both tanks were

Fig. 95. *Closeup of Gorgonian Coral shows strange polyps reaching forth for food. An ordinary hand-held magnifying glass brings many of the reef's strange features into sharp focus when viewed through the glass of the salt-water aquarium. The above polyps are on the purple gorgonian.*

not the same. The fish in one tank would live on and on indefinitely without ever a sign of disease. The fish in the other tank would scratch and itch and soon become covered with parasites. It is not known for certain what actually caused the problem. Perhaps one or two individual fish carried specific parasites or bacteria that multiplied in their tank and these particular organisms were not on the similar fish placed in the other tank. Or perhaps the organisms were in the coral or plants. At any rate, every aquarium is different. One time you can set up a live tank with no problems, other times it will present nothing but problems. Since you cannot successfully medicate an invertebrate tank (except possibly with mild dose of clorox), the solution to a live tank is to have a sterile tank where the fish can be placed and medicated if needed.

The double-tank system has many advantages. It allows you to keep all types of fascinating live corals, plants, crabs, and snails. It also allows you to keep the fish. You can keep some fish in both tanks. If a fish shows signs of disease simply dip him up with a net

Fig. 96. *Another of the author's "Undersea Gardens" which was on public display in 1967 and 1968 in Miami, showing the actual systems described in this book. This aquarium contained only twelve gallons of water yet housed two large anemones, three to five inches; approximately fifty small anemones, one to two inches; one large coral head, live with tube worms and mollusks; two giant tube worms four inches across; live snails; live plants; live starfish and live shells. The water is crystal-clear and a sub-sand filter does ALL the work. The tank is given a weekly cleaning with a Dynaflo motor filter with carbon which is run for a few hours. The tank has held numerous fish in addition, but unfortunately they were sold; but more will be added. It also contains six live rocks!*

Fig. 97. *An Undersea garden with various species of mollusks, gorgonians, crabs, snails, and fish can be as fascinating as the sea itself. The large oyster on the right lived for many months in the aquarium and presented the author with the idea that aquarists some day will grow their own pearls with live pearl oysters imported from Japan. It could become a fabulous hobby.*

and place him in the sterile tank where you may add enough copper to keep the parasites under control. Sometimes a fish will be cured by removing him from the sterile tank and putting him in the invertebrate tank. The parasites on his body may not be able to survive in the live tank and vice versa.

9

The Colorful, Breath-taking Fish

No attempt will be made here to decide which marine fish is the most colorful or which is the most beautiful. If an aquarist has kept Pacific fish for awhile and then suddenly comes across an aquarium filled with beautiful Atlantic fish, they will appear to have more color and beauty than his own collection and of course the same is true in reverse. As the old saying goes, the fish are prettier on the other side. Many times, the true beauty of a salt-water fish is never realized because the aquarist has never seen one in full color. With few exceptions, the marine fish is at its peak color and beauty, when first taken from the sea. If it is kept in good healthy water, and fed a good variety of the proper foods, it can be kept in this fine color indefinitely. However, this is usually not the case, and the aquarist often finds dull, unhappy fish lacking in color or spirit, when he purchases his first marine specimens. Therefore, if possible, marine fish should be sent direct from the collectors to the hobbyist so that he will get them when they are at their best. The pet dealer, since he is in business, should act as the go-between, and handle the order. He should keep a small, but attractive display of the more colorful specimens on hand and take orders, using these as samples. Then his customers will get healthy, fresh-caught specimens, that are full of vigor and that will be able to adapt themselves to the home aquarium. They will live longer for the aquarist and will give everyone more confidence in the fascinating salt-water hobby.

The Queen Angelfish *(Angelichthys isabelita)*
(Queen of the Seas)

One of the most popular, colorful, and graceful fish in the world. This living treasure of the sea is usually the objective of nearly every marine hobbyist and its vivid colors are startling to the novice.

Small two-inch specimens are the most highly colored but as the

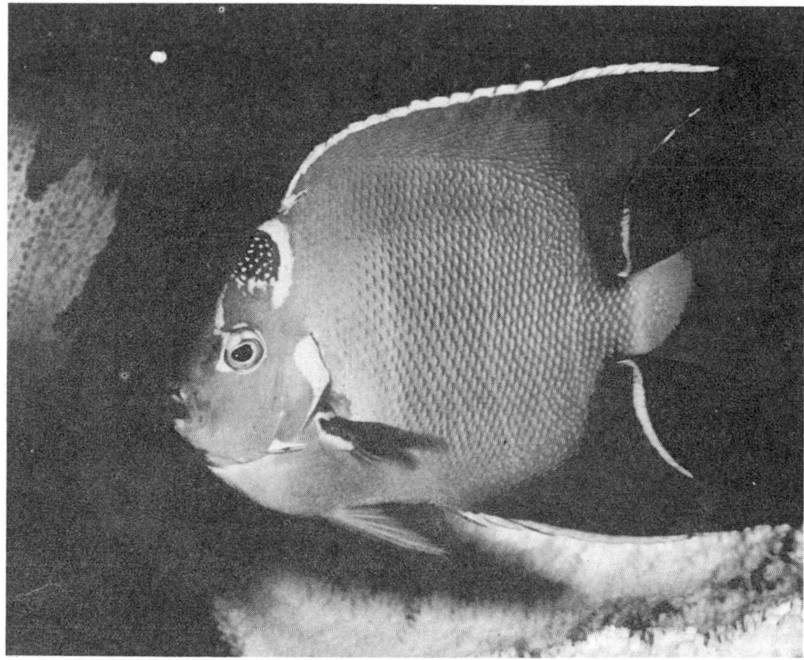

Fig. 98. *Queen of the Seas, the Queen Angelfish* (Angelichthys isabelita) *perhaps the most beautiful fish in the world.*

species matures, the colors are somewhat subdued although they are still beautiful. Young Angelfish live a solitary existence until mating time, and they usually choose to live alone until they are mature. For this reason, just one should be kept in the aquarium, unless there is at least an inch difference in their body length, and then, they should all be introduced to the aquarium at the same time.

The Queen Angelfish, when small, should be given a well-rounded diet of brine shrimp, dry food, fresh chopped shrimp, fish roe, green algae, etc. Tiny specimens less than an inch long, should be fed a constant supply of live brine shrimp in addition to dry food and occasionally they should be fed fish roe, green algae and the other foods mentioned above. Paprika added to their food will help them maintain their brilliant color. Also, finely-chopped greens, lettuce, spinach, etc. will greatly benefit them.

Large Angelfish will seldom eat baby brine shrimp, and seem to be annoyed when this small live food is placed in their aquarium. It gets into their gills and they may panic. Feed them chunks of fresh shrimp, fish roe, and live earthworms, which may be cut into halves or thirds to ease swallowing. Also, tubifex and white worms, may be fed if they can be obtained. Feed balls made up of chopped spinach, fresh shrimp, and dry food, which are well mixed together, and then squeezed into pea-sized lumps, will often give the angelfish proper nourishment and these can often be presented to your pet on the end of a tooth pick.

Blue Angelfish *(Angelichthys ciliaris)*

The commonest of the colorful Angelfish from Florida and one of the best of aquarium fish. The young specimens under two inches are the most colorful and desirable for a salt-water tank. At this age it is difficult to distinguish a young Queen from a young Blue and as color variations exist in both species, the author doubts if positive identification could be made even by an expert. If an adult Queen Angel is found in an isolated coral patch and there are no adult Blue Angels in the vicinity, then it could be nearly certain that any colorful young Angelfish on that patch would be baby Queens, unless of course they were Black or French Angels.

Care and feeding is the same as the Queen and temperament also the same. Just one to the aquarium unless there is a difference of at least an inch in size.

Townsend Angelfish *(Angelichthys townsendi)*

The most vividly colored member of the Atlantic Angelfish. Although there is still some dispute among the experts that this is not a separate species from the Queen Angelfish, the author believes it is. Adult specimens bearing identical markings have been observed on many reefs both off the Florida coast and in the Bahama islands. The adult fish is easily recognized by its outstanding color. Where the Queen Angel is pale blue, the Townsend is a very deep, rich blue, and where the Queen is a pale yellow, the Townsend is a brilliant orange. Even large sixteen-inch specimens have this strong rich color. It is usually an outer reef fish, living close to the Gulf Stream which is another reason the author believes it to be a distinct species. Where the Queen and the Blue will often live close to shore, the Townsend is almost exclusively a clear-water fish and lives with the Rock Beauties, the Jewell fish and others in his class.

Young Townsend Angels can usually be distinguished by their deeper blues and orange hues, although this is difficult until they are at least two inches long.

Two sad features about this spectacular fish are that it is very rare, and the colors fade when it is kept in captivity. Since it lives on the outer reefs, among the fire coral and gaudy sponges and other highly-colored undersea growth, undoubtedly it eats certain food which give it the spectacular color. When kept in the aquarium, even though it may appear to be highly colorful, it will seem dull

Fig. 99. *Young Black Angelfish has transparent tail and swims straight forward in contrast to the weaving motion of the French Angelfish.*

Fig. 100. *Adult Black Angelfish* (Pomacanthus arcuatus).

when displayed with a fresh specimen. This does not necessarily mean that they can't be kept in perfect color. It will just take time and a lot of experimenting on different types of foods to keep this beauty at its best. As marine fish become more popular perhaps some enthusiastic collector or biologist will devise a way of obtaining some of their natural food from the reefs and freezing it for shipment the way frozen brine shrimp and daphnae are handled at the present time.

Black Angelfish *(Pomacanthus arcuatus)*

One of the breath-taking salt-water fish that may have induced you to read this book. Its brilliant yellow and black markings and the magnetic blue pelvic fins contrast so sharply with the white coral in the marine tank that this is usually the first fish noticed in any salt-water display. It lives well, and is comparatively low priced as Angelfish go. Best aquarium size is from three-fourths of an inch to three inches depending upon the size of the tank. Young specimens less than an inch should be fed several times a day and will eat live brine shrimp, dry food, chopped shrimp, etc. All food for these little fellows should be finely shredded so they can eat it with ease.

The Black Angels is at its maximum beauty when two inches long. Larger specimens tend to fade out so that at five inches, the brilliant blue of the pelvic fins is entirely gone, and the bright yellow bands are usually faded out to a uniform grey. At this size, the fish is still quite pretty and becomes very tame. Large Black Angels, although a rich brown and black color, are still beautiful fish. They have long flowing fins and a graceful glide through the water that is beautiful to see. At this large size (which may exceed a foot) they are often seen in mated pairs and their large eyes are capable of expression. Even in the wilds of the reef, the large Black Angel will regard man as a friend and will approach within a foot or two if unmolested. The author once had a mature specimen swim repeatedly into his collecting net, even though it had to turn sideways to fit into the narrow opening.

Black Angelfish sometimes develop a peculiar white patch disease, the cause of which is still unknown. Large patches of the black area will peel off giving the fish an unsightly appearance. This disease is fairly common with the species and doesn't seem to affect the other fish at all. It can be quickly cured by adding one teaspoon of Sulfathiazole Sodium to each five gallons of water in your aquarium. Dissolve the drug in a glass of fresh water first. If disease does not go away repeat the same dosage in three days and raise the temperature slightly. The author has seen Black Angelfish so badly afflicted with this ailment that the body was almost entirely white. Yet, after just a few days of treatment, the fish assumed its normal color.

French Angelfish *(Pomacanthus paru)*

Another breath-taking beauty that is quite similar to the Black Angelfish. At a glance, young specimens appear to be identical, but closer observation will reveal the difference. The most outstanding feature is at the end of the tail, which is square and transparent in the Black Angel, and rounded with a fine yellow band in the French Angel. Also, there is a definite swimming pattern used by the French which quickly identifies it even at a distance. It weaves back and forth in a circular motion very similar to the way a Clown fish swims while the Black Angel swims more or less in straight lines. Also, Black Angels tend to live on the inner reefs near shore, while the French usually prefer the outer reefs near the Gulf Stream.

The French Angelfish is also at its best color at two or three inches and is usually in more demand than the Black because it keeps its brilliant yellow bands much longer. Even at five inches, this beautiful fish has striking color and adult specimens are by no means ugly. Although they lose their vertical stripes at about seven inches, they still maintain a gold edged effect and each body scale will be flecked with this color.

Fig. 101. *Adult French Angelfish* (Pomacanthus paru) *is easily distinguished from adult Black Angelfish by its vivid scale coloring. The adult French Angel is handsomely decorated with gold-trimmed scales whereas the Black Angel assumes an over-all brownish-black color.*

Fig. 102. *Young French Angelfish* (Pomacanthus paru). *Though difficult to distinguish from the Black Angelfish, it will be noted that the young French Angel has a rounded tail with a fine yellow stripe going completely around it, while the young Black Angel has a square tail that is clear at the end.*

Young specimens also get the "White Patch" disease occasionally the same as the Black and of course treatment is the same.

As with other Angelfish, just one should be kept to the aquarium unless there is a difference of an inch in their sizes. Black and French Angelfish tend to be less aggressive than Queens or Blues so if both are to be displayed, the Queen or Blue should be smaller if possible.

There are always exceptions to the rule, where Angelfish of identical size will get along perfectly, especially when they are introduced to the aquarium at the same time, and when they are both given plenty of hiding places.

The Lion Fish *(Pterois volitans)*

This is perhaps the most spectacular fish in the world. It is quite expensive, but such a showy item that it is often desired by the marine aquarist. Eventually, when more are in demand, like other fish, the price of them will be greatly lowered so that more people can afford them. However, even at present, small specimens may be obtained at a cost not much greater than some of the higher-priced fresh-water fish. Since the young fish grow very fast, if fed properly,

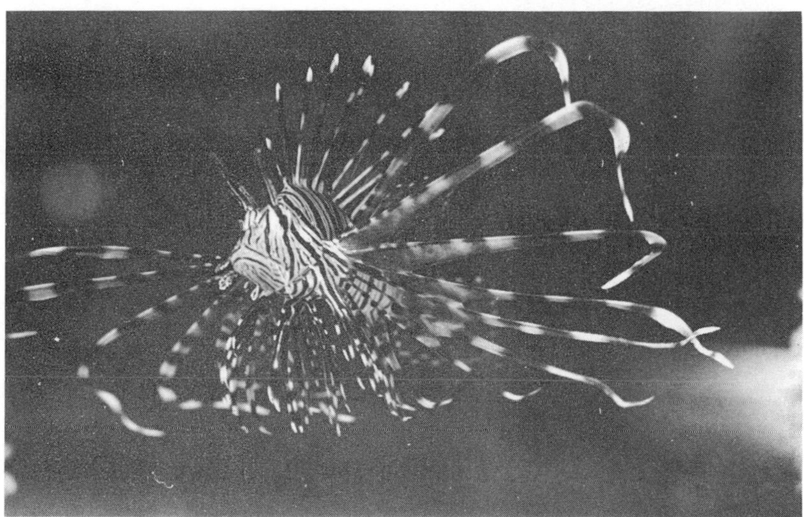

Fig. 103. *The spectacular Lion fish* (Pterois volitans), *also known as the Cobra fish, is one of the most unusual fish in the world. Since it is very poisonous, it should always be handled with great care.*

this might be the answer for the aquarist who can't afford a large specimen.

Lion fish, or Cobra fish as they should be called because of their deadly spines, live very well in the salt-water aquarium, and they can be considered one of the hardiest of marine fish. Many people have kept them well over a year, a fact which helps ease the pain of their high price and they are becoming more available each year as interest in salt water increases.

They should be given an aquarium to themselves for several reasons. One is that they are such a show item, they should be given no competition by having other distracting fish in their aquarium. Also, they will be unhappy with other fish in their tank. Small Demoiselles may nibble at their fins, and others may frustrate the Lion fish by always keeping out of his reach as he attempts to eat them. Probably the most important reason they should be kept to themselves is that they are an expensive fish and shouldn't be risked with other specimens. A healthy Lion fish could be quickly diseased with the introduction of other fish to his aquarium and the guilty hobbyist would certainly feel bad at losing such a rare fish.

The author once kept several Lion fish in a community tank with Sergeant Majors, French Angels, Demoiselles, etc. The results were quite disheartening. The Lion fish spent so much time chasing the elusive Sergeant Majors that they tired themselves out and would not eat small minnows presented as food. They gradually became weak

Fig. 104. *As the Lionfish matures, its body becomes much heavier as seen in this side view. The lengthy filaments over the eyes gradually grow shorter, but never the less, it is still the most spectacular of marine fish in the author's opinion.*

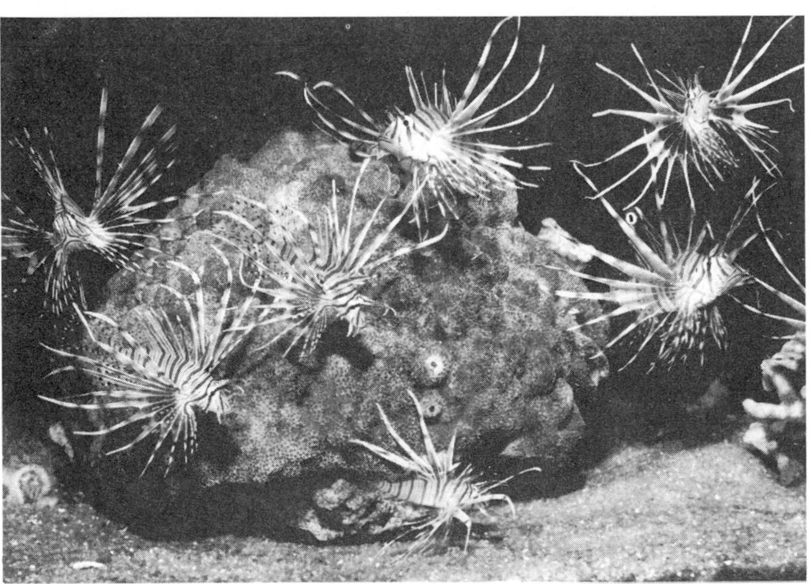

Fig. 105. *Young Lion fish get along peacefully in the same aquarium if they are all placed in the tank at the same time. These exotic specimens are searching around a large clump of live coral for minnows. The author raised twenty-five Lion fish from two-inch babies to these magnificent six-inch specimens in a three-foot-square aquarium, without a single loss.*

from hunger and eventually the Lion fish community tank project was abandoned, and the prized fish given separate homes. The Lion fish feeds primarily on live minnows. Several should be fed at one time until the Lion fish no longer shows interest. Small guppies and other easily-swallowed fish are best and these should be dropped one at a time, in plain view of your pet. If he doesn't eat them, remove them and try feeding again the next day. The Lion fish aquarium should be relatively free of coral so live food cannot hide from its captor. If this is not desirable, the live food may be hand fed by placing it on the end of a toothpick, inserted into the end of a long wooden dowel. Then the food may be moved temptingly in front of the Lion fish until he grabs it. The author once saved a blind Lion fish this way. Since it was unable to see, it couldn't catch its food, and because of its poisonous spines, you can't handle the fish to force feed it. The toothpick extension method was used, and the head of the minnow was inserted directly into the mouth of the starving Lion fish. He promptly swallowed it and further feeding led to complete recovery.

Blindness in the Lion fish is caused by excess light. They are often placed on display and lighted most of the day and sometimes night to show them off. This usually blinds them and the owner often despairs when they suddenly show no interest in their food. He doesn't realize that they are blind and can't see it, so he blames the inevitable loss of this beautiful specimen on everything but the true cause.

If a Lion fish suddenly stops eating, blindness should be checked first. Then if this is not the trouble, the aquarium should be cleaned and a complete change of sea water is usually necessary. This will usually restore its appetite unless of course it has picked up "Ick" or some other salt-water disease.

Rock Beauty *(Holocanthus tricolor)*

A spectacular orange and black fish with beautiful baby blue eyes. This is one of the most stunning members of the Angelfish family and is one of the most highly colored fish in the world.

The best size for the home aquarium is from one to three inches and at this size, it has its maximum beauty. It should be fed plenty of green algae, dry food, brine shrimp, chopped shrimp, etc. with occasional feedings of tubifex worms. Also, paprika should be mixed with some of its food to help it maintain its magnificent color. The author once maintained a specimen on a diet of hair algae which was grown in a five-gallon jar of sea water. This specimen nearly doubled in size in just four months. Out on an isolated reef, a baby specimen was observed very closely and it didn't grow nearly as fast in the natural

Fig. 106. *Young Rock Beauty* (Holocanthus tricolor) *is perhaps the most spectacular of the Atlantic reef fishes. This perfect specimen is about two inches long and has baby blue eyes. The rest of the body is deep orange with a fine red fringe accentuated by a nearly black area in the rear portion of the body.*

state. When first observed it was about three fourths of an inch and seven months later, it had grown to just two inches, which indicates that sometimes a fish will do better in an aquarium than in the sea. Other members of the Angelfish family were observed on a monthly basis and their growth was much slower than formerly supposed. From numerous observations at various locations, it appears that Angelfish grow to about three inches in a year to a year and a half. Of course as stated above, this growth can be speeded up by a rich diet in the aquarium.

Rock Beauties are rare and very shy at all sizes. They should not be kept with aggressive fish and they should be watched closely at feeding time to be certain they are getting enough to eat. Occasionally specimens develop the "White Patch" disease similar to the Black and French Angels and treatment is the same. Also, they are susceptible to a body fungus which appears as white molds on the dark portions of their body. This can be cured by raising the temperature and increasing the aeration for several hours at a time. The sulfathiazole drug should be added if it does not go away. Rock Beauties will do especially well in an aquarium with rich algae growth. They are outer reef fish and need plenty of strong aeration.

Be certain they have a dark secure home in the aquarium where they can hide when necessary. This is very important because this fish can be quickly blinded if given too much light. A large flat shell

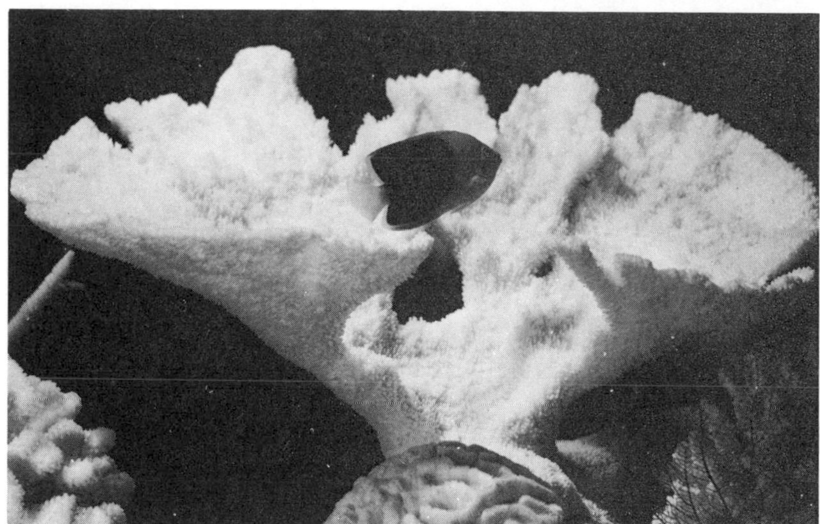

Fig. 107. *As the Rock Beauty matures, the black area in the rear portion of the body increases in size until it takes up a large portion of the body. The coral is an Atlantic variety known as Elkhorn or Fan coral.*

partly submerged in the sand will make a suitable shelter. Bright sunlight especially, will blind this lovely fish and the importance of a dark shelter cannot be stressed too strongly.

If the Rock Beauty does become blinded, and this can be quickly determined by its inability to locate food, the fish should be removed to a separate aquarium which should be kept in the dark except at feeding time. It will be necessary to "hand feed" your pet until he recovers. If it is not possible to remove the specimen to another tank, it is sometimes helpful to coat the eyes with Neoprontosil, a sulfa drug. This can be applied with a cotton swab and should be done every five days.

The Marine Clown Fish *(Amphiprion percula)*

One of the earliest and best known of all the marine fishes, and no doubt one of the most popular. Its brilliant orange and white bands don't seem real. This is one of the first marine fish to become really popular, and lives very well in home aquariums. Some specimens have been kept as long as five years and it has already been spawned by at least one individual and perhaps more.

It is a peaceful fish and travels in little schools around the aquarium. It readily eats dry food as well as most aquarium foods including chopped shrimp, brine shrimp, fish roe, etc. and is well established in the fish world. Formerly quite expensive, it may now be obtained

Fig. 108. *The marine Clown fish* (Amphiprion percula) *is a very popular fish. They live well in a properly maintained aquarium and have been kept for several years by many aquarists. In the natural state, these beautiful creatures live among the tentacles of large sea anemones and are often called the anemone fish. It is startling orange and white in color.*

Fig. 109. *Marine Clownfish hovering above a large Pacific sea anemone which is their natural home in the sea. They swim right down into the stinging tentacles and apparently are immune to the stings which would kill other fish.*

at a modest price. Tiny inch-long specimens may be safely kept in a two- to five-gallon aquarium, and they will be the envy of all aquarists who see them.

In the natural state, they live in and around huge sea anemones, and occasionally they may be seen on display in large aquariums, living with their deadly friend. Although they will live with the Florida Anemone, they do not take to it, and will swim near but not into this anemone. It still makes a beautiful sight and constitutes one of the most attractive marine aquarium displays. Their peculiar habit of living with the Sea Anemones, has given them the name of the Anemone fish, a name preferred by most ichthyologists.

This will probably be the first colorful marine fish to be spawned and raised on a large scale so that in the future, the price of them will be low enough for everyone. The author suggests keeping five large Clown fish in a fifty gallon aquarium situated where it will get some sunlight, for those attempting to raise this fish. Then place several

Fig. 110. *The Maroon Clownfish* (Amphiprion tricintus) *is rarer than the common clown* (A. percula) *and much less peaceful. In fact it is extremely quarrelsome with other maroon clowns and two should not be kept together unless they are carefully observed. The smaller clown to the right is the Golden Clown* (Amphiprion akallopisos). *It is also called the Orange Skunk Clown but the author feels the name unjust for such a handsome fish.*

layers of coral against the sides so that the fish will have privacy if needed. By choosing five adult specimens, you are almost sure to have a pair, and by providing the layers of coral, you will give the mating pair a chance of privacy. The sunlight will encourage algae, which should be allowed to grow so that if young are born, they will have some minute food organisms in the water. Should a pair show signs of spawning, remove the other Clown fish, and watch for eggs. Then, if eggs are deposited, remove parents the day they hatch and hope for the best.

Clown fish may be kept with most other marine fish and for some peculiar reason, Angelfish and other Atlantic fish will pay little attention to them. They should be included in every marine aquarium and no doubt, they will always be a marine favorite.

Clown fish sometimes develop body fungus which appears as tiny white lumps on the orange part of their bodies. It is usually caused from chill and can be cured by raising the temperature to about 85 degrees for a few hours at a time, and increasing the aeration. Also, avoid too much bright light as they seldom hide and they can be blinded. If practical, it would be wise to turn off the aquarium light at feeding time as they usually rise to the surface to eat the dry food.

Neon Goby *(Lactinius oceanops)*

A beautiful blue salt-water aquarium fish with such a friendly dis-

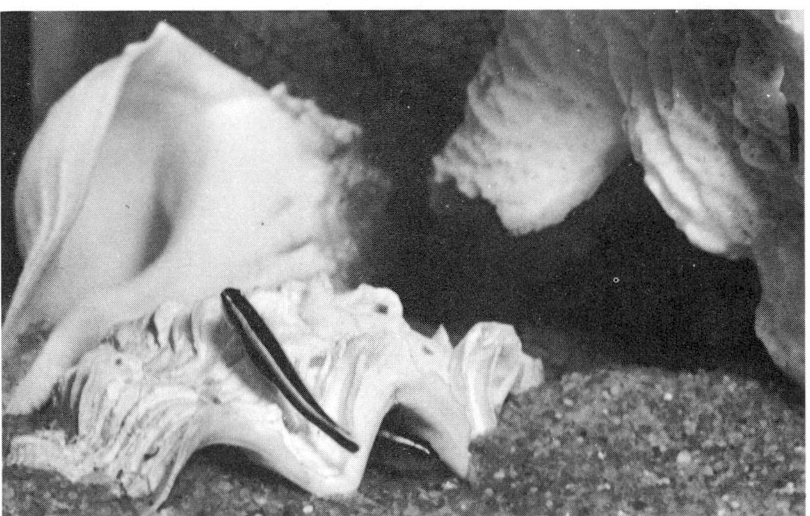

Fig. 111. *A mated pair of Neon Gobies* (Lactinius oceanops) *makes a home under a shell in one of the author's aquariums. Several days later, they produced a cluster of approximately one hundred eggs on the upper surface of the shell.*

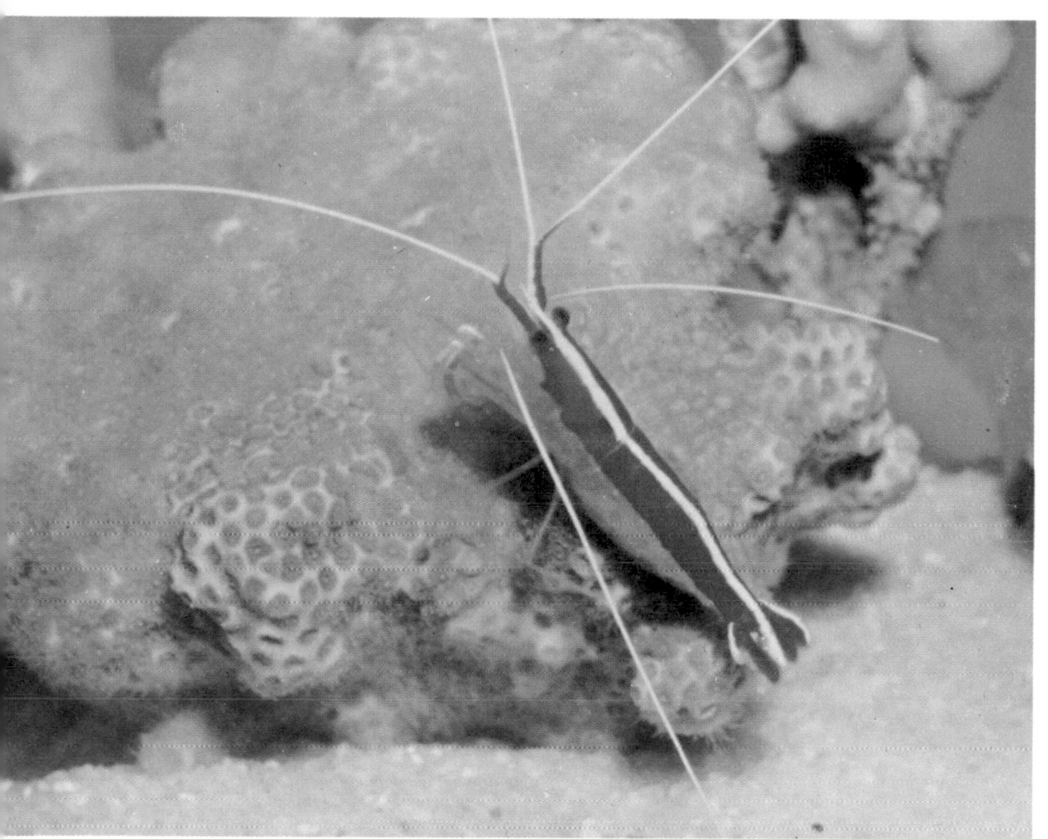

The fiery red, Scarlet Cleaner Shrimp is one of the most spectacular of invertebrates for the aquarium. They live well and like the coral shrimp, they are sometimes obtained in mated pairs.

Giant plume worms and orange coral give this aquarium a natural, undersea look. Despite their fragile appearance, the plume worms are very hardy and seem to contribute to the general health of the aquarium itself.

position that it is liked by all the fish in the sea as well as by the aquarist. This was one of the first colorful salt-water fish ever to be spawned in the home aquarium. Not only was a spawn produced, but the eggs were hatched and the young raised to the free swimming stage.

The first spawning was with a mated pair which were taken from one of the author's aquariums and presented to Dick Boyd, an employee at Coral Reef Exhibits. Mr. Boyd succeeded in spawning the pair not once but several times. The author spawned several pair shortly after that and succeeding in raising the young to the free swimming stage. Since then, many people from various parts of the country have also spawned the Neon Gobies and undoubtedly this also will be one of the first colorful salt-water fish to be raised on a large scale.

Several may be kept in the aquarium at one time, and they should be given shells to hide under in the aquarium. They may be kept with most other fish including Sea Horses, Cowfish, and most other marine fish with the exception of large Cardinals, Porkfish, and other fish that may tend to devour them.

In Ed Fisher's book on Marine Tropicals, he predicted that the Neon Goby would probably be the first marine fish to be spawned successfully in the home aquarium and he was right.

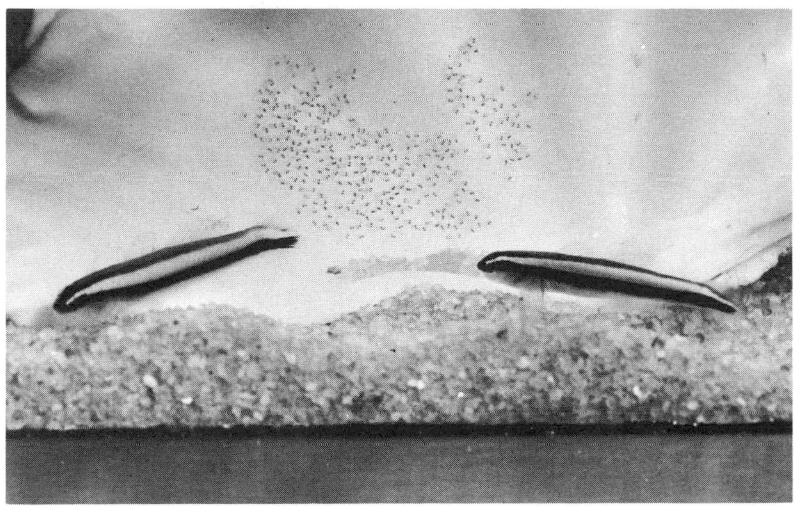

Fig. 112. *After about six days, the bright blue eyes of the unborn Gobies are clearly visible to the naked eye. Both parents attend the nest and take turns fanning the eggs to prevent fungus. The shell was upturned here for photograph and was carefully replaced. Eggs hatch in about ten to twelve days.*

Fig. 113. *The Neon Goby checking a large Tomato Clownfish* (Amphriprion ephippium) *for parasites. Although the goby is a cleaner fish, it will not rid the aquarium of all parasites for it feeds on specific types only.*

The little Neon Goby is the friend of all the fish in the sea. Even giant Barracuda will visit his home and lie perfectly still in the water for hours while the little blue gobies swim up and down his fearsome body searching for parasites. Huge Moray eels, Parrot fish, Grouper and practically every fish on the reefs will all visit the Neon Goby's home to have their parasites extracted.

Your beautiful Angelfish and other marine fish will want their parasites removed so be sure to include several Neon Gobies for them. You will witness a strange spectacle when you see your pet Angelfish hover motionless beside the Goby's home waiting for the little blue servant of the sea to perform his duty.

For those wishing to spawn the Gobies, the procedure is very similar to the spawning of any egg layer. First obtain a mated pair of Gobies. Place them in a small aquarium filled with fresh sea water, and condition them on live brine shrimp, dry food, fish roe, etc. Place a flat shell or coral in the tank so that they will have a dark secure home, and when mating season approaches, you will notice that the female is filling out heavily with eggs. Do not disturb them other than feeding, and soon you will see them tending their nest. The *Tradacna* shell shown in the illustration is best because it allows you to see the eggs without disturbing the nest so that their growth can be watched daily.

Both Gobies will attend the eggs, and they will constantly hover on them to keep them from getting fungus. Sometimes, if the male is especially active, he will eat the eggs so they should be watched closely. If this happens and you actually see him eating the eggs, remove him and the female will usually take care of the eggs until they hatch.

This usually takes from ten days to two weeks and the female should also be removed as the eggs hatch or she may devour the young. Baby Gobies are transparent but even at birth, they have a bright blue spot at their eye and one at the base of their tail. They will carry a yoke sack at first and will have difficulty swimming until about five days. After that they will be free swimming and in ten days they will be quite active and will be eagerly searching for food. The author fed his newly hatched Gobies marine infusoria gathered from heavy algae growth, and introduced egg yolk through the infusion method.

Neon Gobies spawn twice a year and may produce several spawns in rapid succession during the spawning season. This is usually in the spring and fall. About 100 babies are born at a time and when the eggs are a week old, the bright blue eyes can be easily seen with the naked eye. This fish should certainly be included in every salt-water aquarium and for the aquarist who accepts a challenge, the Neon Goby will give it.

At one month, the gobies are thin slivers of blue and can eat freshly hatched brine shrimp with ease. Also they should be fed fine dry food, fish roe, and fine shredded shrimp. They grow rapidly if aquarium conditions are right and in three months time, they will be about a third grown. After that they grow slower until at one year, they are fully mature. At this stage, they usually leave the family group and seek a mate and the whole procedure is repeated. It is a beautiful sight to see a mother and father Goby surrounded with their offspring. They all live together in one big happy family until the babies are fully mature. Only then do they leave home. It's almost the same as the human race.

Probably this same procedure could be carried out in a home aquarium if it was large enough. The author has tried leaving the parents in with the nest until the eggs hatched and quite often it was successful. The day the eggs hatched, adult brine shrimp were introduced to the aquarium and the Gobies ate this rather than their young. Although no conclusive evidence was obtained, it seemed that the Gobies would usually eat their eggs for the first one or two spawnings and then at the last spawning, they would hatch them out. They took excellent care of their nest at all times and usually all the eggs would hatch with the exception of one or two. In one instance, a pair spawned in an aquarium with a Rock Beauty and they allowed me to up-turn the shell every few days to make color movies of the event. I repeated this until the eggs had hatched and still the parents made no attemp to destroy the nest.

Neon Gobies prefer a temperature of 70 to 75 degrees and do not stand up well with quick temperature changes. They will sometimes get "Ick" or white spot and it is fatal to them unless quickly cured. They require good aeration and if signs of white spot or "Ick" develop, raise the temperature to 85 degrees for several hours at a time until signs of the disease disappear. Also keep the salinity at around 1.022 or slightly less.

The Marine Jewel Fish *(Microspathodon chrysyrus)*

The most magnificent member of the Demoiselle family is the Marine Jewel fish. This fiery beauty is a deep midnight blue with light blue diamonds glistening over its entire body. Furthermore, it is an amazingly hardy fish that is especially suited to the marine aquarium. It will eat dry food, brine shrimp, green algae, fish roe, or practically any fish food, and makes itself right at home in the aquarium.

The Jewel fish comes from the outer reef right next to the Gulf Stream. It lives in the deadly fire coral, which is so poisonous that a

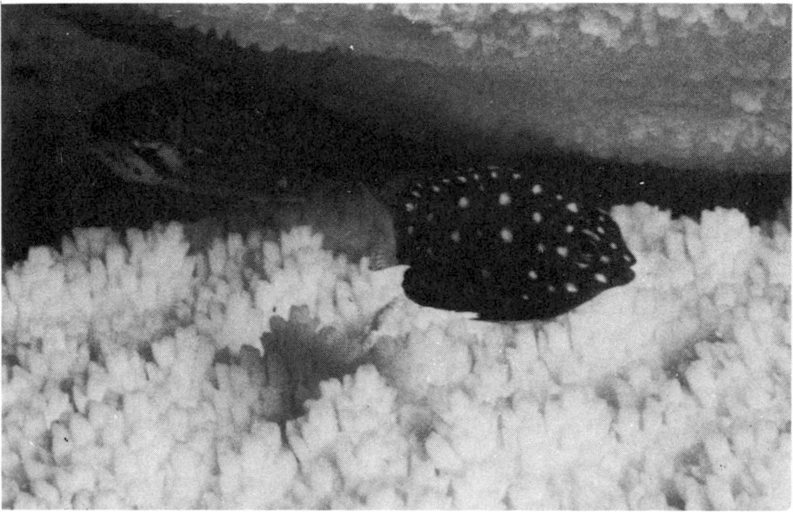

Fig. 114. *The fiery Marine Jewel fish* (Microspathodon chrysyrus) *has a deep blue body with numerous diamonds that sparkle in the sunlight. When content, and viewed in the right light, this fish sparkles as though his body was covered with living jewels.*

bad contact with it would no doubt prove fatal to a human. Consequently, it is a rather expensive fish. It lives well however, and its beauty can hardly be described.

Best aquarium size is from one half inch to an inch for at this size the body is nearly covered with the "Jewels." As the fish matures, which is at about four inches, its tail turns a brilliant orange, and the blue spots gradually fade so that at the large size, they are not nearly as attractive. This fish should be given plenty of aeration and good water circulation and the salinity should be maintained at 1.022 to 1.025.

Just one should be kept in the aquarium unless it is a very large aquarium in which case two or three may be kept if they are all introduced at once, and if there is a difference of at least an inch in their sizes. They should be watched closely and if there is fighting, the offender should be removed.

The Cardinal Fish *(Apogon maculatus)*

A brilliant red fish with a gold stripe through the eye. It is one of the few nocturnal salt-water aquarium fishes. Although it normally hides during the day, it will soon learn to come out at feeding time and its rich red color will contrast nicely with the white coral. Its large mouth is developed for swallowing small fishes, so beware! Don't keep small Gobies, Beau Gregories, or other little fish in with this fellow or they will soon be nothing but a memory. Feed chunks of fresh shrimp and live earthworms. Brine shrimp will seldom be eaten unless they are adult size in which case they will be eagerly devoured.

The Cardinal fish likes to hide and must be given a dark hiding place or it may be blinded. Just one should be kept in the aquarium unless they are small specimens. Then several may be kept together if they are all introduced at the same time.

Scarlet Back Demoiselle

Another member of the Beau Gregory family that is similar in habit and reputation. This beautiful little fish is sometimes called the "poor Man's Jewel fish." When very small, its body is covered with little blue spots and its back is a flaming red, making it a highly colorful fish.

Best aquarium size is about a half inch and just one to the aquarium is the rule. If more are kept, there will be constant tension and the fiery red color will disappear. This is also a hardy fish and as it seldom exceeds three inches, it is a good aquarium fish. It will eat dry food, brine shrimp and most other aquarium foods and as it is

Fig. 115. *Atlantic and Pacific fish will live contentedly in the same aquarium, if properly introduced. In the center is the dazzling Blue Demoiselle* (Abudefduf caeruleus) *from the Pacific and below is Neon Gobie from the Atlantic reefs.*

also an inexpensive fish, it is an excellent one for the beginner. Does best at a salinity of 1.022.

Blue Demoiselle *(Abudefduf caeruleus)*

A very colorful Pacific Demoiselle with a brilliant blue body so bright that it glistens. Like the Blue Reef fish, it can turn the color on or off depending on its mood.

It will eat dry food readily and will also eat chopped shrimp, brine shrimp, and most aquarium foods. Best aquarium size is about one inch for at a larger size it is very aggressive. One or two in the aquarium is usually the limit and these should be watched closely to see that they don't fight. This is a very active fish and will add much activity to the aquarium. There is also a yellow Demoiselle which may belong to the same family.

The Orange Demoiselle

An active little fish from the outer reef that is a brilliant orange with a black spot on the tail. It is sometimes mistaken for a young Rock Beauty because of its color, but its actions are a dead giveaway for the experienced collector. It darts in and out of crevices in true demoiselle fashion and is well suited to the aquarium as it is exceptionally hardy.

Best aquarium size is about one inch or less and like the other demoiselles, just one should be kept in the tank unless it is a very large aquarium. It will eat most aquarium foods and is especially fond of dry food. Occasionally green algae should be added to its diet, as well as fish roe, brine shrimp. Lives best at salinity of 1.022 to 1.025.

The Sergeant Major *(Abudefduf saxitilis)*

This is perhaps the most common salt-water aquarium fish. It is very hardy, an excellent feeder, and in addition, it is inexpensive as well. Furthermore, it is one of the few marine fish that is compatible with members of its own kind. It is definitely a school fish and may be kept in small groups or three or four to as many as several dozen in a larger aquarium. It adds much activity to the marine tank and will eat dry food, brine shrimp, chopped shrimp, and most aquarium foods. Best size for the small home aquarium is a half inch or at least less than an inch. They grow very fast and larger specimens may be aggressive if placed with timid fish. Specimens over two inches

Fig. 116. *The Sergeant Major* (Abudefduf saxitilis) *is one of the fastest and most alert fish on the reef. Though a most common fish, they can be most difficult to collect. Ever alert, these specimens are hovering near the top of the tank in anticipation of a handout.*

should have at least a fifty gallon aquarium and even then, there may be quarrelling so they should be watched closely. However, if they are obtained small and grow to this size in the tank, they will usually be compatible. Basic color is yellow and black but the entire body color may vary from almost black to nearly white depending on the mood and health of the fish. Generally, they become dark if aquarium is improperly lighted or if suffering from toxic poisoning.

The Beau Gregory *(Pomacentrus leucostictus)*

The Beau Gregory, sometimes called "Little Yellow Belly," is the first colorful fish noticed by the amateur collector. Its brilliant blue and yellow body give it immediate attention and it is an excellent aquarium fish. Very often when the author has returned from a collecting trip, a curious crowd would gather about the dock to view the catch. They would look at the Angelfish, Butterfly fish and suddenly exclaim: "What is that beautiful fish?" I would look expecting to see them pointing at a pretty Blue Angelfish, or a brilliant red Cardinal fish, but no, they would be pointing at the little yellow and blue Beau Gregory. It seldom failed.

Yet, this charming little fish has not been too popular as a marine aquarium fish. A few "experts" gave it a bad name and they slighted one of the nicest salt-water aquarium fishes of all. They said it was "mean" and a fighter and other bad things. But it isn't so bad, if given half a chance.

First, it is one of the least expensive of the salt-water fish. Second, it is one of the most beautiful, and third, it is one of the hardiest! What could be better than that? It is true that large Beau Gregories are mean and aggressive, but so are large Jewel fish, Sergeant Majors, Blue Demoiselles, or any other Demoiselle. So just obtain a small specimen, and you will have a gem of the aquarium. The author has kept many small Beau Gregories together in one aquarium, and as long as they were all introduced at the same time, and were given plenty of food and hiding places, they behaved like perfect little gentle-fishes. It's usually the large fellows over an inch that are nasty. But even these make good aquarium fish if just one is kept to the aquarium, and if they are kept with fish larger than themselves. Also, contrary to popular belief, they do not lose their color when they get big, but actually have more color, except when they get very old. The author has collected many specimens nearly three inches long that were in superb color. Of course these large specimens would raise havoc in a peaceful aquarium, but put them in with large Angelfish, or Porkfish and they will be kept in line.

There is nothing more beautiful in the fish world than a tank full of baby Beau Gregories a quarter of an inch long. They will look like living jewels as they dart in and out of their hiding places. Each one will pick out a little hole in the coral and that will be his home to guard and protect.

The author has raised many baby Beau Gregories to maturity which takes about a year and cannot praise them too highly. They are certainly beautiful with their flaming blue and yellow bodies and their little freckled faces. If several are to be kept in the same aquarium, they should all be introduced at the same time and they should be obtained at a size of one half inch. They grow fast and will do better if allowed to grow up in the aquarium. Keep their water at 1.022 or less and give occasional feeds of green algae. They will also eat dry food, brine shrimp, chopped shrimp, fish roe, and practically any food you give them. It is important that they have plenty of hiding places in different parts of the aquarium so that they will feel secure. Baby Beau Gregories should be handled very gently for they can be very easily frightened to death.

The Butterfly Fishes

No matter how beautiful the marine aquarium is, it will aways be enhanced by the addition of one or two Butterfly fishes, and no really

Fig. 117. *The Four-eyed Butterfly fish* (Chaetodon capistratus) *is by far the most popular fish in its group. Its delicate markings and prominent false "eye" near the tail, make it a marine favorite.*

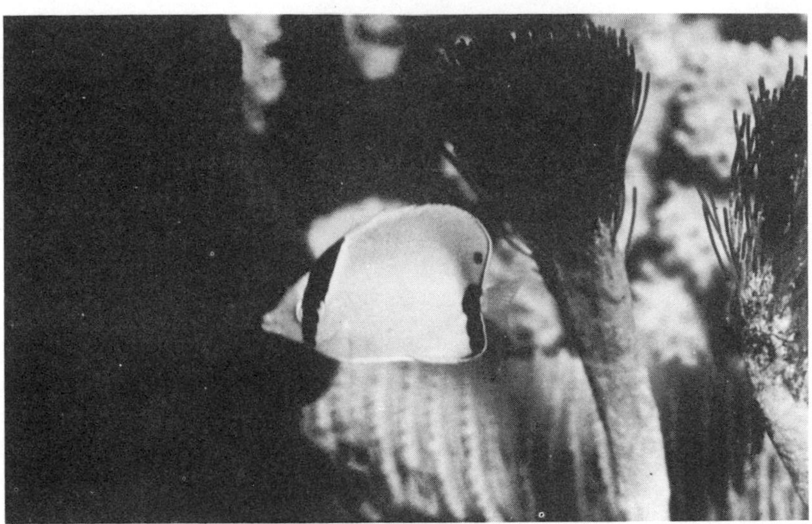

Fig. 118. *The Least or Painted Butterfly fish poses beside* penicillus, *a marine algae or plant. Although not quite so showy as other Butterfly fish, this species is by far the hardiest and eats dry food as well as most other aquarium foods.*

complete salt-water display can do without them. What they lack in color, they make up in petite behavior, delicate markings, and an all around attractive appearance so that it is easy to understand their popularity. Four or five Butterflys, properly displayed with sea fans and finger coral, will make such an attractive display that the gaudier fishes will not even be missed, for these delicate shy little beauties, are a symbol of the reefs and they have won their place in the aquarium field.

Unfortunately, most Butterfly fish are poor feeders and live only a few months in captivity. However, this situation is rapidly changing, for we are learning much more about these desired fish so that eventually, they will live as long as the hardiest of marine fish. Actually, the Butterfly fish is very hardy. It ships exceedingly well and nearly always dies of slow starvation in the home tank. An example of their hardiness is "Dingo," the travelling Butterfly fish. Dingo was a four-eyed Butterfly fish who was captured in Jamaica, B.W.I. by Capt. Lawrence Holloway and flown to New York to the Holloway's home aquarium. Dingo was a shy feeder at first, but soon discovered that the Holloways weren't going to feed him just brine shrimp, like everyone else, for instead he got a good variety of food, the most important of which was tubifex worms. Dingo developed a passion for them and soon frew fat and saucy and lived a record time in their aquarium. Then the Holloways decided to move to Florida and

Fig. 119. *The Banded Butterfly* (Chaetodon striatus). *Note coral-encrusted sea fan which may be cleaned and treated like coral and will handsomely decorate the aquarium.*

Dingo was carried down in a small plastic bag inside Mrs. Holloway's handbag. He made the trip fine and was transferred to another aquarium in the deep South. At first all went well, but as time went by, Dingo lost weight due to the fact that his precious tubifex worms couldn't be obtained in Florida, and had to be flown down by special connections. Dingo refused all other food including white worms, and several times, when his shipment of tubifex worms arrived dead, Dingo would go hungry until another precious cargo would be obtained. He was truly neurotic, and would rather starve than eat anything else, which is exactly what he did, for when it became impossible to obtain his precious food, Dingo slowly faded away after living well past the year mark in captivity.

Other aquarists have kept the Four-Eyed Butterfly fish for considerable lengths of time, and once the feeding problem is solved this beautiful fish will live a long time in the home aquarium. In addition to tubifex worms, Butterfly fish will sometimes eat white worms, micro worms and other foods of this type. They will also occasionally eat brine shrimp and finely chopped fresh shrimp, but they will seldom do well on these foods and must be fed the small worms to maintain them for any length of time.

Besides the Four-Eyed Butterfly fish, there is also the Common Butterfly, the Banded Butterfly, and the Least or Painted Butterfly. The Least Butterfly belongs in a class by itself for it is the hardiest of

Fig. 120. *Long-Finned Butterfly fish* (Heniochus acuminatus) *is very hardy and eats chopped shrimp, dry foods, and other foods. This specimen doubled its size in just a few months. Brown Clownfish hides under protective ledge of coral.*

Fig. 121. *Two fish often confused by the aquarist are the Moorish Idol* (Zanclus cornutus) *on the right, and the* Heniochus acuminatus *or Long Finned Butterfly on the left. Both are very hardy in the aquarium if healthy, undrugged specimens are obtained. Of the two, the Heniochus is the hardiest.*

all the Butterfly fish and eats dry food as well as most aquarium foods. It will compete with the Sergeant Majors for food and will eat chopped shrimp, brine shrimp, fish roe, etc. It can easily be kept past the year mark and has been kept several years by good aquarists.

In addition to the above-mentioned Butterflies which all come from the Florida coast, there is also a wide variety of Butterflies from the Pacific, some of which are extremely beautiful. Their general habits are similar to the Atlantic species and unless they can be coaxed to eat well, they will not last long in the home tank. Perhaps some of them will prove to be as hardy as the Least Butterfly, but only experimentation on the part of the aquarist can determine this for at present, little is known about the Pacific Butterflies in relation to the home aquarium.

The Moorish Idol *(Zanclus cornatus)*

A breath-taking Butterfly fish from Hawaii and also the western Pacific. It is unique in shape with slender snout and extremely long dorsal fin. It is perhaps one of the most highly publicized marine fish and is the main subject of many artistic designs featuring marine life. Although extremely rare in this country, continued interest in salt-water fish will encourage more dealers to import them so that eventually the larger aquariums will keep them on display. Like most Butterfly fish, it is a delicate feeder and should be given an aquarium to itself so that it will have the full show, and also will not have to compete with more aggressive fish for food. It grows to a fairly large size and a mature specimen should have at least a fifty gallon aquarium. It is a great show fish and one of the most fascinating of all marine fish.

Royal Gramma *(Gramma loretto)*

The aristocrat of the Atlantic marine fish and a beautiful one at that. This rare treasure looks as though it had been dipped in Easter egg dye and then had mascara added to complete the makeup.

The body is a brilliant reddish purple from the front to about half-way down the back, and the rest of the body is a flaming yellow with a few freckles added for looks. Fine red lines about the face give it a most decorative quality and perhaps give it that expensive look, for this is the highest priced marine fish from the Atlantic Ocean.

It is a rare, deep-water fish from the outer Bahama island and is seldom seen on.display except in the largest of aquariums. Once settled in the home tank, it will do surprisingly well and eats dry food with gusto. It will also eat brine shrimp, fish roe, green algae, chopped shrimp, and a variety of other foods.

Fig. 122. *The exquisite Royal Gramma* (Gramma loretto) *is one of the most highly-colored and expensive marine fish.*

Just one to the aquarium is the general rule unless there is a little difference in their sizes, in which case several may be kept together if they will get along. They should be given a flat shell or coral for a home and although they may hide at first, they quickly become tame and will soon be out at feeding time with the other fish.

Too much light may blind them as they are unaccustomed to it. Also, since they are so expensive, they should not be kept with demoiselles or aggressive fish. This fish also likes plenty of aeration and does best at salinity of 1.022.

Be sure to cover the aquarium because they are jumpers, and it would be an expensive disappointment to find them dead on the floor in the morning.

Yellow Tang or Blue Tang *(Acanthurus unicolor)*

The Yellow Tang is a graceful addition to the marine aquarium that will add much vitality to your display. It is a very fast fish and one of the most difficult to collect. Small specimens under three inches are best for the home tank for at this size, they are not quite as nervous and will adapt to the aquarium very well. Young specimens are usually bright yellow and as the fish matures, the yellow gradually turns to blue. However, there is still some controversy about this as it is generally assumed that there are no adult Yellow Tangs off the Florida coast. In many years of collecting, the author is

Fig. 123. *The Royal Gramma* (Gramma loretto) *in typical pose, emerges from its home in a hollowed-out piece of red pipe organ coral. It is considered by many to be the most exquisite of all Caribbean fish.*

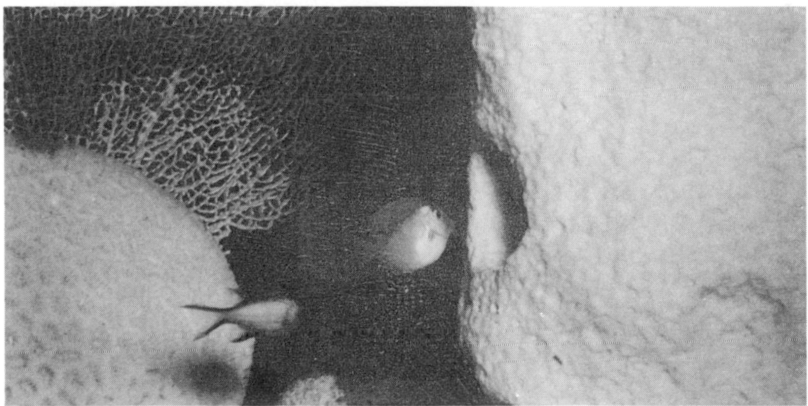

Fig. 124. *The iridescent Blue Reef fish* (Chromis marginatus) left, *and the graceful Yellow Tang* (Acanthurus unicolor) *right, are seldom seen in aquariums. This beautiful display consisted of only two pieces of coral, yet, with a large gold sea fan placed in back, it made a fine exhibit.*

not quite certain of this for Yellow Tangs have been observed in adult sizes many times. Also, the young have been observed in both colors at the same sizes, which might indicate that it is possible for the yellow fish to be a separate species in some instances. One thing against this is the fact that when mature, the Blue Tangs will school and to date no one has ever reported a school of Yellow Tangs off our coast so perhaps the general assumption is right. At any rate, for identification, the young tang is referred to as a Yellow Tang and then called a Blue Tang when it turns color.

It is a very nice aquarium fish and a good feeder. It will eat dry food, green algae, chopped shrimp, tubifex worms, and most aquarium foods. Some paprika should be mixed with its food to help it maintain its color. The young yellow specimens are quite striking and in addition to the rich yellow color, the body is generally outlined with a fine red line.

The Pacific Yellow Tang *(Zebrasoma flavescens)* is a true yellow even at the adult size, but it is difficult to obtain specimens at present. All tangs are members of the Surgeonfish family and are equipped with a sharp scalpel or knife which fits in a sheath near the base of the tail. The fish erect this spine at will and it can inflict serious damage to a careless handler.

The Blue Reef Fish *(Chromis marginatus)*

A graceful swallow-tailed fish from the quiet depths of the outer reefs. Its body is a brilliant magnetic blue that can be turned on and off at will. So bright is the color that it can be clearly seen fifty feet below the surface of the water on a quiet day.

It attains a length of about seven inches and since it comes from the outer reefs, it must have strong aeration in the aquarium. This is a rather rare fish and it is somewhat shy. Aggressive Demoiselles should not be kept in the same aquarium or they may quickly tear its delicate fins to shreds. Large specimens five inches or over should be kept in a fifty-gallon aquarium and although this fish will spend most of its time out in the open, it still should be provided with a home so that it will have a place of safety at night.

Feed chunks of fresh shrimp, earthworms, and adult brine shrimp. Also fish roe and tubifex worms if available. Several small specimens may be kept in the aquarium at one time, but larger specimens prefer to stay by themselves, although two or three will sometimes school together.

The Porkfish *(Anistoremus virginicus)*

One of the very few marine tropicals that travels in schools. This

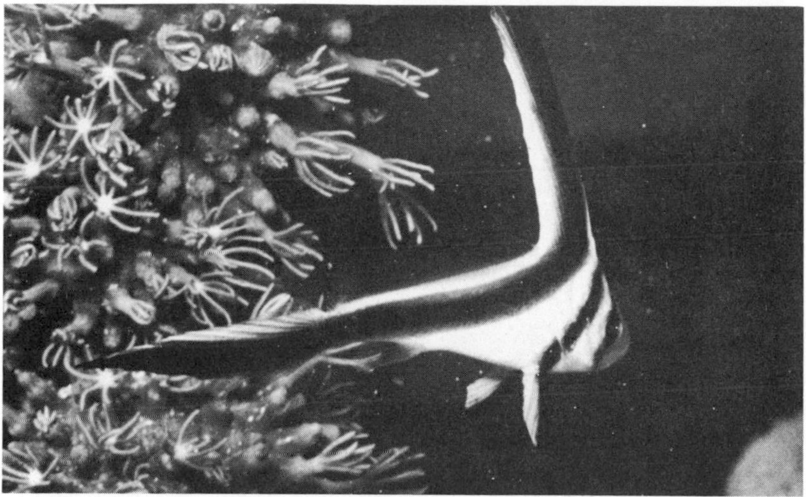

Fig. 125. *The Jackknife or Ribbon fish is a spectacular marine beauty. It travels in small schools and because of its delicate fin structure, it should not be kept with aggressive fishes. The tremendous dorsal fin of this strange fish can be pointed in any direction and used to ward off other fish.*

pretty orange and black striped fish is rather common off the Florida coast. The young specimens do well in a ten or twenty gallon aquarium and several may be kept together. They will eat chopped shrimp, small minnows, earthworms, and dry food and as they mature, they develop wide vertical stripes across their head which gives them a beautiful appearance and they are hardly recognized as the same fish. They grow to a size of at least six to eight inches and of course at this size they will need a very large tank. They should not be kept with small Demoiselles, Gobies, etc. or the smaller fish may be eaten.

Rare Pacific Gems

From time to time, exotic, highly colored marine beauties will become available to the salt-water aquarist. Most of the species that reach this country will be relatively hardy, as delicate specimens are rarely shipped, due to the tremendous distances involved. Young Angelfish and Butterfly fish in particular are extremely colorful and many are truly spectacular. Most command a rather high price, due to the complications involved in getting them from the depths of the sea in some far distant ocean, which may be ten or fifteen thousand miles away, to your home aquarium. The author always gazes at a prized gem from the Pacific with awe. It is almost inconceivable that a tiny salt-water fish could be captured in the depths of the sea, prob-

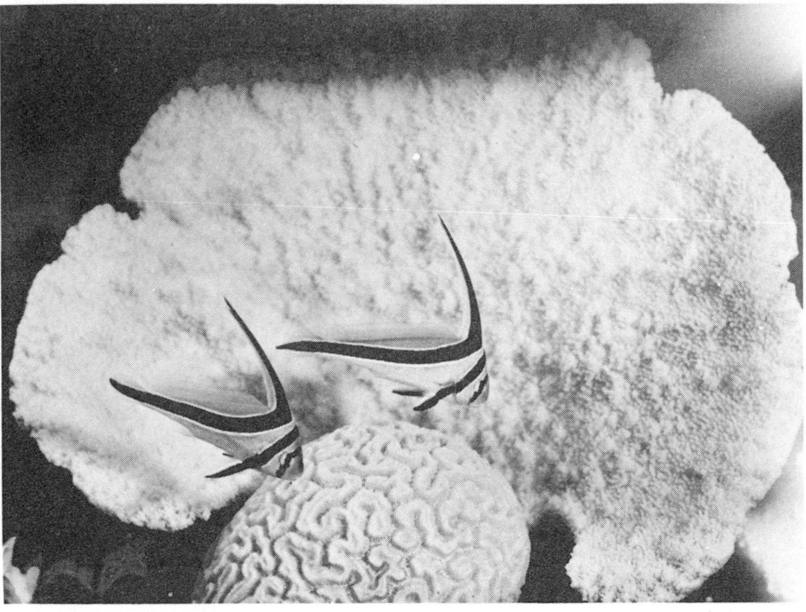

Fig. 126. *The Adult Ribbon Fish or Jacknife* (Eques lanceolatus) *is even more spectacular than the juvenile species pictured in Fig. 125. These perfect specimens were collected in the bay near Miami.*

ably brought to a staging area, transferred by native boats to a motor vehicle which brings it to an airport, then shipped halfway around the world to a major city, where it eventually finds its way to someone's aquarium. The most amazing part is that the little creature can go through all this and still survive; and some people say salt-water fish aren't hardy!

Due to the rather high price of the rarer Pacific fishes, the amateur aquarist, needless to say, should by-pass them until he has gained considerable experience with the less expensive specimens. Some of the very colorful Angelfish may consume a half week's pay, and it would be folly to purchase them unless you are capable of keeping them in good condition. Angelfish and Butterfly fish may require specialized feeding, and if the aquarist does not have a variety of foods available he may become distressed as his precious marine beauty slowly withers away from lack of proper nourishment. A few pieces of live coral may prove most helpful here, as it will allow the fish to nibble upon certain types of reef vegetation similar to that found in its natural state. The author has saved many rare Pacific fish in this way. Some were extremely emaciated when acquired, but after they were carefully transferred to fresh sea water and fed large quantities of brine shrimp and fine chopped shrimp, and had nibbled on clumps of live coral in the aquarium, their health was restored and

Fig. 127. *Jet black and white* Dascyllus melanurus *shows in startling contrast to the smoky corals in the marine tank. This beautiful fish comes from the Pacific reefs. Its close relative* Dascyllus trimaculatus, *is also jet black but instead of the stripes, it has three small spots on a coal-black body.*

Fig. 128. *Pacific Blue Angelfish* (Pomacanthus semicirculatus) *is a striking fish of deep, luminous blue. Although it was formerly quite rare, it is now being brought into the country in larger numbers for the marine aquarist.*

Fig. 129. *The author's first adult Emperor Angelfish* (Pomacanthus imperator) *to arrive alive in the shipping bag, after a 10,000 mile journey from the Far East. This spectacular beauty is among the most prized of rare Pacific gems and is probably second only to the Regal Angelfish although both are equally spectacular in their own way. This stunning beauty resides in a four-foot-long all-glass tank with a large Spotted Panther Fish, a Platax Batfish, and a Golden Striped Grouper. The sea fan is cured for tank use.*

Fig. 130. *The exquisite Copper-Banded Butterflyfish* (Chelmon rostratus) *is a spectacular gem from the Indio-Pacific area. It is very hardy in the aquarium if a healthy, undrugged specimen can be obtained. Unfortunately many are still being shipped in drugs and these are doomed to slow death in the aquarium regardless of how well they are treated by the aquarist.*

Fig. 131. *A Long-Nosed butterflyfish from Hawaii* (Forcipiger longirostis) *is a real gem in the aquarium. It is very active and probes into the crevices of coral for food. This species is found throughout the Indo-Pacific.*

eventually their colors became as vivid as they were when they were first taken from the sea.

Some of the most popular Pacific fish include the Pacific Blue Angelfish *(Pomacanthus semicirculatus)* and the Imperial Angelfish *(Pomacanthus imperator)* which is also called the Koran. Both are quite hardy with bodies accentuated with white bands and colors varying from deep blue to pale purple. The Blue Angel has slightly curved bands similar to the Atlantic French or Black Angelfish, while the Koran has concentric bands with a white banded bull's-eye near the base of the tail. Other exotic Pacific marines are the yellow Lyre Tail Wrasse, the Twinspot Wrasse *(Coris angulata),* Spiny Butterfly, Longnose Australian Butterfly *(Chelmon rostratus)* as well as other exotic Angelfish, Clown fish, Trigger fish, Tangs, and numerous Demoiselles. In fact there are hundreds, perhaps thousands, of spectacular salt-water fish from faraway reefs that will eventually find their way to the aquarist with an interest in salt-water fish keeping. Much of this is due to modern jet transportation, which greatly reduces the time element, a critical factor in shipping fish.

The Jawfish *(Opisthognathus sp.)*

Both the Yellowhead Jawfish and the Pearly Jawfish are captivating

Fig. 132. Platax pinnatus *is the most spectacular of Pacific Batfish. Its body is jet black, outlined in red. It grows to large size and requires a fifty gallon tank for comfort.*

Fig. 133. *The graceful Batfish* (Platax obicularis) *curls its huge dorsal as it turns in the aquarium. This species is the most commonly available and it grows to a large size. It bcomes very tame, quickly accepting food from your fingers. This specimen increased in size from just a few inches tall to nearly a foot in just a little over a year.*

Fig. 134. *Pacific Mud Skipper hops about on land or rests partly in and out of the water as shown here.*

as aquarium specimens. They are unique among the exotic fishes in that they "dance" on their tail as they hover above the bottom. They have large, expressive eyes and they seem to be able to turn their heads to follow the aquarist as he walks by the aquarium.

Fig. 135. *Mud Skipper resting on a rock in a shallow aquarium. These interesting creatures live about mangrove roots, climbing out on land to catch flies and other insects. If fed properly, they are very hardy.*

Fig. 136. *The beautiful, semi-transparent Convict Goby spawns readily in the aquarium. It is especially interesting because the development of the eggs may be clearly observed through the transparent body of the fish. The Convict Goby matures at about an inch and a quarter and is very hardy.*

Fig. 137. *Adult Marine Clown fish present a striking picture in the aquarium. The orange and white colors of this spectacular beauty contrast so vividly that it doesn't look real. This group forms almost a perfect circle around a ledge of live coral in one of the author's tanks.*

Fig. 138. *The Cubbyu or High Hat* (Eques acuminatus) *is an inexpensive and interesting addition to the marine aquarium. An inoffensive fish, it should not be kept with aggressive specimens, and it does best in the aquarium if kept with members of its own kind so that it will not have to compete for food. It will eat finely chopped shrimp, brine shrimp, worms and small minnows. Small specimens under two inches have enormous dorsal fins, which grow shorter as the fish matures.*

Fig. 139. *Two monarchs greet each other in the aquarium. The Emperor Angelfish at the left and the spotted Panther Fish on the right. The author raised a panther fish from two-inch size to seven inches in a little over two years. This large specimen is fringed with orange.*

Fig. 140. *The exquisite Pearly Jawfish* (Opisthognathus sp.) *is the favorite of many aquarists who are quickly captivated by its shy behavior. The beautiful little fish lives in small colonies just off the edge of the deep reef where it dances above the sea floor on its satin-like tail.*

It is a small, delicately hued fish with fins that resemble exquisite lace. Of the two more common species, the yellowhead is the more colorful. Both come from deep water so the aquarium should not be brightly lighted. The bottom of the tank should contain at least two or three inches of sand, and they should be provided with a number of tridacna shells to hide under. They will enlarge an area under the shell by carrying huge mouthfuls of sand to the shell opening. In the ocean, they live in deep tunnels which they make by moving the rock and sand with their large mouths. The tunnel is dug straight down vertically and then it usually curves under a rock where they enlarge a little area so they can turn around. It is a thrilling sight to see a colony of them hovering above their homes on the sea floor. As you approach, they dart into their holes. Then if you move away you will see them peek out to see whether or not you have left.

If you have a deep aquarium of a couple feet or more in depth, you could put six inches of shell or rock over a sub-sand filter and the little fellows will make tunnels just as they do under the sea. Several may be kept in the tank if they are all introduced at the same time. They are very hardy but they must be handled cautiously when first acquired as they are very excitable. They should be placed in the aquarium with the light off and then each one should be gently pushed under a shell so that it can quiet down. The aquarium must be tightly covered at all times as they are extreme jumpers. Even small openings around filter stems should be blocked or you will find your little pet on the floor in the morning.

Jawfish sometimes injure their tails shortly after being collected if the collector doesn't handle them properly. The tail becomes red, worn, or even bleeding. It is best to examine the tail closely before you purchase them. If it is simply red then it will probably heal once they have been placed in a good home. But sometimes the tail may be badly damaged and infected and it will take considerable treatment to cure it. It may be painted with merthiolate once or twice a week. The tank should also be treated with copper to avoid bacterial buildup.

They are shy fish and shy feeders. It is best to keep them in a tank by themselves but they can live in a community tank if tank mates are selected properly. They will eat adult frozen brine shrimp as well as chopped shrimp. Usually they like to see the food fall to the bottom where they will swim up to it and engulf it with their large mouth. They generally show little or no interest to food that is lying still on the bottom. If their food isn't eaten right away, it should be removed from the tank with the fine filter net or regular net. This is an ideal aquarium fish and will probably be one of the first to spawn in the home aquarium. Already a few people report that they have observed the little fellows carrying a large mouthful of eggs in

Fig. 141. *The Coral Catfish* (Plotosus anguillaris) *is a fine scavenger in the aquarium and constantly digs in the sand for food. However, it is extremely poisonous, perhaps fatal, and belongs in a display tank in a store or public aquarium, rather than the hobbyist's tank, except for special study.*

Fig. 142. *The Wrasse family presents some of the most colorful and interesting of all fish. There is literally no end to their variety and color. Some are bright yellow, others may be bright green. One is startling white and red so much unreal that it appears to be painted. The above specimen comes from deep water and is bright blue and yellow. It is still unnamed and the author calls it the Fairy Blue Wrasse.*

Fig. 143. *The Scarlet Hogfish or Cuban Hogfish* (Bodianus pulchellus) *is a deep-water species from Florida and Caribbean waters that was not discovered until the scuba gear became fashionable for collecting in the deeper waters. The fish is brilliant red and yellow and of quite large size making it most desirable for the aquarium.*

Fig. 144. *An immature High Hat is a very delicate fish yet it can be reared by a good aquarist. It should be fed large quantities of newly-hatched brine shrimp and should not be kept with any aggressive fish. Small high hats a half-inch to an inch flit about a coral ledge like tiny fireflies. The very small specimens have enormous dorsal stringers but are so delicate they must be handled with utmost care to get them home alive.*

Fig. 145. *Young Squirrel fish* (Holocentrus ascensionis) *have red and black stripes and hardly resemble their parents. The two specimens here relax under a magnificent cluster of Elkhorn coral.*

Fig. 146. *The Ballet! Two Yellowhead Jawfish do a graceful ballet dance in the aquarium.*

Fig. 147. *The Opera! The same jawfish appear to be singing. Some aquarists call these cute little fish the "people" fish because of their expressive faces and interesting antics.*

their aquarium home. Perhaps the time is not too far off that someone will succeed in raising the young. Jawfish mature at four or five inches, which makes it an ideal fish for the home aquarium. In addition to the Pearly and Yellowhead Jawfish, there is also a larger shallow-water species known as the Marbled Jawfish. This species, while interesting, is not nearly as exotic as the smaller, deep-water fish. It has a huge mouth, opening an inch and a half to two inches, and it will swallow your finger clean up to your wrist if you reach into the tank. It has absolutely no teeth so it cannot harm you. Its living habits are similar to the other jawfish.

10

Oddities from the Sea

The salt-water aquarium should by no means be limited to the highly-colored species, for there are a tremendous number of grotesque, and extremely interesting creatures from the sea that will utterly fascinate the marine aquarist, Although many of these may be kept in the community tank along with your other fish, some of them, due to their "peculiar" habit of eating everything that moves, should be kept in an aquarium to themselves. There is such tremendous variety of interesting denizens of the deep, that only the more popular types which would be available to the aquarist, will be mentioned here. No doubt in the future, as more people keep salt-water aquariums, a much greater variety of these bizarre creatures will be on the market so that they will be available more each year as the hobby progresses.

The Octopus

No fish book could ever be complete without the Octopus. This amazing creature is reputed to be quite intelligent and although at present, it does not live well in the aquarium, it is so fascinating that aquarists will continue to attempt keeping them until its civilization problems can be solved. It will look well, eat well, and usually die very quickly when confined to an aquarium. Aquarists all over the country are trying to find out why? Some authorities maintain that it dies from fright, others from confinement, but all unanimously agree that it is difficult to keep for any length of time. Its average life span in the aquarium will vary from a week to occasionally a month and in a few extreme cases up to six months.

The Pacific species seems to do much better in confinement, but since it comes from colder water, it must be slightly refrigerated in the home to maintain the normal temperature it is accustomed to.

The Pigmy Octopus will usually outlive all other members of the

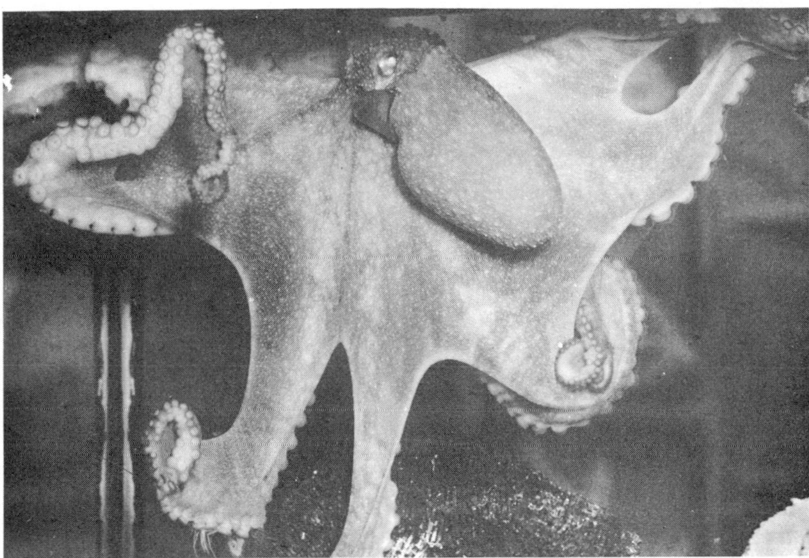

Fig. 148. *The Octopus can become very attached to you. This huge specimen gingerly accepted food from the author's hand.*

Fig. 149. *Powerful suction discs help the Octopus hold its prey.*

species and is the only hardy member of the group. It is quite small and has an adult spread of about three inches which makes it very desirable for a small aquarium. It usually lives in empty sea shells and presents an amusing sight when it climbs part way out of the shell to catch its food. Small live crabs, sea snails, and shrimp will all be readily eaten and enjoyed by this interesting fellow.

The fate of the large Octopus is usually from lack of water, for he will nearly always climb out of the aquarium and die on the floor. For this reason, not only must the equarium be tightly covered, but the cover should also be heavily weighted so that your beloved pet cannot slide the glass to one side to climb out. The Octopus will usually eat fresh shrimp tails, small crabs, and live snails or mollusks. Uneaten food, or food he has discarded, should be removed from the aquarium. He should be given a secure coral home, so arranged that he can get completely out of view if necessary and then the challenge is on. How long can you keep him?

The Incredible Boston Beans

Few people have ever had a live "Bean" swimming madly about their aquarium because they could only happen in a salt-water aquarium and until recently, this small insignificant bean-like fish, was not available to aquarists in other parts of the country. The author began shipping them to various pet shops and tropical fish stores and the response was terrific! Everyone re-ordered them and all agreed that they were sensational!

"Boston Beans" are actually baby cowfish and trunk fish and in this infant stage, they look just like a tiny black bean. To see one on land is like looking at a little blob of dirt, but place it in the aquarium and it will swim madly about. Tiny, almost invisible fins propel

Fig. 150. *The incredible "Boston Beans," look like tiny black beans swimming madly about the aquarium. In reality, they are baby Trunkfish and Cowfish.*

its round, hard body, and it's hard to believe your eyes when you see one. Then you have to laugh for it is really amusing. Close examination will reveal a tiny oriental face with almond eyes and small pointed mouth. It is such a ridiculous little fish, and such a charmer that you can't help but like him when you see this energetic little fellow swim bravely about the aquarium.

Despite their small size, the "Beans" do quite well, and will eat brine shrimp, as well as finely-shredded fresh shrimp. They make a fine addition to the Dwarf Sea Horse aquarium as they eat the same food and they are proportionate in size to the horses. Their water should be kept slightly weak at about 1.018 to 1.020 and feeding should be done several times a day as they eat continuously at this size. The author knows of one person who raised a "bean" from a tiny quarter inch size baby to nearly three inches long in the course of about three years and though a great accomplishment, it shows what can be done with care and patience.

The best aquarium size is from a quarter to a half inch in diameter

Fig. 151. *Two Cowfish* (Lactophyrs tricornis) *swim over to inspect a sea horse in one of the author's tanks. Small cowfish make an interesting addition to the aquarium but they should be obtained in the half-inch to one inch size. Large cowfish require a very large tank and are very excitable.*

and the smaller specimens appear more incredulous. They should be kept in a small aquarium to themselves, so that they may be observed as the center of attraction, otherwise, they would appear insignificant and not show up at all if placed in an aquarium with larger fishes.

Cowfish *(Lactophrys tricornis)*

Although the cowfish doesn't actually "Moo," is does vaguely resemble a cow with its long nose and authentic set of horns. It is an excellent aquarium fish and lives fairly well in the home tank.

Best aquarium size is from one to three inches and at this size, it can be kept in a ten- or fifteen-gallon aquarium with other fish. It will eat chopped shrimp, earthworms, and occasionally accepts dry food. Small specimens under an inch will usually eat live brine shrimp and should be given a large quantity of food. Larger specimens are easily obtainable, but they need a good sized aquarium, as they swim rather fast when they become excited. The aquarium should always be kept covered as they are inclined to jump when frightened and have even been known to knock the cover glass from the tank when they leap. This is one of the main difficulties in keeping them for the aquarist will invariably find his pet on the floor in a semi-petrified condition. A person walking by the aquarium or the room light suddenly turned on. will usually send this normally quiet fellow scurrying blindly across the tank. It will often bump into the end glass and dent or occasionally bend its horns. This does not necessarily mean that the cowfish is difficult to keep. Just use a little discretion and always approach his aquarium slowly, and avoid turning the aquarium light on suddenly if the room is dark. Always turn on the room lights first. This same procedure should be used with all aquarium fishes.

Cowfish are especially suited for display with large Sea Horses and the two are found in nature in close association. They get along fine and make a fine exhibit.

The Large Sea Horse *(Hippocampus punctulatus)*

Everyone has heard of Sea Horses but until recent years few people had ever seen them alive in an aquarium. In the past they were difficult to obtain. Now thanks to modern shipping methods, and a general increase in salt-water aquariums throughout the nation, Sea Horses are becoming increasingly popular. They are so unique among fishes, with their strange, horse-like appearance, their prehensile tail, and their ability to swim with no apparent means of locomotion, that it is small wonder they are so much in demand.

Large Sea Horses will make an ideal aquarium pet and they have been kept in the home tank for well past the year mark by the au-

Fig. 152. *A pair of large Sea Horses* (Hippocampus punctulatus). *The male is easily distinguished from the female by his leathery pouch.*

thor as well as other aquarists. One or two will live happily in a five gallon tank and several may be kept in a ten- or fifteen-gallon aquarium. They don't take up much room because they usually fasten their tail to the nearest object and remain there until feeding time, or until disturbed. They are undoubtedly the most entertaining and amusing pet in the entire fish world and are entirely harmless. A large Horse will tightly wrap his tail about your fingers as you lift him from the aquarium and his fate will be in your hands. Never keep him out of the water for more than a few seconds and avoid playing with him unnecessarily.

Feeding the large Sea Horse might present a problem and this should be seriously considered before a pair is obtained. They will eat only live swimming food and except in rare instances, will they accept other food. Their natural food is a tiny half-inch long shrimp that lives in the sea. If you live by the seashore, these may be obtained by running a fine net through the grass in shallow water, or by shaking out the floating sea weed. Only the small shrimp should be collected so that it can be swallowed whole by your pet. In addition to this food, they will also eat baby minnows, live adult brine shrimp, baby guppies, mosquito larvae, daphnae, and other small

Fig. 153. *A pregnant male Sea Horse. Note the enormously swelled pouch in the lower portion of the body.*

swimming insects or crustacea. Occasionally, a Horse can be trained to eat the adult, frozen brine shrimp if it is carefully thawed, and allowed to drift about the aquarium in a life-like manner. If this can be successfully accomplished, then your feeding problem will be solved. Freshly hatched brine shrimp will seldom if ever be eaten by the large Sea Horse. It is just too insignificant a food for such a large fish and the author has often seen Horses literally starve in an aquarium filled with this small live food. But, place a small minnow or other normal food in the same tank and the Horse will immediately eat it. Yet, freshly hatched brine shrimp is nearly always recommended as food for these creatures by most literature. Of course, there are exceptions when a large Sea Horse will actually eat this tiny food, but this is not usually the case.

Medium Sea Horses, which range in size from an inch and a half

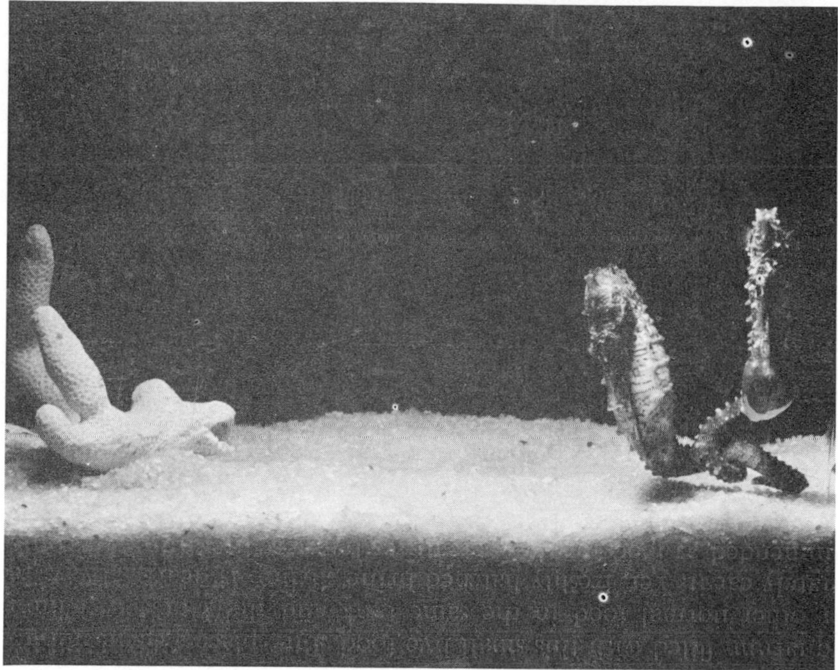

Fig. 154. *A pair of large sea horses about to mate in the aquarium. The female on the left is swollen with eggs while the male's pouch is inflated with sea water. In the actual transfer of the eggs, the female deposits them into the male's pouch where they incubate and develop into fully developed baby horses.*

to three inches, *will* eat the freshly hatched brine shrimp and this is no doubt where the misleading information arises. The aquarist who would have difficulty obtaining a steady supply of live food, can still successfully keep the medium Sea Horse, and maintain it largely on a diet of freshly hatched brine shrimp. As this smaller horse grows, it should eventually be fed baby Guppies, adult brine shrimp, and larger foods required by the adult horses.

Large Sea Horses will occasionally mate in the aquarium if kept to themselves, if there is a male and female. Sexing the species is simple, for the male has a leathery pouch at the base of the tail on the under side, and this is not present on the female.

"Loaded" or pregnant males may often be obtained and these will give birth to several hundred little horses in the home aquarium. It is quite a sight to see so many little horses in an aquarium at one time. They will swim rapidly about their new home, wrapping their tails around any object within their grasp, including other horses and will begin searching for food shortly after they are born.

Those attempting to raise the babies are in for a huge project. They have ravenous appetites and eat nearly continuously. Since the average "herd" of horses usually is around four hundred, and the average single horse may eat 3,000 to 4,000 brine shrimp in a single day, simple arithmetic will soon have the daily consumption of brine shrimp at about 1,500,000 which is a lot of shrimp. Nevertheless, it can be done, but since the Horses will require larger food as they mature, and will need constant changes of fresh sea water, the project should only be attempted by those who have access to these items. A detailed account of this tremendous project which was actually carried out, may be obtained from the Steinhart Aquarium in San Francisco, California.

Sea Horses are normally brown but occasionally may be obtained in a variety of colors. The author has personally collected brilliant red specimens, so vivid that the authentic color was doubted by scientists. Beautiful golden yellow Horses have also been collected by the author and these are much more common than the red species. In addition, there were many other hues varying from almost white to nearly black, and these color phases may often be seen in the aquarium as the Sea Horse is capable of changing its color to a remarkable degree. If placed in a tank with all white sand and white coral, the Horse will usually assume these colors and will not show up very well. To keep him in his natural brown color, place several cured sea fans and a Sea Horse Tree or two in the aquarium. A nice collection of marine plants, like the *Penicillus* and *Udotea,* will usually make the horse feel at home. Avoid large dense pieces of cluster or lace coral in his aquarium as this will provide hiding places for his live food and he will have difficulty in catching it.

Fig. 155. *The blessed event over, Dad seems weary but proud of his huge family. A Sea Horse may have from two to seven hundred babies depending on the size of the adult male.*

The Flame Scallop (Lima scabra) *with its fire red interior, is a favorite for the aquarium. It is very active in addition to its brilliant color. It is also known as the file shell because of the rough outer covering of the shell. The author gave it the name of Flame Scallop in his early years of collecting.*

The stunning Marine Jewel fish (Microspathodon chrysyrus) *is an aquarium favorite with both dazzling color and sparkling personality. When viewed in sunlight its brilliant blue spots sparkle like gems.*

Another color phase of the seahorse is this gold specimen.

Rare, fire red seahorse in one of the author's tanks. The normal color of the Florida seahorse (Hippocampus punctulatus) *is brown but occasionally a bright red specimen is found (about one in a thousand). The red horses live among the bright red fire sponges. The author worked with Dr. Paul A. Zahl on an article on seahorses in which the red sea horse was the central theme. Jan. 1959 issue.*

Fig. 156. *Young and medium-sized Sea Horses are often covered with hairy growths called "Cerri" which helps to camouflage them in the sea grass where they live.*

Large open pieces of staghorn or finger coral are best for Sea Horses and these should be used sparingly, so that the horses will be in plain view. But as stated before, these should be bolstered with the brown cured sea fans and sea horse trees so that your pet won't turn all white.

When your Pet Sea Horse passes on, and the author hopes this is from old age, you may still keep him with you indefinitely by drying the body in the sun for several days. Then coat it with clear shellac and you will have a permanent memento suitable for jewelry or wall decoration.

The Dwarf Sea Horse *(Hippocampus zosterae)*

This is the "guppy" of the salt-water world and is the beginner's fish. It is exceptionally hardy, subsists entirely on live brine shrimp, which are available everywhere, and it has live young. Furthermore, it may be kept in a fish bowl even without aeration if desired. It is also very inexpensive. With all these fine points in its favor, it is small wonder that it is the most popular of all marine fish and the author feels that eventually, it will be as common as the goldfish.

Since Dwarf Sea Horses are quite inexpensive, and also quite small, many aquarists prefer to keep them in a small two gallon aquarium by themselves. Here they may be observed at close quarters and their food concentrated in sufficient quantity so that they will never be hungry. The water should be kept at a salinity at

Fig. 157. *A small one or two-gallon aquarium will provide a comfortable home for a dozen Dwarf Sea Horses if an air pump is used to keep the water in motion.*

Fig. 158. *The Dwarf Sea Horse is the "Guppy of the marine world." It is extremely hardy, inexpensive and has live young, like its fresh-water counterpart.*

1.020 and aerated sufficiently so that the brine shrimp will be kept alive until consumed. This tiny food should always be present in the aquarium. It may be hatched in a quart jar and the live shrimp may then be siphoned through a handkerchief and fed to the Horses. Some aquarists prefer to hatch the eggs directly in the Sea Horse aquarium and with this method only the highest quality eggs should be used. This variety of eggs will usually hatch in less than a day and often in eight or ten hours so that your pets can start feeding as soon as the shrimp leave the egg cases. This latter method is sometimes quite messy as the unhatched eggs cluster the aquarium, and although these may be removed with a fine daphnae net, it still is a cumbersome job.

"Loaded" or pregnant male Sea Horses, are also available in the Dwarf Sea Horses, and these will have their young shortly after they are placed in the aquarium. These may be easily raised to full size by a good aquarist, provided they are kept in fresh sea water and that it is changed at least once a month. Undoubtedly most of you readers know that it is the male that has the young in the Sea Horse family. The eggs are conceived by the female and during the mating process, she transfers them to the male's pouch where they mature into little Sea Horses. Average herd for the dwarfs are from thirty to sometimes a hundred in a large male and like their larger cousins, they are perfectly formed at birth, and immediately swim about in their search for food. The average size of the adult dwarf horse is from an inch to an inch and a half. They come in a wide range of

Fig. 159. *Miniature sea palms and plants decorate the Sea Horse aquarium and provide hitching posts for the horses.*

Fig. 160. *The tiny Pigmy Pipefish is fully mature at two inches and makes an ideal tankmate for the Dwarf Sea Horse. It is very hardy and comes from Florida waters.*

Fig. 161. *A colony of Dwarf Sea Horses living in a ten gallon aquarium well planted with green plants. Under such ideal conditions, the little horses will actually spawn and reproduce. They will also assume a variety of colors from green to yellow as they do in their natural habitat.*

Fig. 162. *Dwarf Sea Horses may be kept in a fish bowl but the water must be aerated daily. An aquarium air pump with sub-sand bowl filter is best, but if one is not available, the bowl may be aerated by dipping up a glass of water from the bowl and pouring it back from a height of a foot or more so that it bubbles the water strongly as shown here. This should be done several times a day.*

Fig. 163. *The Pipe fish is a close relative of the Sea Horse and gives birth to live young. There are many varieties and they range in size from a few inches to well over one foot. They often swim vertically to imitate a blade of grass and change color to match their surroundings.*

colors, from bright green to gold, yellow, brown, black and white. However, like the larger horses, they soon turn white when placed in an aquarium with white sand and coral. To preserve their natural colors, they should be kept in an aquarium with green algae, either growing on the glass, or in plants, and they should be provided with one or two small cured sea fans and a Sea Horse tree. The latter, is the skeleton of the whiplike Gorgonias that grow on the reefs and makes a perfect hitching post for the little Horses. Further information about the Dwarf Sea Horses may be obtained from the book, *Keeping the Dwarf Sea Horse*, an *All Pets Publication,* also by the author.

The Pipe Fish

A close relative to the Sea Horse and an interesting addition to the marine aquarium. Pipe fish come in a wide assortment as there are many different species, and they do quite well in the home tank. The male has the young, like the Sea Horses, and the young are nearly transparent at birth, but still able to eat newly hatched brine shrimp. They can be raised to maturity depending on the species.

Best aquarium size is about two or three inches for at this size they can still eat live brine shrimp. They must have live food like the Sea Horses, and will seldom eat other foods, unless it is free swimming. Larger Pipes can be fed baby Guppies, Mollies, live daphnae, mosquito larvae, etc.

The Pipe fish is much more active than the Sea Horse so that if large Pipe fish are kept with large Sea Horses, the "Pipes" will eat most of the food before the Horses even know it is dinner time. Since Pipe fish are very inexpensive, the aquarist is often tempted to overload his aquarium with them and the live food problem becomes difficult unless only the small Pipes are selected. One species in particular, *(Corythoichthys albirostris),* formerly thought to be practically extinct until the author discovered them in large numbers, is extremely hardy and has a rather comical face, with colored stripes and a peculiar "headdress." This particular type is perhaps the hardiest member of the entire family and can be kept without aeration in some instances. It has the further advantage that it does not grow very large so that even adult specimens will eat live brine shrimp, making their food problem a cinch. Pipe fish do best in a salinity of 1.018 to 1.020. Small Pipes are a fine addition to the Dwarf Sea Horse tank as they eat the same food and are very compatible.

The Moray Eel

There are always some aquarists who prefer to keep the more

Fig. 164. *Rarely photographed, the bug-eyed Dragonette* (Callionymus sp.) *is the ideal tank mate for the dwarf sea horse. It is hardy, inoffensive, and most interesting, for when it erects its huge dorsal fin it looks like a miniature sea dragon. The author was the first in the nation to collect them for aquarium use.*

dangerous specimens in their home tanks and this is understandable for although fierce and certainly capable of severe biting, the Moray eel holds a definite amount of fascination to the hobbyist as well as general public. These dreaded monsters of the deep are well known for their ferociousness and as any skin diver can testify, they are definitely not playthings.

Large Morays are among the most fearless creatures of the sea and the author, who has encountered many thousands of them on his undersea trips, can give proof of their voracity. They are one of the few fish in the sea that cannot be frightened away once they have decided to attack and they will stand their ground lunging savagely at their victim. Normally, they are quite peaceful, but periodically, perhaps due to a mating instinct, they will emerge from their homes and swim up to meet a skin diver who might invade their domain. It is a fearsome sight, especially when the attacker is a giant green Moray six or seven feet long. The author once battled a specimen this size for nearly two hours and was saved from serious injury by using a large collecting net to ward off each strike. The net was

Fig. 165. *Closeup of the moray shows a mouthful of teeth which can inflict a painful bite to the careless aquarist. Morays are very hardy but are great jumpers and most aquarists lose them because they jump out of the aquarium at night and die on the floor. Their tank should be tightly covered with no escape holes.*

Fig. 166. *Moray Eels make interesting pets for those who want something different. This species, the Black Edge Moray* (Gymnothorax nigromarginatus) *adapts itself well to the aquarium. Its feeding habits are interesting as it feeds entirely by smell, swimming rapidly about the tank until it locates the food with its sensitive nose. Toadfish is its tankmate.*

torn to shreds and all of the eel's teeth were knocked out in the battle, but still it would not give up. The author finally retreated to the boat.

Best aquarium size for the Moray, either the green or speckled, is around eighteen inches to two feet. They will be quite comfortable at this size in a twenty-five-gallon aquarium and will eat shrimp tails, small minnows, and good-sized-chunks of fresh scallop. Use an outside filter with carbon, and remove all uneaten food promptly from aquarium. Be especially watchful for food which has been swallowed and then thrown up, as this can quickly foul the aquarium unless quickly removed. Best feeding procedure is to drop the shrimp tail in plain view of the Moray and then prod it close with a long stick. If he doesn't eat it, remove it and repeat feeding next day.

Moray eels are especially active at night. They will perform a weird ceremonial dance after dark and the aquarium must be tightly covered or they will climb out. Even tiny openings where filter stems enter the tank must be covered or your pet will crawl out and die on the floor. Most Morays in captivity die in this fashion as they are very hardy and will live for years under proper aquarium conditions.

The Moray should always be handled with a large net when transferring from one aquarium to another, and they are not too difficult to handle as long as they don't become excited. When one does, it may leap to the floor, snapping at everything in sight. Then it is dangerous, for its teeth can inflict a serious wound, which is highly infectious.

Occasionally, if a Moray does succeed in jumping out of an aquarium, it may still be saved if it hasn't been out too long. Simply return it to its aquarium and prod it so that it will swim about the tank. This forces water through its gills and helps it to recover. The author has saved many specimens in this manner.

The Nurse Shark *(Ginglymostoma cirratum)*

A genuine live shark that lives very well in the home aquarium. It not only has a long lifespan in the aquarium, but it soon becomes a pet, allowing you to scratch its back or stuff food into its mouth.

The best aquarium size is around twelve inches and at this size, the entire body is spotted, giving the fish an attractive appearance. As the creature matures, the spots disappear and the body assumes an overall grayish brown color. Small specimens may be kept in a twenty- to thirty-gallon aquarium, but as soon as they reach a length of eighteen inches, they should be moved to at least a fifty-gallon aquarium where they may be kept at least a couple of years or until they get too large for that.

The basic food for the Nurse shark is fresh shrimp. This should be

Fig. 167. *Baby Nurse sharks* (Ginglymostoma cirratum) *live quite well in the aquarium and make fine pets. The young are handsomely spotted.*

Fig. 168. *Remora, or shark sucker, attaches itself to the back of a Nurse shark. Occasionally, while diving, Remoras have attached themselves to the author's back and were easily captured by easing them off into a net.*

fed cautiously at first and the whole shrimp tail should be used. Drop the food directly in front of the shark and push it towards his mouth with a slender rod. If he is hungry he will snap up the food quickly, otherwise, the food should be removed from the aquarium and the procedure repeated the next day. If, after a week the shark still hasn't eaten, it will usually be necessary to force feed him by grasping him firmly with one hand and pushing the food well into his mouth with the other. Then he should be released slowly so that he will not become too excited. Usually, after one or two force feedings, he will eat by himself. When he really becomes tame, he will come to the top of the aquarium and stick his head part way out of the water at feeding time. A small shark will generally eat several shrimp tails at a meal and when he no longer shows interest, feeding should be discontinued.

In addition to shrimp, the shark will eat fresh scallops, small crabs, and minnows. An outside filter with activated carbon or charcoal should be used on their aquarium to remove milky juices associated with their food.

If kept in an aquarium without sand, baby sharks will occasionally develop a severe skin rash on the under portion of their body. This may be cured by Sulfathiazole ointment made with a mixture of Sulfathiazole Sodium and castor oil. Apply this oily paste directly to the infected area every two days until the rash has disappeared.

Nurse sharks, contrary to popular opinion, will bite savagely. They attack more skin divers than any other shark, and although the attacks are seldom fatal, they often require hospital treatment.

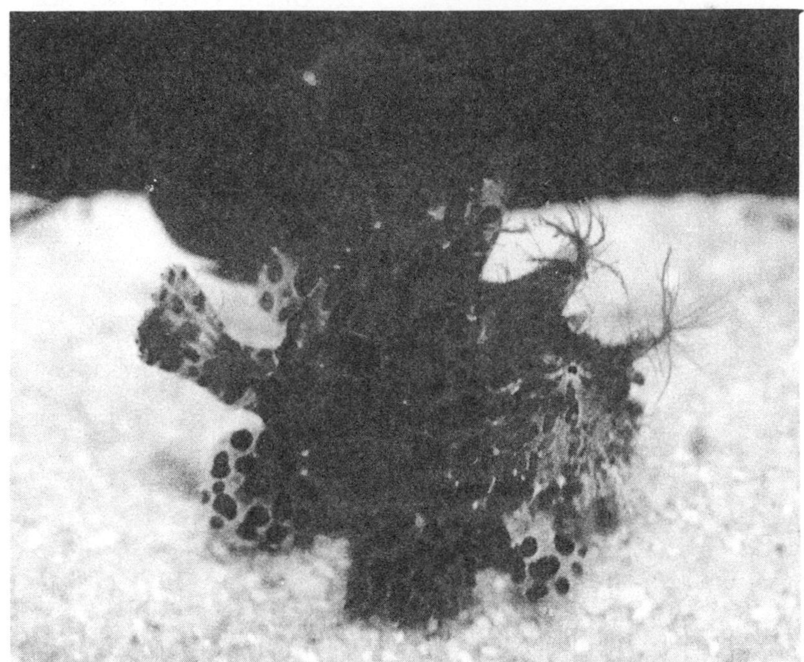

Fig. 169. *The Anglerfish* (Antennarius) *has a tiny fishing rod and lure attached to its nose, and actually "angles" for its food. It is one of the most interesting and unusual fishes in the sea and lives quite well in the aquarium if conditions are proper.*

Even baby sharks have well-defined rasping teeth which can easily tear the skin painfully. Handle them with care always grabbing them firmly about the middle and keep their open mouth away from the tender parts of your arm. It is doubtful if any damage would be suffered should a small specimen clamp down on your fingers, but if you are curious enough, you should perhaps try it.

The Angler Fish *(Antennarius)*

A close relative of the Sargassum fish, the Angler fish is unique among all fishes, in that it is equipped with a fishing rod and lure. So well is this developed, that the species is actually able to "fish" for its food. Now what would be more interesting in a marine aquarium than to see a fish fishing? It is certainly a spectacle to watch.

The Angler fish is at present, seldom obtainable for the marine hobbyist. But it is such an unusual creature that the author felt it should be included in this book. It is not extremely rare, its scarcity is just due to the fact that at present, no way has been found to obtain them in quantity and no doubt, as the market for them increases, a suitable supply will be had.

Like its cousin the Sargassum fish, the Angler fish is also a master at camouflage. It often makes its home around a piece of sponge and can duplicate the color of the sponge so exactly that it is almost unbelievable. The author once had a brilliant red specimen which maintained its color for many months until green plants were placed in the aquarium. The Angler fish picked out a large plant for its home and promptly began to change green. As I was making a movie sequence of the fish, this color change just wouldn't do, so I removed the plants and the Angler returned to its normal red coloring.

The Angler fish will do quite well in the aquarium but it is such a hard job to obtain specimen, that it should be given a tank all to itself so that it will be the entire show. It will soon pick out a favorite spot in the aquarium where it will remain motionless for hours at a time, scarcely breathing, so that the fish will think it is part of the aquarium decoration. Then as its food approaches it, the Angler will watch closely and when its "meal" is the proper distance away, it will

Fig. 170. *The Angler fish* (Antennarius sp.) *walks slowly about the aquarium in search of food. Plant-like growth is a marine algae* (Penicillus capitatus). *Also known as Merman's Shaving Brush.*

Fig. 171. *The Angler wriggles a worm-like lure to attract a live minnow who is approaching from far right. Sea Horse also shows interest in the lure.*

Fig. 172. *The minnow swims in fast to grab the worm-like lure and is engulfed by the Angler fish in one quick gulp. Anglers will also eat large Sea Horses if no other food is present.*

extend its "fishing rod" and jiggle the tiny lure temptingly in front of it. The unsuspecting minnow will make a pass at the bait and an enormous mouth will open and engulf it so fast that the eye can scarcely follow.

Angler fish must have live food and they scrutinize their food so closely, that it is difficult to fool them into eating dead fish, even when it is drawn through the water in a life-like manner. All live minnows must be floated in a small jar in the aquarium so that they will be gradually introduced to the temperature and water of the aquarium. This is of utmost importance because the Angler usually won't feed until he is well adjusted to the aquarium. His food must also be adjusted to the aquarium so that it will swim about in a normal fashion. Otherwise, the minnows will show no interest when the Angler presents them with his "bait" and the great show will be lost. The Angler fish can become quite tame and he will allow you to corral or herd the minnows right into his mouth. This will require some practice on your part as the fish must be very gently moved toward the waiting monster. Then as soon as they are in range, he will angle briefly and swallow them whole in a fierce gulp that will leave you shaking. Thus you will see one of the greatest spectacles in the world, a fish, fishing.

Fig. 173. *The Porcupine fish* (Diodon hystrix) *has a relatively smooth skin when not inflated. It can be inflated by holding it against the glass with a net. The net must be small for if the fish inflates inside the metal rim of the net, it may be fatal. Porcupine fish become great pets in the home aquarium and wag their tails like puppy dogs when they see their master.*

The Porcupine Fish *(Diodon hystrix)*

The Porcupine fish is often confused with the Spiny Boxfish as both are quite similar. One of the main differences in addition to bodily appearance is that the Porcupine fish is almost exclusively a reef dweller while the Spiny Boxfish nearly always lives in the bay close to shore.

This is an excellent aquarium fish and will live a long time with proper care. Best aquarium size is from one to eight inches. If any fish is capable of distinct facial expression it is the Porcupine fish. It will actually appear to smile when you approach the aquarium. Its eyes will brighten and it will "wag" its tail like a young puppy. With these characteristics, it is a small wonder that this fish is such an aquarium favorite. Combined with the fact that it can be kept well past the year mark, it will eventually become one of the most popular of marine fishes.

Young "Porkies" will eat small chunks of chopped shrimp, baby minnows, and adult brine shrimp. They will also eat earthworms and this is sometimes preferred over the shrimp but the shrimp

Fig. 174. *Porcupine fish fully inflated. When not in use, the sharp spines are covered by a sheath of skin and lie flat against the body. Besides the needle-sharp spines, the Porcupine fish can also inflict a crushing bite.*

should constitute their main diet as it is necessary for their growth.

Although the Porcupine grows to a length of nearly three feet, good-sized specimens of five to seven inches are nearly always available for the home aquarist. These will live comfortably in a twenty-five to fifty-gallon aquarium and are a little difficult to feed at first. They can usually be tempted to eat by giving them whole shrimp either live or frozen, and these should be dropped in plain view so that your pet will see them. Porcupine fish are great "thinkers" and spend a great deal of time in deep thought. They will rest in a corner of the aquarium with their head under the shelter of coral and stay there until they are hungry or the spirit moves them. Then they will swim eagerly about the aquarium in search of food. Full-sized Guppies or other minnows are often relished as food by these charming pets and this should be remembered so that you won't put this fellow in with your expensive fish. He would probably eat them regardless of their value; so keep him accordingly!

Because of their large eyes, the porcupine fish can be easily blinded. Be certain to give him a large flat piece of coral, so arranged that it makes a ledge or shelf in the aquarium under which "Porky" can hide if he wishes. Also, don't keep his light on unnecessarily because of the danger of blinding. As with Spiny Boxfish, and other fish that require chunks of fresh shrimp as their main diet, an outside filter filled with activated carbon should be used on his aquarium, to remove the milky residue which comes from this food as it is being chewed.

Spiny Boxfish *(Chilomycterus schoepfii)*

A very hardy and active marine aquarium fish. Its fierce appear-

Fig. 175. *"Grumpy," a rare member of the Spiny Boxfish family.*

ance is not in keeping with its character for actually it is a peaceful and lovable fish. The large eyes and interesting facial expression make it an aquarium favorite.

Best aquarium size is from one half inch to three inches. Larger specimens, though readily obtainable do not generally do well as they often shy away from regularly obtained foods and often starve to death.

The tiny specimens under an inch are by far the most spectacular, particularly for a small aquarium and anyone who has kept one will undoubtedly remember it above all their other pets. Spiny Boxfish quickly become tame and will eagerly accept food from a tooth pick or fingers. They will eat chopped shrimp eagerly and this should be dropped in plain view so that they can see it fall to the bottom. This is important as they are accustomed to chasing their food. Once they are eating, they will usually pick up the food from the bottom, but at first it must be dropped in front of them so they can see it fall. In addition to chopped shrimp, they will eagerly devour earthworms and are especially fond of these. Baby specimens under an inch should be fed live brine shrimp; tubifex worms, and white worms in addition to finely chopped fresh shrimp. Spiny Boxfish will seldom eat dry food and must be fed the foods mentioned above. Also, when the specimen is over an inch, it will seldom eat brine shrimp as they are too small to bother with. Small minnows and Guppies are also eaten by the larger specimens.

Fig. 176. *Spiny Boxfish* (Chilomycterus schoepfii) *inflated. It does not inflate as full or as readily as the Porcupine fish, except when very small. It may be distinguished from the Porcupine fish by its spines which always remain erect. Despite its ferocious appearance, it is quite harmless and may be safely handled if grasped from behind. Keep fingers away from its powerful beak as it can pinch badly.*

Fig. 177. *The common Spiny Boxfish examines its rare cousin and stares in disbelief.*

The Spiny Boxfish may be obtained quite large for special displays. At this size feeding is more difficult but they will usually eat earthworms and large chunks of fresh shrimp which should be served with the shell left on. They like to crush their food. In the natural state they feed almost exclusively on small scallops which they chase through the water. They also eat Dwarf Sea Horses as this is a natural food although they prefer the former. Small snails can sometimes be used as food if dropped so that the fish can see it fall.

The Sargassum Fish *(Histrio)*

Here is the ultimate in camouflage, for this interesting creature looks almost exactly like a piece of seaweed. It is one of the most interesting fishes in the sea and fortunately is not rare so that it can usually be obtained by an enthusiastic aquarist.

It does not grow very large and can usually be had in sizes from a half inch to three inches. The smaller sizes are recommended as the fish grows very fast and the youngest specimens seem to be able to adapt themselves to life in the aquarium much better. This is one of those bizarre fishes that should be given an aquarium to itself, or kept in a two or three gallon fish bowl, provided with aeration.

The Sargassum fish will eat anything that moves, including other Sargassum fish, just so long as the other fish is slightly smaller than itself, so that it can be swallowed. Consequently, it can readily be seen why it should be confined to separate quarters. If another aquarium is not available, the swallowing monster may be kept in with your prized beauties by isolating him to one corner of the aquarium

Fig. 178. *Living in the floating sea weed, the Sargassum fish blends perfectly with its surroundings.*

with a sheet of glass. Another satisfactory method is to keep him confined in a plastic live well or breeding tank which is perforated so that the water will circulate through it. These are often used for live-bearing, fresh-water fish and are available at most pet shops.

Sargassum fish may also be kept in an aquarium with fish that are much longer than themselves so that they can't possibly swallow their associates. Large Sea Horses are especially suited for a combination display for neither will bother the other. However, do not keep Sargassums with the Dwarf Horses as they will soon grow large enough to eat the small horses.

Feeding the Sargassum fish is relatively simple. They will eat small Guppies or any little fish. Also they will readily consume live earthworms, and since these are often more available, it is a good food for them. They should be fed a live fish periodically though to maintain a proper food balance. The Sargassum fish will also eat chunks of fresh shrimp which should be served on the end of a toothpick. Carefully touch the shrimp against the Sargassum's nose and he will usually grab it viciously and your food problem will be solved. The swallowing capacity of the Sargassum fish, although fantastic, still has its limitations. It certainly cannot swallow a fish two or three times its size as reported by one national magazine. It may attempt to swallow a fish larger than itself, especially if it is hungry, but it cannot accomplish the impossible. Small minnows about one half the length of the Sargassum's body are best for food as it can easily swallow and digest these. It will usually eat two or three of these at a meal and after a couple of days, it will be ready for another meal.

Fig. 179. *The Sargassum fish swims down from its lair to attack a Demoiselle that was placed in its aquarium as food.*

Its digestive system works very fast and its food is quickly converted into flesh, hence its rapid growth.

Mrs. L. M. Holloway, an outstanding marine aquarist, recently raised a baby Sargassum fish to maturity, a process which took about ten months. She started with a tiny one half inch specimen which she kept in a one and a half gallon aquarium and fed the little fellow faithfully two or three times a week until it finally grew so large that it had to be moved to a five gallon tank so that it would have room to swim. "Sarah Gassum" as her pet was cleverly named unintentionally by a friend was kept on a diet of chunks of fresh shrimp, supplemented with an occasional minnow and grew to immense proportions. It was a fascinating pet and the Holloways, who have kept many marine fish, still look upon this fish as the most interesting in the sea. The aquarium was equipped with a sub sand filter only, and this both aerated and filtered the tank. Every two or three months, the water was changed and the sand removed and washed. Other than that, the fish had little care and grew to the maximum size of five inches!

Although Sargassum fish do best in natural sea water, they still may be successfully maintained in the artificial solution provided it is mixed with some fresh sea water. They are amazingly hardy and

Fig. 180. *The strange Sargassum fish seems to be able to hypnotize its prey, for often the intended victim will become paralyzed with fear when approached, and make no effort to escape. Note the frightened appearance of this Demoiselle. It was quickly swallowed by the hungry Sargassum fish even though both fish were nearly the same size.*

the usual case of death in the aquarium is due to the salt water "ick" which is introduced to them when feeding live minnows. Live fish intended as food, should be floated in the aquarium in a small jar so that it will become adjusted to the temperature in the aquarium. This is not necessary in a small tank however, if the Sargassum fish will eat the food in a few minutes, for then the disease could not start. Uneaten minnows should be promptly removed from the aquarium.

Sargassum fish have an amazing ability to change color and can become almost snow white if kept in an aquarium with coral. An excellent "plant" to keep with them is the artificial growth commonly sold as Aqua Fern. This should be obtained in the neutral color which is usually brown. Cured sea fans are also excellent for this strangest of all fishes.

An interesting experiment regarding the Sargassum fish's ability to swallow was performed by Carl Zinn of Miami. Mr. Zinn placed twenty-five Sargassum fish in a large fish bowl and asked the author over the phone if he wanted them. By the time the fish were delivered which was about a week later, there was only one large Sargassum Fish left. "This proves that the Sargassum fish will eat each other," reported Carl, laughingly.

11

Interesting Crustacea, Invertebrates and Scavengers

This field includes perhaps the widest variety of specimens that could conceivably be kept in the home salt-water aquarium. So numerous and diversified is this group that only a very few will be mentioned in the following text and although many not included in this book would make excellent additions to the aquarium, they should always be obtained in the smaller sizes as these are less likely to wreak havoc upon a peaceful aquarium.

In general, salt-water snails, mussels, clams, scallops, etc. are very unsatisfactory in the home aquarium, except for special study. In this case, they should not be kept with the regular display as they often burrow into the sand or coral where they die and foul the water. Like all rules, there are many exceptions, and an aquarist who is also interested in shells, can derive much pleasure and education from keeping the various shells alive in a small aquarium, as described further in this chapter.

Also, there is a wide variety of crabs, many of which are extremely vicious if kept with fishes, but if kept to themselves in a small bowl or aquarium, they are interesting to study. This one field alone could present a fascinating aquarium study for not only is there a fantastic variety of colors and shapes in this group, but they sometimes grow to gigantic proportions, some species having a spread of over twelve feet!

The Arrow Crab

The Arrow crab, also called Spider crab, or Daddy Longlegs of the sea, is an interesting addition to the marine aquarium. Also, it is a fairly good scavenger for it will pick up small uneaten chunks of

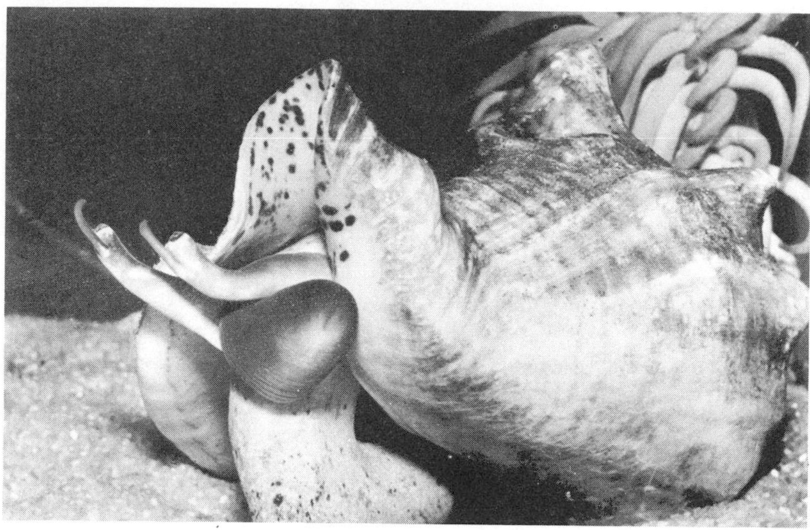

Fig. 181. *Live conch extends its stalked eyes and mouth in search of food. Large projection at the bottom is its "foot," which contains a single claw by means of which the creature drags itself along the sea floor.*

Fig. 182. *Miniature Mangrove jungle is constructed in the aquarium. Under-gravel filter keeps water from becoming stagnant. Sand is piled unevenly to depths of six inches or more. Hollow depression in sand makes small pond. Coral rock gives natural look and allows Mangrove Crabs or Fiddlers a place to sun and dry themselves.*

Fig. 183. *Close-up of miniature Mangrove swamp shows Fiddler crabs living in contentment. They will signal each other with their huge claws.*

food from the aquarium bottom. Although there are many spider crabs, this species is the best, not only because of its decorative quality, but also because it is readily obtainable from pet dealers handling marine fish.

Best size for aquariums are the smaller specimens with a three inch spread or less. Large Spiders are apt to be aggressive and may kill some of your prized fish. But the small specimens, unless absolutely starved will seldom .bother anything and are mostly interested in protecting themselves.

An interesting fact about the Arrow crab, discovered by the author, is that it often carries extra food on the end of its nose, which is especially adapted with "hooks" so that the crab can impale the food, and save it for future use. This proves especially valuable in some marine aquariums where an over-cautious aquarist has removed every last trace of food that was not immediately eaten. At least the Arrow crab won't be hungry.

The Arrow crab will do fairly well in the salt-water aquarium if certain precautions are taken to protect him in his hour of need. This is when he has shed his skin. At this time he is highly vulnerable to attack by all the aquarium residents. His body is extremely soft and his tank mates know it. Sometimes, if the fish are well fed, they will not molest him, but this is seldom the case and he should be isolated with a sheet of glass for a day or two until he has regained his armor.

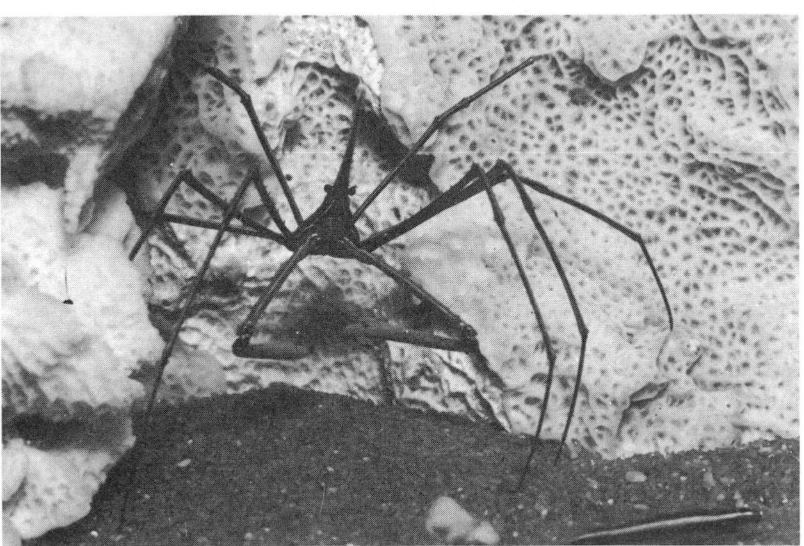

Fig. 184. *The Arrow crab or Spider crab, is often called "The daddy longlegs of the sea." It is an excellent scavenger and often carries extra food on its nose.*

The Arrow crab, like other crabs, will eat small chunks of fresh shrimp, and also is fond of algae which should be fed periodically. They should not be kept with Porcupine fish, Spiny Boxfish, Trigger fish, Blueheads, or Wrasse. Although this species is quite hardy, toxic cement or metal poisoning seems to be fatal to them. If they should suddenly act logey, and refuse to eat, they should be placed in a glass bowl with fresh sea water and given an algae-covered rock to nibble on.

The Banded Coral Shrimp *(Stenopus hispidus)*

This is perhaps the most colorful crustacean commonly available to the marine aquarist. It is startling red and white like the familiar peppermint candy cane and has a huge antenna usually as long or longer than its own body. Coral shrimp add color and interest to the salt-water aquarium. They are fairly inexpensive and live quite well if kept with fishes that will not molest them. They seem to be especially susceptible to toxic poisoning in the aquarium which chiefly comes from the cement. Therefore all-glass aquariums, or the plastic type, is recommended for them. They will eat chopped shrimp, chopped worms, and green algae and will seldom bother the other fish except in self-defense. Like other crustacea, they will shed their skin periodically and the cast-off skin is a perfect likeness of the owner. At first glance, the aquarist will think he has a new

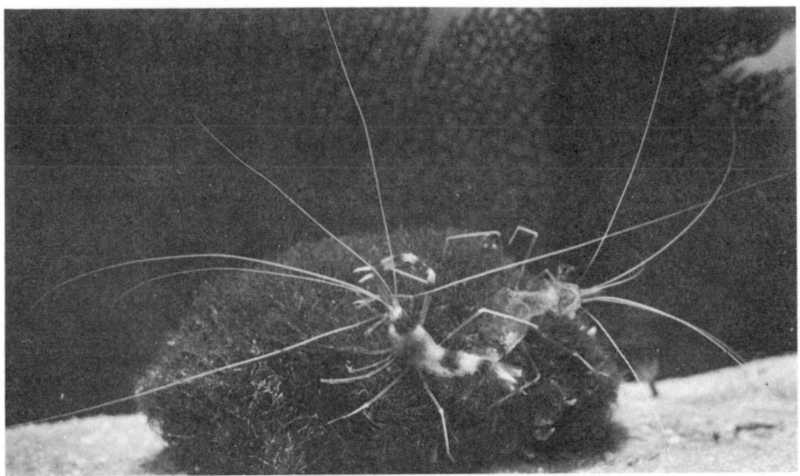

Fig. 185. *The Banded Coral shrimp* (Stenopus hispidus) *is a beautiful red and white crustacean. It sheds its skin periodically, a process which enables it to grow. This photograph shows the skin actually leaving the body.*

Fig. 186. *Coral shrimp is at left, shedded skin is on right. The discarded outer skin is so life-like that there appears to be another shrimp in the aquarium.*

Coral shrimp in the aquarium. Then upon closer inspection, when the skin is discovered to be lifeless, the hobbyist will mourn thinking his interesting pet has died. Until finally, the actual specimen will be discovered in back of the coral in better health and color than ever. Such things as this makes the salt-water hobby one of the most interesting pastimes that can be had. The author once had a mated pair of Coral shrimp in a large community tank and the female shrimp was heavily loaded with eggs. At feeding time, the male came forth and battled with the fish for food. Then after obtaining a good-sized portion, he returned to the female sharing the food with her. In this manner, his mate, carrying the eggs was not exposed to the dangers of the aquarium and could remain safely in the coral even at feeding time. The author has witnessed this same procedure several times with various pairs so it was not merely an unusual incident.

Coral shrimp may be obtained in mated pairs as they nearly always live this way when mature. The female is much larger than the male and when carrying eggs, the undertail portion of her body will be bright green, making it easy to sex them. Coral shrimp have spawned many times in the author's aquariums and the young are transparent and about one quarter inch long. They should be separated immediately from their parents who will quickly devour them.

Fig. 187. *Giant Sponge Crab lives its early existence in the finger coral. It has a metal-like body covering and moves with slow, jerky movements that appear somewhat mechanical. It grows to a length of nearly two feet and is an interesting aquarium specimen. Also called Scavenger Crab.*

Fig. 188. *Hermit crabs are so named because they go off to live by themselves. They make interesting scavengers for the marine tank. Note anemones attached to shell for camouflage.*

Scavenger Crab

This is one of the most peaceful and gentle members of the crab family, yet, they are highly colored and very attractive. As the name implies, they are true scavenger crabs and their claws are especially adapted for this purpose, being cupped-shaped at the ends for scooping up the sand. They will seldom if ever molest the fish and are quite hardy.

Best aquarium size is about two- to four-inch size with claws extended. Large specimens a foot or more may be obtained and present a fearsome sight, for at this size, their body is quite large and their gargantuan spread gives them the appearance of giant spiders.

They will usually eat small chunks of shrimp or other food that falls to the bottom and are especially fond of algae. A small algae covered rock placed in their aquarium will become their temporary home until they have stripped it clean. Then they will move on to more lucrative pastures.

Small specimens are usually dark green or red, while the larger specimens are nearly all a brownish red color. This species was introduced to the aquarium hobby by the author.

Sea Anemone

The sea anemones are often called "the beautiful living flowers of the sea." They have been in much dispute in regards to marine aquariums, and so much nonsense has been printed about them regarding their lethal qualities that most aquarists have shunned away from these beautiful creatures.

Actually, the anemone isn't so bad and it can be safely kept in the marine aquarium right along with the fish, if it is a healthy specimen, and if the aquarium is constantly aerated and filtered. The author has kept many hundreds of anemones in aquariums under all kinds of conditions and finds them an asset to the salt-water tank. They always draw immediate attention when placed on display and if properly fed and cared for, they will last for years. However, they do have their limitations, and because perfect specimens are not always obtainable, they are not recommended to the salt-water aquarist until he has had considerable experience. For the novice, it is recommended that the anemone or anemones, be kept in a small five- or ten-gallon bowl to themselves until he has learned how to care for them and can recognize when they are in good health.

Sea anemones will usually do much better in an aquarium that is using a sub-sand filter as this allows drainage under the sand and this is natural with their environment. Very often in an aquarium aerated with air stones only, the anemone will get over the stone and become inflated with air. This often kills it and a dead anemone can quickly foul the water in the aquarium. This is what has given this beautiful creature its bad name.

Fig. 189. *Beautiful pink-tipped sea anemones from the Florida coast. These are often called "the living flowers of the sea."*

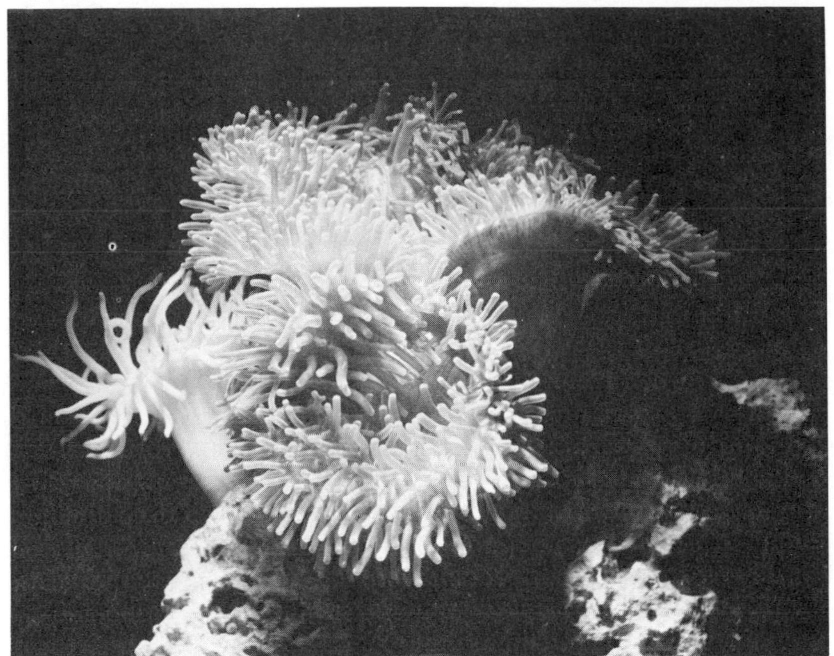

Fig. 190. *A beautiful Pacific anemone* (Stoicactus sp.) *such as this perfect specimen, will provide a happy home for the clownfish and perhaps induce them to spawn. The smaller anemone on the left is a Florida pink-tipped anemone which gives an indication of the huge size of the Pacific species.*

The author has kept as many as fifteen large sea anemones in a five-gallon aquarium for months on end without any outside filter or air stones. The water stayed crystal clear and the anemones stayed in perfect condition. A sub-sand filter, that ingenious device of our modern aquarium age, did all the work. Of course, this crowded condition is not recommended, but was merely tried as an experiment to help disprove some of the statements about anemones.

Won't anemones kill my fish? This question is often asked by the marine aquarist who is interested in these beautiful creatures. Actually, the anemones will kill the fish under certain conditions, and there is no guarantee that they won't occasionally catch a pretty specimen. So, if you have a rare, expensive beauty, don't put him in with the anemone because with the creatures from the sea, anything can happen. As a rule though, if one or two anemones are placed in a fifteen- or twenty-gallon aquarium, it is very unlikely that they would catch any fish, as long as the fish remain in a healthy condition and there is no serious fighting in the aquarium. There are certain fish that should not be kept in with anemones because of their habit of burrowing under the sand. These fish may come up directly under an anemone and be seriously stung. This includes

Fig. 191. *A forest of sea anemones! Those who feel anemones are difficult to keep would stare in disbelief at this tank of dwarf anemones which numbers in the hundreds. Not only did the anemones live, they multiplied ten fold in a period of a little over a year. Good light and lots of live brine shrimp as well as good aeration is essential to their well being.*

the Wrasses, Slipper Dicks, Blue Heads, and other members of this general group. Also, Sea Horses, because of their habit of wrapping their tails about round objects, should not be kept wtih anemones. Very small aquariums, in which the anemone takes up a major portion of the area, should not be populated with fish as there would be little chance for the fish to dodge the dangerous tentacles.

Certain fish actually thrive with anemones and the Clown fish is well known for its ability to swim right inside the anemone without harm. There is also a beautiful "Clown shrimp" from the Atlantic side that lives among the tentacles of the anemone in a similar association.

Anemones should be fed small chunks of shredded shrimp once a week, and the food should be dropped directly into their extended tentacles. Food which has been discarded by them should be promptly removed from the aquarium as it can foul the water.

When purchasing an anemone, be certain to inspect the base. This is often damaged by an inexperienced collector. If it is torn badly, do not accept it, as it probably will die when placed in your aquarium. Badly puffed anemones as well as those which are flat with fine,

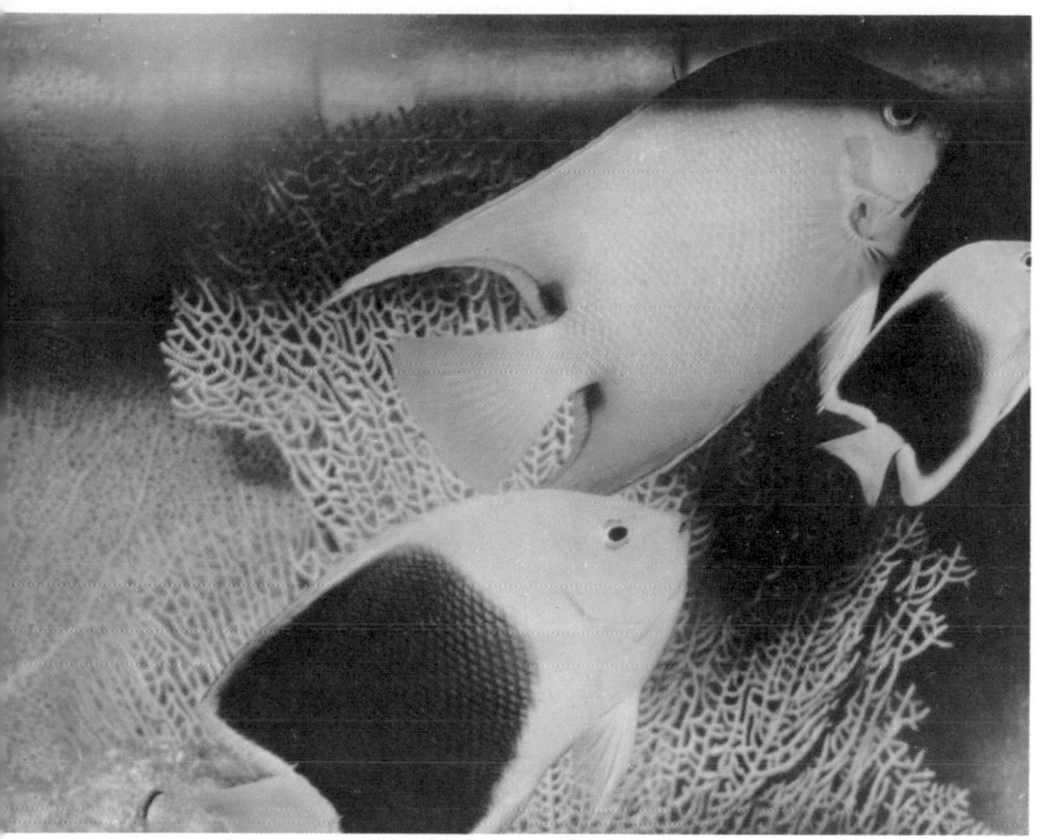

Feeding time in the aquarium! Gorgeous Rock Beauties and Townsend Angelfish rise to the top of the tank to be fed. Salt-water fish are more alert and have much more personality than the average fresh-water fish. They can recognize the aquarist at a distance of ten or twenty feet away from the aquarium, especially if he is holding a familiar food container.

An experimental tank with deep-sea crinoids and live corals. This fascinating aspect of the marine hobby is a challenge to the aquarist who would venture into the wondrous field of keeping deep-sea specimens.

The Spanish Hogfish (Bodianus rufus) *is a colorful fish from Florida and the Caribbean. Young specimens are often mistaken for the Royal Gramma.*

Fig. 192. *This colorful little shrimp spends its life in the stinging tentacles of a sea anemone. Its powerful feet enable it to walk across the tentacles without sticking to them.*

Fig. 193. *Strange orange and white Clown Shrimp lives in the tentacles of the Atlantic Stinging Anemone* (Stoicactus sp.). *The white spotted clown shrimp is at the upper left portion of the anemone. Several transparent shrimp may also be seen crawling about the anemone.*

stringy tentacles, should also be avoided. In short, if you can't get a good healthy anemone, then do without one, rather than take a chance with a poor specimen.

Anemones usually give off a heavy scum shortly after they are removed from the ocean. This usually forms about the base, where they attach to the aquarium, and it can be "peeled" from the anemone when it forms and removed from the aquarium. This is a cleansing process in which the anemone is discarding decayed grass and other impurities from its body. Once this scum is removed, it will seldom if ever reappear in the aquarium. Good circulation in your aquarium will assure you of healthy anemones, for these creatures must have constant aeration or they will die. If the air should suddenly go off in your aquarium, the anemone would probably be the first to die, and then it could quickly lead to the pollution of whole aquarium. But certainly this cannot be blamed on the anemone for it is trying to stay alive and it will add much beauty to the salt-water aquarium.

The Basket Starfish *(Gorgonocephalus agassizi)*

Probably the weirdest creature from the sea that can be obtained

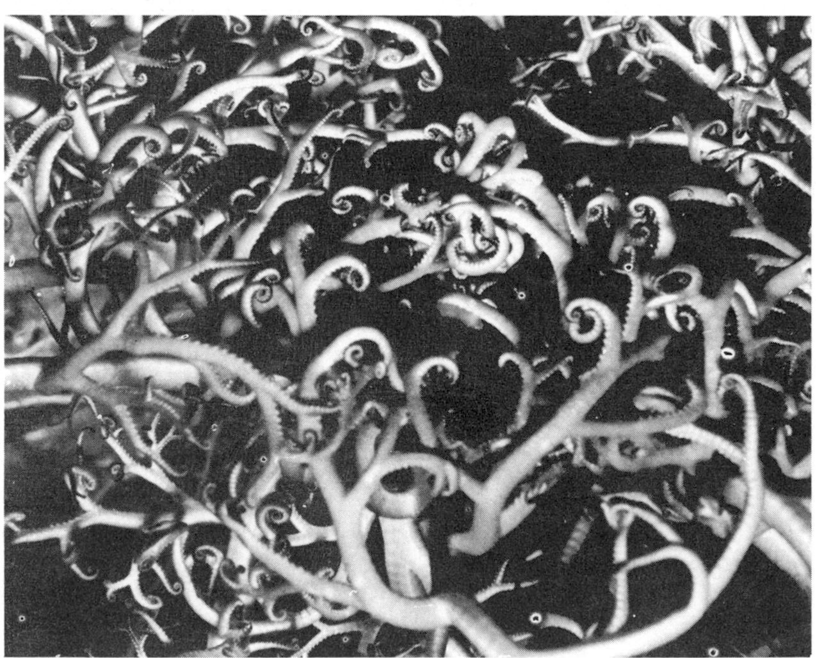

Fig. 194. *The weird Basket starfish, a horrible mass of wriggling, clawed arms, is one of the strangest creatures in the world and is seldom seen in public displays.*

occasionally by an aquarist, is the Basket starfish. It looks like something that shouldn't be alive, something too horrible to behold, yet, when you see one in the aquarium, you can't help but marvel at this strange creature. It looks like the "Thing" science fiction writers write about or a strange living creature from outer space. Yet, it is not extremely rare, it is just seldom if ever displayed and it's probably just as well.

The Basket star has hundreds of arms all centering about the main body cavity, and each arm is divided into hundreds of "clawed hands" so that when the whole creature starts moving, all in unison, it makes you wonder how such a strange thing can exist. It may wrap itself into a ball about the size of a grapefruit, when it is sleeping, but rap on the glass, and a dozen strange arms will suddenly shoot upward as though springing from a trap. Disturb it further, and it will unfold and unwind until it is a tremendous fern-like creature completely filling a twenty-gallon aquarium. The arms will thrash back and forth wildly, trapping anything that gets entwined in its "clawed hands" and the center body cavity will expand rhythmically, like the giant nerve center of a strange machine. Then after

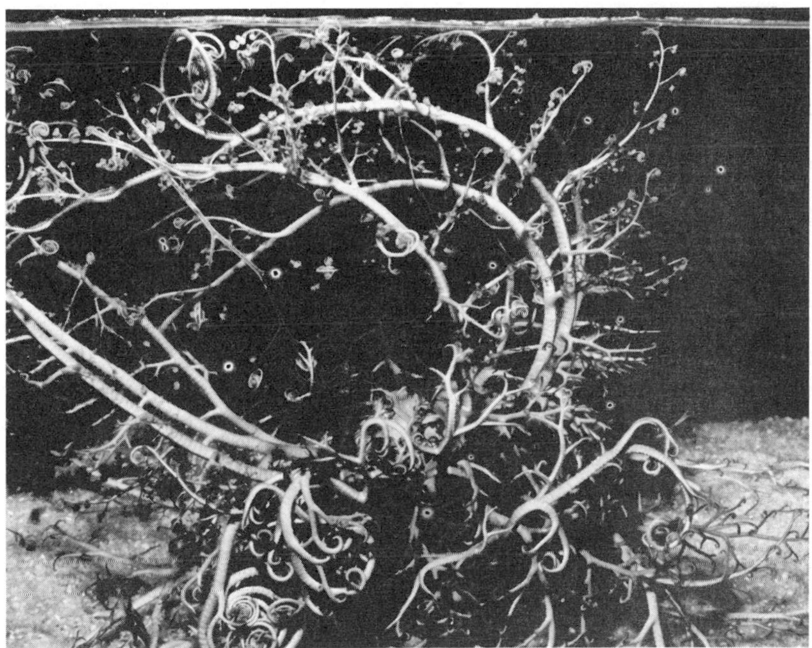

Fig. 195. *Huge fern-like arms flail about as though attacking some unseen enemy. As you watch this incredible thing you become almost hypnotized by the rhythmic pulsations of the central body which directs the movements of thousands of tiny fingers that coil and uncoil in perfect coordination.*

an hour or two of fierce thrashing, it will suddenly tire and slowly roll into a tight ball and go back to sleep. Only in the sea could such a strange creature exist!

The average life span for the Basket starfish is unfortunately just a week or two at the most. It doesn't do well in the aquarium and commits suicide when it seems doomed to confinement. It will tear itself to pieces in a horrible manner befitting its weird nature, but it is such an intensely interesting creature that the author feels it worthwhile as an aquarium specimen. After all, what television show lasts a week?

Perhaps in future years when more people have kept this strange creature, someone will learn the secret of keeping it alive, and it will open a new field of fascination for the whole country.

Nudibranchs, Snails, and Scallops

The small Nudibranchs or sea slugs as they are commonly called, are often highly colored and if there is a rich coating of algae growing on the glass or coral, they will do quite well in the aquarium. They should be introduced to the tank the same as fish so that they are accustomed to the changes of temperature and pH when placed in the aquarium. Some are a brilliant green while others are orange and blue and the fancier reef specimens may be pink, sky blue, or most any color. Some aquarists make a special study of these beautiful creatures and keep them in small glass containers heavily covered with growths of algae.

Large Nudibranchs, like the Sea Pigeons, or Sea Hares as they are also known, should not be placed in the community tank as they give off a heavy slime which may foul the water by trapping uneaten food. Also this larger type needs tremendous quantities of algae and eats constantly so that it often keeps the aquarium in a rather dirty condition. When seen out in the sea, Sea Pigeons remind one of a cow grazing contentedly on the sea bottom. They live well in the aquarium, but as stated before, they need such tremendous quantities of algae unless one lives by the sea, keeping them would prove rather difficult.

Ordinary salt-water snails or other living sea shells, are often kept in small separate aquariums by the marine hobbyist. Some of the sea shells have brilliant mantles far exceeding in beauty, the handsome shell they leave behind. If more conchologists were aware of this, they would keep the live shells in their aquarium to study. Then if the creature dies, they would still have the shells. This is an interesting field of exploration and those attempting it should bear in mind that most snails eat algae, roots, or decayed vegetation so these should be present in the aquarium. Also, since most of the animals

Fig. 196. *Giant Cowry covers his beautiful, shiny shell with a bristling mantle. These interesting shells are a favorite of collectors, but how many have ever kept one alive in an aquarium? Actually, they live quite well and make a very interesting study.*

Fig. 197. *Live Horse conchs live well in the aquarium. In fact keeping them is simply a matter of placing them in a well set up tank with sub-sand filter and a few algae rocks. They will live for a year or more with little attention. This fine specimen was collected by the author's son, Paul Straughan, on a family collecting trip.*

Fig. 198. *A beautiful live cowrie crawling about a dense bed of green algae. Keeping live sea shells opens up an entire new field for the aquarium hobbyist, particularly the shell collector who may wish to watch and observe his specimens. Eventually even live sea shells will be raised either in the aquarium or in protected beds in the sea.*

living in shells give off a strong mucous or slime, they should not be kept in the aquarium with your prized fish lest they pollute the water. One or two tiny shells like the Flamingo Tongue, or similar-sized shells certainly would do no harm in a ten- or fifteen-gallon tank if it is watched closely and removed promptly if it dies.

Large Cowries which reach a length of five inches, should always be kept in a separate aquarium as these give off a very heavy slime. However, they live well and will eat lettuce and other leafy vegetables. A sub-sand filter is recommended with all snails or other shells as it will greatly reduce chances of pollution.

Brilliant red scallops known commercially as Flame Scallops *(Lima scabra)* are sometimes available to the aquarist and they will add a dash of flaming red to the salt-water tank. However, they must be watched closely and if they fail to blossom forth, they should be quickly removed from the aquarium. They are not recommended in an aquarium with expensive hard-to-replace specimens because of the danger of pollution if they die unnoticed in the aquarium.

Fig. 199. *The egg cases of a murex growing on a penicillus plant is easily transplanted to the aquarium where the young will hatch out. Raising them is not easy but it will be done in time. Egg cases of many shells, skates, squids, fish, even the giant whaleshark, may be found under the sea and most will hatch out in the aquarium if conditions are proper. They should be handled and transported with the utmost care to avoid damage to them.*

The usual procedure with most aquarist is to keep oddities like this in a small glass tank by themselves, rather than chance them in their main exhibit.

Sea Urchins and Starfish

Sea Urchins are not generally very satisfactory in the marine aquarium because of their tendency to hide. They will live quite well however, and eat algae as well as small chunks of chopped shrimp which should be pushed directly under them. The short-spined sea urchin and the club urchin live the best and they should be kept in an aquarium with little or no coral. Long-spined sea urchins found on the reefs, will not do quite as well, nevertheless, they can be kept at least a few months and are a great curiosity. They will also eat similar foods.

The common starfish is also an interesting addition to the salt-water aquarium because so many people have seen the dried speci-

Fig. 200. *Live Star Shells in the aquarium make shell keeping even more fascinating. In a single afternoon on a shallow reef, one can obtain enough live shells to stock all his tanks and perhaps his neighbor's tank also.*

mens, yet few have seen them alive and crawling about an aquarium. They will eat small chunks of shrimp which should be tucked under them once a week. Brittle stars, Serpent stars, etc. although very colorful and unique, do not do well in the aquarium as they hide most of the time. Those wishing to keep them should place them in an aquarium with no coral, and with just a large flat shell raised slightly from the bottom. The starfish will hide under the shell which can be tipped over when you are viewing your display.

Large starfish, the type often seen dried in window displays, may also be kept in the aquarium and do quite well despite their size. They will usually need a fifteen- or twenty-five-gallon aquarium and care should be taken when transferring them, that the suction discs are not torn when they are removed from their container to place them in the aquarium. They will also eat chunks of shrimp which should be pushed under them so that they can find it.

In the past few years, the keeping of invertebrates in the home aquarium has almost equalled the keeping of exotic colorful fish. In fact, it would not be surprising to see this phase of the hobby actually pass the keeping of the exotic fish. The two main reasons for this are that the invertebrates are much easier to collect than the

Fig. 201. *Drum-type fish bowl equipped with new miracle under-gravel filter made especially for fish bowls. All-glass container with sub-sand filter is excellent for laboratory- or home-study of invertebrates or other specimens that may require pure sea water and a completely non-toxic container. A single pump could operate up to a dozen bowls.*

fishes, and they are generally less expensive. In addition, many are far easier to keep alive since they present few problems with disease or parasites.

Anyone can collect invertebrates. He doesn't even have to know how to swim. All that is needed is a bucket to carry the specimens home and a small net to scoop up specimens that might sting or nip one's fingers. It just requires a trip to the sea shore, and whether one lives in the tropics or in the cold climate, he will find a wealth of invertebrates at his doorstep. These include a tremendous variety of sea urchins, starfish, nudibranchs of every color and description, live snails and molluscs, crabs, shrimp, sea anemones, live corals, live rocks, and an unending variety of plume worms and other sea worms all of which are of great interest in the aquarium. Little wonder that the keeping of invertebrates is becoming so popular.

Practically every rock under the sea will house some type of live marine creature. They may be crabs, snails, tunicates, anemones, barnacles, or the rock itself may be encrusted with algae, beautiful tube worms and molluscs either attached to the outer surface or living within the rock itself. Just bringing a single live rock from

Fig. 202. *The strange Mantis shrimp with its four eyes and powerful pincers, is an amusing addition to the marine tank. It comes in assorted colors and has the habit of carrying or moving large quantities of sand about the aquarium. It should be handled with a net as its sharp claws can inflict a serious wound. Shrimpers call it the "thumb splitter."*

Fig. 203. *The Squat lobster, or Spanish lobster, is a harmless and interesting addition for the marine hobbyist who wants something different. It is very hardy.*

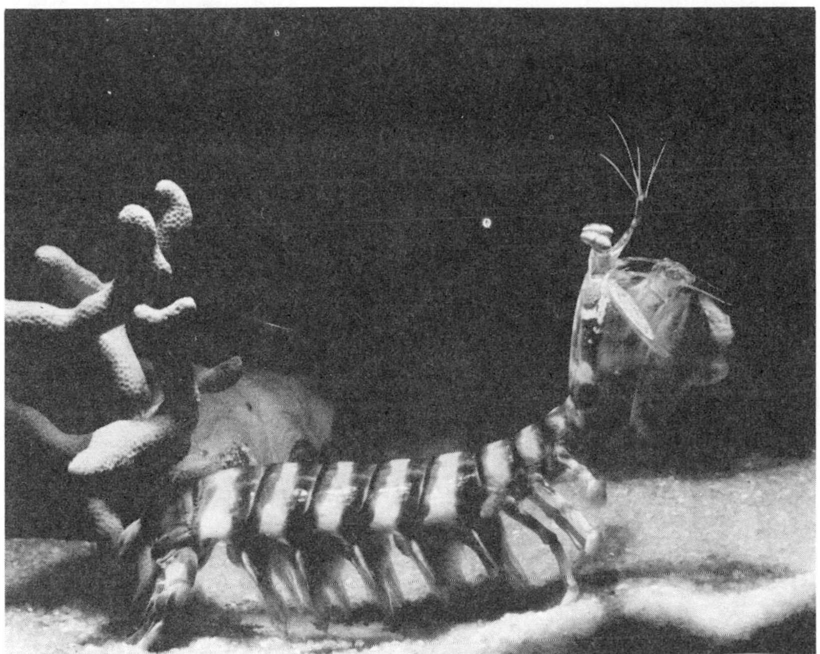

Fig. 204. *The Mantis Shrimp is a real oddity for the aquarist who wants something different. Large specimens one foot or more in length are spectacular creatures whose gymnastics in the aquarium will constantly delight the aquarist. He may lie on his back or peek at you from in back of a coral head.*

the sea and keeping it in a bright, clean aquarium can provide hours of fascination for the aquarist. It is almost unbelievable, the variety of life that can live in a single rock, particularly one that has been picked up in an area rich in life. One rock may easily contain nudibranchs, brittle starfish, crabs, molluscs, algaes, tube worms, mantis shrimp, small fish, barnacles, and many other forms of marine life all of which may make its appearance quite by surprise to the aquarist. Occasionally, many of the rocks from the reefs may contain live specimens of the bright red pectin shells which are highly prized by shell collectors. Other rare shells are likely to show up on rocks gathered from deep reefs by divers equipped with scuba gear. Very often live shells may be born right in the aquarium for their eggs or very minute forms of the shell may be living in the rock when it was collected. But rocks are only a small part of the fascinating invertebrate field. There are also the live corals which are equally as fascinating though more difficult to keep. This opens up an entire new field in salt-water aquarium keeping. It is as endless as the sea

Fig. 205. *Closeup of Mantis Shrimp shows double eyes and huge pincers or claws with which it can slash out with lightning speed.*

Fig. 206. *Male Fiddler Crab has one huge claw that he raises and lowers in slow, jerky movements to signal his mate. The underportion of the claw is white so that when it is raised it can be seen from some distance. The movement of the claw somewhat resembles a musician playing the fiddle.*

Fig. 207. *Female Fiddler Crab carries a cluster of eggs under her tail. The female is slightly smaller than the male and does not possess the large claw or "fiddle" of the male.*

itself, for even when one has kept all the live corals from the local reefs, then there are the Pacific Reef, the Indian Ocean Reefs, not to mention the deep reefs which have been completely untouched in so far as keeping their corals is concerned. In addition, the deep reefs have their own specific species of corals, tunicates, starfish, and shells, many of which have not yet even been identified.

Most invertebrates are quite hardy and easily adapted to the aquarium. They may be kept in a fish bowl, a two to five gallon aquarium, or of course a larger aquarium if desired. Sea shells, small starfish, small sea urchins, etc., will do nicely in a five gallon tank which should be equipped with an undergravel filter and a small inside or outside filter containing carbon to keep the water sparkling clean. With invertebrates, one can have as inexpensive an aquarium as he desires. An ordinary two gallon fish bowl can become an invertebrate tank by simply placing a bowl type undergravel filter inside and covering it with a couple inches of silica sand. Attach an air line to it so that it gives off a strong surge of bubbles and your bowl is ready for invertebrates. A more elaborate invertebrate tank is a five or ten gallon aquarium. The new all-glass tanks are by far the best containers for invertebrates because they afford a clear, undistorted view of the fascinating creatures of the sea. These too should be set up with undergravel filters, and an aquarium light should be used so they may be observed at various times of the day, particularly late evening when many nocturnal species may decide to come out.

12

The Salt-Water Community Tank

Many different varieties of salt-water fish may be safely kept in the same aquarium, with proper knowledge of their living habits. It must be remembered that marine fish are quite often quarrelsome, that they require more air, and in addition are much more costly than the familiar fresh-water tropical fish. In view of this, it is always best to avoid crowding them, unless you live by the sea and have ready access to both sea water and live specimens. A very broad rule would be one fish for each two gallons of water. Then the size must be considered. If the specimens are very small, an aquarium can easily accommodate many of them. Best results are obtained when all the fish are placed in the aquarium at the same time. They will grow accustomed to their new home together and usually will seldom fight unless there is more than one of the same species. Demoiselles in particular will not tolerate another of their own kind in the same aquarium. They will generally attack the intruder immediately, nipping the fins and very often killing it in a very short while. For this reason, much care must be taken when selecting marine tropicals for your aquarium. Choose one fish of each species when first setting up your exhibit. If more than one of the same kind is desired, be sure there is about an inch difference in their sizes, and they will usually get along. Exceptions to this rule are Sergeant Majors, Neon Gobies, Porkfish, Clown fish, and Wrasse. These fish travel in schools and several may be kept in the aquarium at one time, and their showy colors presents a wonderful exhibit, as they travel about the aquarium in small groups.

Angelfish are solitary individuals. Just one should be included in the aquarium, unless the other differs in size by at least an inch as stated above. The Blue Angel is much more pugnacious than the Black or French Angel and when the two are to be kept in the same aquarium, it is best to have the Blue Angel the smaller of the two. It is possible to keep many Angelfish in the same aquarium without any fighting, should it be necessary to do so.

The secret is confusion. Place a dozen or more Angelfish in one aquarium, and they will encounter each other so often that they will not have a chance to get their tempers up. This is especially helpful to dealers who cannot very well have a separate aquarium for each of their Angelfish.

Generally, quarreling will start soon after the aquarium has been set up, if any is to take place at all, or when a new specimen is introduced to the aquarium. Watch the fish closely and if any serious fighting takes place, remove the offender at once. Introduce new specimens when you do your general cleaning for when the aquarium is all stirred up the fish are not likely to notice a newcomer among them.

Large Demoiselles, Beau Gregories, Orange Demoiselles, Large Jewel fish, or any others belonging to the same group should not be kept in the marine aquarium, unless by themselves. They are extremely pugnacious and will fight and kill many of the smaller fish in the aquarium. The Beau Gregory in particular has earned a bad name for himself as many large specimens were shipped throughout the country to unknowing aquarists. Word soon got around that this fish was just no good as it was too quarrelsome and its reputation was ruined. Actually the Beau Gregory is a very beautiful and charming fish. Its colors will compete with the showiest of all marine tropicals and it can be kept in the community tank, if it is obtained small, with a body size no larger than one inch long. Obtained at this size, it can do little harm and will add vitality to the aquarium. The same applies to the other Demoiselles. Keep them under an inch when you get them, and they will usually grow up with the other fish into one happy family.

Fish with large mouths like the Blue Hamlet, Cardinal, Sargassum fish, etc. should not be kept in the community tank unless the other fish are large enough so that they cannot be swallowed. Also large Hermit crabs, large Spider crabs, or any large crabs should be kept in an aquarium by themselves as they will eventually catch one of your prized pets. Always try to obtain small crabs for your display. They will be easier to manage and will seldom bother the fish.

One or two sea anemones can safely be placed in the community tank if it is over eight gallons and these will live peacefully, indefinitely. The only time the anemone would bother your fish, is when you have the tank too crowded and a large fish is chasing one of the other fish. In their frantic effort to escape, the fish will accidentally come in contact with the stinging tentacles of the anemone and it may kill them. Wrasses, like Blueheads, Slippery Dicks, and other members of the same family, that sleep under the sand, occasionally come up out of the sand directly under an anemone, with harmful results to them. Therefore, it is best to eliminate anemones if you intend to keep the Wrasses, in any quantity, or just keep one anem-

Fig. 208. *A large, well-balanced aquarium. Small school of Sergeant Majors at top, Porcupine fish, center, Butterfly fish, Porkfish and anemones are at lower right. Note the beautiful coral formations. A salt-water aquarium of this magnitude represents an investment of several hundred dollars and is not recommended for beginners.*

one in the tank, and watch it closely.

Sea Horses should not be kept in the community tank. They are such slow swimmers that they probably would starve to death. Also the fish may pick on them and being so defenseless, they will suffer. There are a few fish that may be kept with the Sea Horses and it will liven up their tank with color. Neon Gobies, red Cardinals, small Spider crabs and small Sargassum fish will all live peacefully with the Sea Horses. Do not keep Puffer fish, Filefish, large Spiny Boxfish, Porcupine fish or sea anemones with Sea Horses. Puffers and Files especially will promptly eat the fins from your pet Horses and they will be unable to swim.

Generally, the community tank will do better if the specimens are obtained on the small size as there will be less quarrelling, feeding will be easier and the fish will be in their best color.

Listed below are suggested combinations for community tanks. If you decide to keep unusual specimens, like Moray eel, Octopus, Gorgonias, Sea Pigeons, Sting rays, Lion fish, etc., keep them in a separate aquarium. It doesn't have to be a large tank, but don't put them in with your community tank. Remember, if a large fish dies, you may lose all the others. When the occasion demands, Sea Horses, Sargassum fish, etc. may be kept in the community tank if they are separated with a piece of glass.

Fig. 209. *A large number of young Black Angelfish may be kept in the same aquarium with little fighting if they are all introduced at one time and if they are given places to hide.*

Suggested Combinations for Salt-Water Aquariums

The following groupings are meant merely as a guide to the beginner and are subject to wide variations and inter-groupings. There is no guarantee that these specimens will positively live in perfect harmony and if any fighting ensues the offender should be immediately removed.

Two-gallon Aquarium

12 Dwarf Sea Horses
2 small Pipe fish
2 very small starfish

or

1 Angelfish ½ inch size
1 Beau Gregory less than ½ inch
1 Neon Goby
1 Sergeant Major ½ inch size

or

1 sea anemone

or

2 Banded Coral shrimp

or

3 small Clownfish
2 Neon Gobies
1 small Hermit crab

or

1 Sargassum fish 1 inch long

or

2 medium Sea Horses
4 Dwarf Sea Horses

or

1 Jewell fish ½ inch
1 French Angel—same size
2. Neon Gobies, small

Five-gallon Aquarium

3 Neon Gobies
1 Angelfish 1 inch size
3 Sergeant Majors ½ inch size
1 Beau Gregory ½ inch
or
1 Butterfly fish
2 Neon Gobies
1 Clownfish
1 Black Angel 1½ inches
3 Sergeant Majors ½ inch
1 Hermit crab
or
3 Clownfish
3 Sergeant Majors
3 Neon Gobies

3 Sergeant Majors
or
2 large Sea Horses
1 Sargassum fish 1 inch
or
50 Dwarf Sea Horses
or
1 Queen Angel 1 inch
1 Spider crab, small
or
3 sea anemones
or
6 Boston Beans
3 baby Spiny Boxfish
3 baby Hermit crabs

Ten-gallon Aquarium

1 Black Angel 2 inches
1 Queen Angel 1½ inches
4 Sergeant Majors ½ inch
2 Coral shrimp
1 Beau Gregory ½ inch
or
3 Butterfly Fish 2 inches
3 Neon Gobies
1 Black Angel 1½ inches
1 Queen Angel 1 inch
1 Hermit crab 1 inch

or
4 large Sea Horses
2 Spiny Boxfish 1 inch
1 Cowfish 1 inch
or
3 Porkfish
1 Black Angel 1½ inches
1 Queen Angel 1 inch
2 Coral shrimp

Fifteen-gallon Aquarium

6 sea anemones
1 Spider crab
2 Beau Gregories ½ inch
or
6 Clownfish
1 Black Angel 1 inch
3 Neon Gobies
1 small spider crab
1 sea anemone
or
1 Nurse Shark 12 inches
or
6 large Sea Horses
1 Cowfish 1 inch
1 Spider crab

or
1 Lion fish 4 to 6 inches
or
1 Porcupine fish 5 inches
3 Porkfish
3 Wrasse
2 Hermit crabs
or
1 Moray eel 14 inches or less
or
4 Butterfly fish
3 Neon Gobies
1 Black Angel 1 inch
2 Clownfish

Thirty-gallon Aquarium

1 Queen Angel 4 inches
1 Black Angel 3 inches
5 Neon Gobies
5 Sergeant Majors ½ inch
1 Demoiselle

or

1 Porcupine fish 6 inches
5 Wrasse
6 Hermit crabs

or

1 Moorish Idol 4 inches
5 Neon Gobies
3 Clownfish

or

8 Clownfish
3 *Dascyllus Trimaculatus*
4 Neon Gobies
1 small Spider crab
1 Black Angel 1½ inches

or

2 Moray eels

or

5 Dascyllus Aruanus
1 Black Angel 1½ inches
2 Coral shrimp
3 Clownfish
1 Least Butterfly fish

Fifty-gallon Aquarium

3 Moray eels

or

10 Clownfish
1 Black Angel
2 sea anemones
5 Neon Gobies

or

1 Lion fish

or

1 French Angel 6 inches
1 Queen Angel 3 inches
1 Black Angel 1½ inches
8 Sergeant Majors
1 Orange Demoiselle
3 Neon Gobies
1 Spider crab
Scavenger crabs

or

8 Dascyllus assorted
1 Least Butterfly
2 sea anemones
5 Clownfish
1 Black Angel 1½ inches

or

1 Nurse shark up to 20 inches

or

1 Queen Angel 5 inches
1 French Angel 4 inches
10 Sergeant Majors ½ inch
4 Neon Gobies
2 Beau Gregories
3 Clownfish

or

1 Moorish Idol
5 Neon Gobies
3 Clownfish

or

10 sea anemones
2 Spider crabs
3 Beau Gregories

or

6 Butterfly fish
6 Neon Gobies
2 Coral shrimp
5 Hermit crabs
1 sea anemone

or

10 Large Sea Horses
5 Spiny Boxfish 1 inch
5 Neon Gobies
3 Cowfish 1 inch

Five hundred-gallon Aquarium

1	Adult French Angel	5	large Moray eels
1	Adult Queen Angel	12	Neon Gobies
1	assortment of smaller fish	6	anemones
	or		or
1	mated pair of Angelfish	1	mated pair Moorish Idols
	or		or
25	Florida lobsters	3	large common Butterflys
	or	1	Rock Beauty
1	Large Pacific sea anemone		assortment of smaller fish
7	Large Clownfish		or
	other smaller Demoiselles	25	Spiny Boxfish
	or		other small fish

A very broad rule for marine displays would be one inch of fish for each two gallons of water. It is better to have less fish and keep them well fed than to overload the aquarium.

13

Miscellaneous Specimens for the Aquarium

Although there are a great many colorful and interesting marine fish and specimens not listed in the preceding pages, just because they were not depicted does not necessarily mean that they are not good aquarium fish. The author tried to include most of the more popular types which are normally available to the marine hobbyist, through his local aquarium dealer or by ordering direct from the collectors in Florida and on the West Coast.

Unusual specimens which can sometimes be obtained include baby Stingrays, which believe it or not will become so tame that they will wrap their flippers gently around your hand to obtain small bits of fresh shrimp, their favorite food; also weird Batfish, Electric rays, baby Barracuda, baby sea turtles, Trumpet fish, Cornet fish, Tripletails, Bermuda Chubs, grass Porgies, and a large variety of Gobies and Blennies. Most of these can be kept a considerable length of time by a good aquarist and since most are rarely available, they are very interesting when obtained.

Tiny Stingrays four or five inches long are especially interesting. They will bury themselves in the sand with only the eyes visible, and when food is presented, they will quickly emerge. As stated above, they become very tame, but though small, they are capable of inflicting damage with the sharp spine at the base of the tail and they should be handled accordingly. They will usually eat fresh shrimp and grow quite rapidly and are one of the most unusual pets from the sea. Larger specimens a foot or more in length are much more common and quite easily obtained by a collector.

The Batfish and electric Stargazer are two rather rare fishes and obtaining them might be quite difficult. For the aquarist who wants something really odd, these creatures will fill the bill. Other unusual

Fig. 210. *Sharp-nosed Reef Puffer has a comical expression and unusual tactics. It may swim backwards, sideways, or hover motionless in the water. If it so chooses, it may also squirt water in the surprised aquarist's face.*

Fig. 211. *Rainbow Goby with diamond-shaped tail is quite rare and is occasionally collected by the author who gave it this name.*

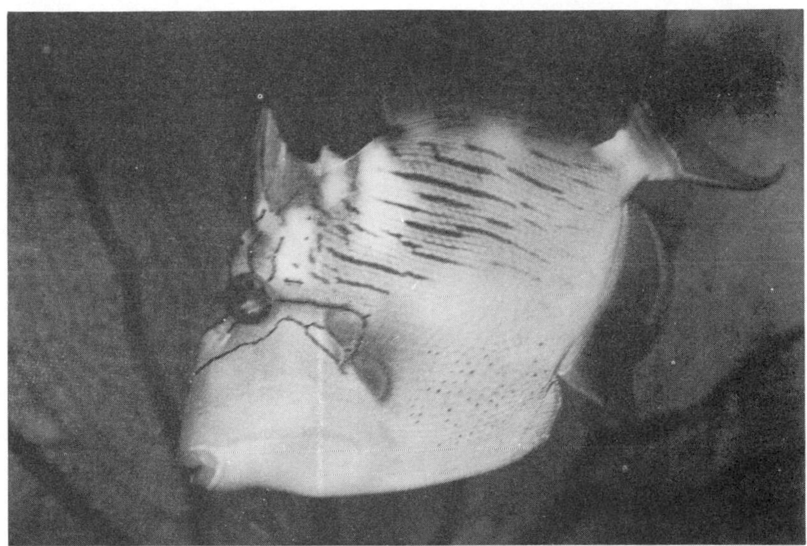

Fig. 212. *The vicious Queen Triggerfish* (Balistes vetula) *quickly becomes tame in the aquarium and when young will cradle itself contentedly in the palm of a befriended aquarist. Large specimens can inflict a severe bite and must be handled accordingly.*

Fig. 213. *A baby sea turtle swimming to the bottom of the tank after a chunk of fish. Sea turtles are much more alert and intelligent than the common fresh-water turtles sold as pets. Natural coral sand of high calcium content should be used in their aquarium, according to Warren Zeiller of Miami Seaquarium. The turtles will eat the sand when grabbing their food and this will add important nutrients to their diet keeping them in good health.*

salt-water residents are the comical Trumpet fish, the Moonfish, Lookdowns, Goatfish, Lizard fish, Squirrel fish to mention a few.

Parrot fish, while extremely colorful, are not too well suited for the small home aquarium. With the exception of the rainbow Parrot and the red Parrot, most of them do not have much color until they are quite large. Their diet consists mostly of live coral and although they will live for a while in confinement, they usually lose most of their brilliance.

One of the most unusual associations of fish with other forms of life, is that between the deadly Portuguese Man of War jellyfish, and the *Nomeus* or Man of War fish. This attractive little fish makes its home in the tentacles of jellyfish, and lives a precarious existence among the "high tension wires" of this dangerous creature. The *Nomeus,* which normally feeds on zooplankton and other tiny foods that drift through the sea, is not a good aquarium fish and dies very shortly after confinement. It has a beautiful silver-blue body with large pectoral fins which probably are used to keep the dangerous tentacles of its host away from its own body. Continued experiments with this unusual fish will no doubt prolong its life in the home aquarium.

Baby Flying fish and baby Dolphin and once in a great while, even a baby Sailfish, can all be kept in a home aquarium for varying lengths of time. All must be fed live brine shrimp, and as they grow very fast, they must be fed huge amounts. The Flying fish should be kept in an aquarium to themselves that is tightly covered so they

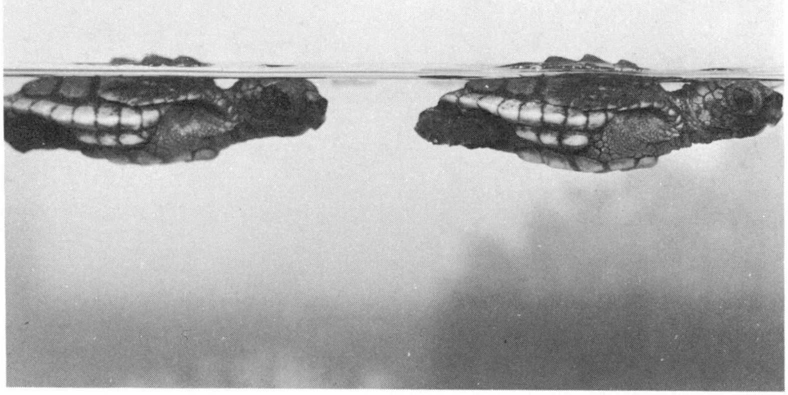

Fig. 214. *Baby sea turtles are lovable pets. They become so anxious to see their owners, that they will swim on their back at his approach. They are easy to feed and will eat chopped shrimp, small minnows, or worms which may be placed on a toothpick and inserted into their open mouths.*

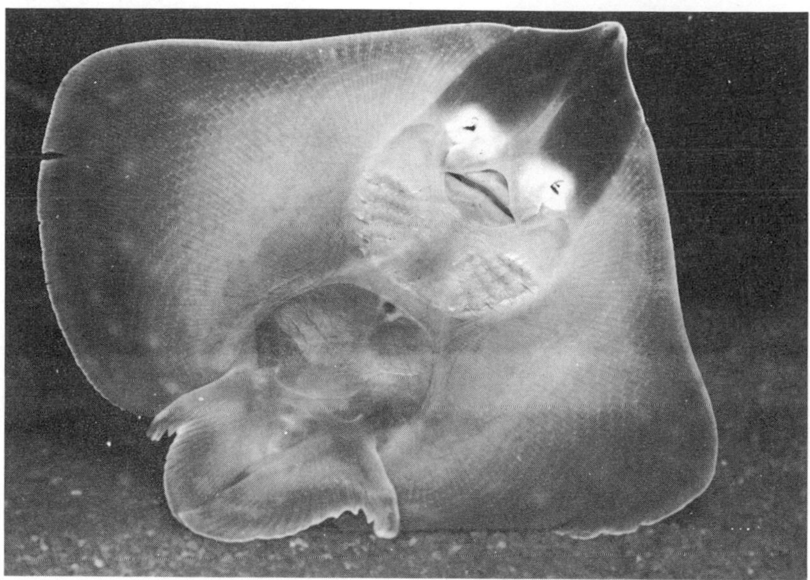

Fig. 215. *Small Rays four or five inches long will live well in the aquarium and accept food readily. They will also become tame and nestle into the hand of the aquarist. Underside of this specimen bears ghost-like appearance.*

won't leap out. They must be given good aeration and tremendous quantities of food should be present at all times. Mr. F. G. Wood of Marine Studios, Florida, has been experimenting with them for some time and at present time holds the record for their longevity. The baby Dolphins will also eat dry food which should be floated at the surface and they are surprisingly hardy despite their diminutive size. Baby Sailfish are so seldom collected that the author will not hazard a guess as to their life-span in the aquarium. They certainly would be a sensational specimen to exhibit for even in the small eight- or ten-inch size they are equipped with a tiny sail like their parents. Probably the rarest creature of the open sea that could be kept in the aquarium is the sea Moth, a strange insect-like creature that swims about the surface like a moth or butterfly. The author once chased one from the bow of a boat in the Bahamas, but lost it when it submerged in the open sea. Green or Pearly Razor fish are sometimes available to the aquarist and their peculiar habit of diving under the sand makes them an amusing addition to the home tank. They live well in the aquarium and of course, sand should be kept in its tank so that it will feel at home. They will eat regular aquarium foods including brine shrimp and chopped shrimp.

Fig. 216. *The Atlantic Long-Nosed Batfish is a strange bottom dweller and is equally as fascinating as the short-nosed batfish. This one became so tame that it would hop to the front of the aquarium to greet the author and would take live minnows from the author's hand.*

Fig. 217. *Deadliest of all fishes is the Stonefish* (Synanceja sp.) *whose thirteen poison dorsal spines along the back can bring horrible death to an unwary bather. This specimen would bury itself in the tank with just the eyes protruding above the sand. Stone fish are not recommended for children! In fact pet shops should not sell ANY poisonous fish to minors.*

Fig. 218. *Two weird denizens of the sea are the sea robin in front and the batfish in back. The sea robin makes a loud noise that may startle an aquarist who is unfamiliar with it, especially at night for the noise can be heard throughout the entire house.*

An innocent looking but deadly fish, to the other aquarium residents, is the Spotted Trunk Fish. This comical little fellow with the hard shell and white-spotted body has the peculiar ability of poisoning everything in the aquarium including itself if it becomes irritated. So powerful is this poison that it can even kill other fish in an open live well out in the ocean where the water is constantly changing. The author lost many fine specimens until the truth was learned about this strange little fish. At one time an entire collection of Jewel fish, Rock Beauties, and other hard-to-get specimens were lost in minutes when one of these innocent-looking trunk fish was placed in their containers. The fish died almost instantly and the mystery was not solved until sometime later when a Spotted Trunk Fish was thrown into a floating live well. The other fish died immediately and after that the Trunk fish was strongly suspected. Tests in aquariums with common fish soon proved that this fish was a killer when aroused. The poison it extrudes is so powerful that it will kill even the hermit crabs. Usually, when the fish gives off its poison, it is the last to die and apparently is immune to its poison but dies from the slime and pollution caused from the dead fish.

Fig. 219. *Another interesting batfish is this deep-sea species whose body is nearly as flat as a pancake. This interesting little fellow was caught near Miami where it was washed into shallow water probably by one of the hurricanes.*

Despite its poison, the Spotted Trunk fish is a real charmer and lives well in the aquarium. It will eat chopped shrimp, brine shrimp, and most aquarium foods, including green algae. It can live in the community tank and will not give off the poison unless threatened with a net, or by an aggressive fish. Another fish suspected of this same type of poisoning is the Trumpet fish and probably other members of the Trunk fish family.

Pistol shrimp, or Sixteen Gun Salute shrimp, as the author calls them, are interesting crustacea that are out of the ordinary as far as conventional specimens are concerned. They have massive claws like the Maine lobster and they have the uncanny ability of snapping their claws so loud that it can be heard clear across the room. If one is held in the hand the clicking of the claw will sting sharply as the noise is caused from concussion and it can raise a welt on the flesh when it hits. The Sixteen Gun Salute shrimp lives inside sponges and is said to stun its prey by snapping its claw close to the intended victim. The author's first experience with these unusual shrimp was quite surprising. Several had been collected and were distributed to various aquariums and finally the clicking started. It sounded exactly

Fig. 220. *The weird Batfish hops around the aquarium on tiny "feet." It "angles" for its food with a tiny fishing lure on its forehead and swallows small minnows, marine worms and other edible matter.*

Fig. 221. *Head-on view of weird Batfish.*

Fig. 222. *The Lookdown is one of the most unusual aquarium fishes. It is bright silver in color and as thin as a sheet of paper.*

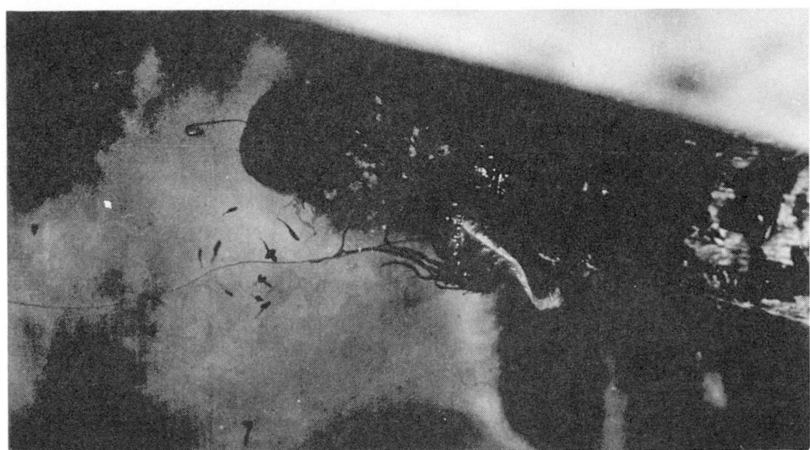

Fig. 223. *The Portuguese Man of War fish* (Nomeus) *gather about the deadly tentacles of their host who has drifted into a piling. These beautiful little blue and silver fish do not fare well in the aquarium.*

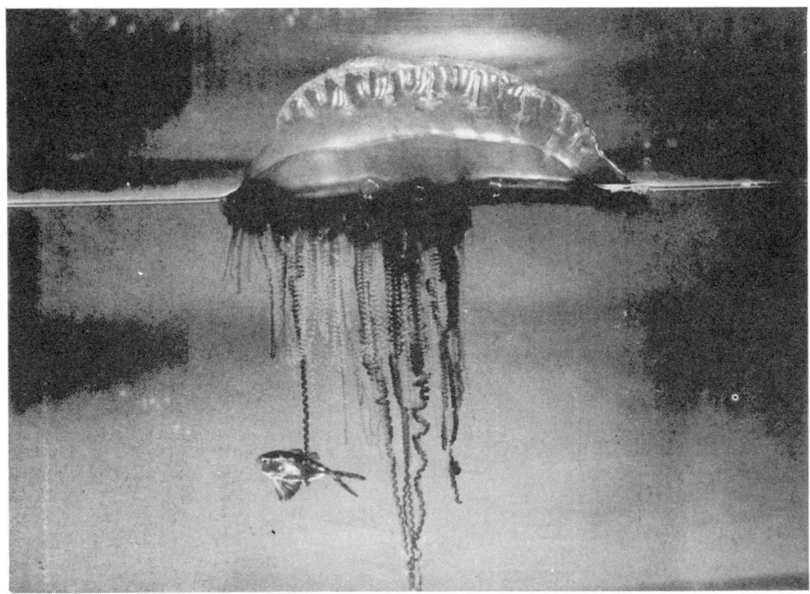

Fig. 224. *Only the Man of War fish can swim beneath the tentacles of the Portuguese Man of War Jellyfish. Other fish are quickly stung to death and devoured by the horrible creature. The author was nearly killed by a recent encounter with the stinging jellyfish.*

Fig. 225. *The Sixteen Gun Salute Shrimp was given this name by the author because of its ability to make a loud noise by snapping its huge claw. If it snaps its claw in a metal container it sounds like a small cannon. It is also called the Snapping Shrimp or Pistol Shrimp. It lives well in the aquarium, and although seldom seen it often disturbs the quiet of the night with its loud noise.*

as though the glass had cracked and the aquariums were all checked carefully for leaks. More clicking and still no leaks soon led to the discovery that something in the aquarium was making the noise and it was traced to the amazing shrimp. The author promptly named him the Sixteen Gun Salute shrimp in memory of old Navy days.

Another interesting member of the shrimp family that is rapidly becoming popular is the Dancing shrimp. This beautiful red- and white-striped crustacean grows to a length of about two inches and does not have any claws like the Banded Coral shrimp. They often gather in large groups and can be displayed this way, which makes a fine display, for they will rock back and forth in unison as though keeping time with the rhythm of the sea. They will eat green algae and chopped shrimp and live well.

Small Snappers, Groupers, Grunts, and other fairly common fish will live well in the home aquarium and can usually be obtained without too much difficulty. The Grunts are the most common and are often used as food for the Lion fish and the Sargassum fish. They nearly always travel in schools, and since this is the exception rather than the rule in marine aquarium fish, they will make a fine display when exhibited with one or two colorful specimens. Some Groupers are highly colorful, including the Rock Hind which has brilliant red spots, and the Golden Grouper, a small highly-colored member of the family that come chiefly from the Bahamas. The small Spanish Hogfish *(Bodianus rufus)* is another highly-colored fish that may be obtained occasionally. It is a brilliant blue and yellow and has a rather slender shape which is characteristic of the Wrasse family to which it belongs.

It will be some time before the marine hobbyist has exhausted the interest and pleasure of the Atlantic salt-water fishes, but if he does, he still hasn't scratched the surface because there are a few more oceans to be exploited. The vast Pacific with its fabulous Great Barrier Reef, a gigantic paradise of fantastic reefs well over a thousand miles long, is so loaded with colorful marine fih that it may take several lifetimes before they can all be brought to the attention of the aquarist. Already, the spectacular Lion fish, the extremely beautiful and popular marine Clown fish, and a variety of Demoiselles,

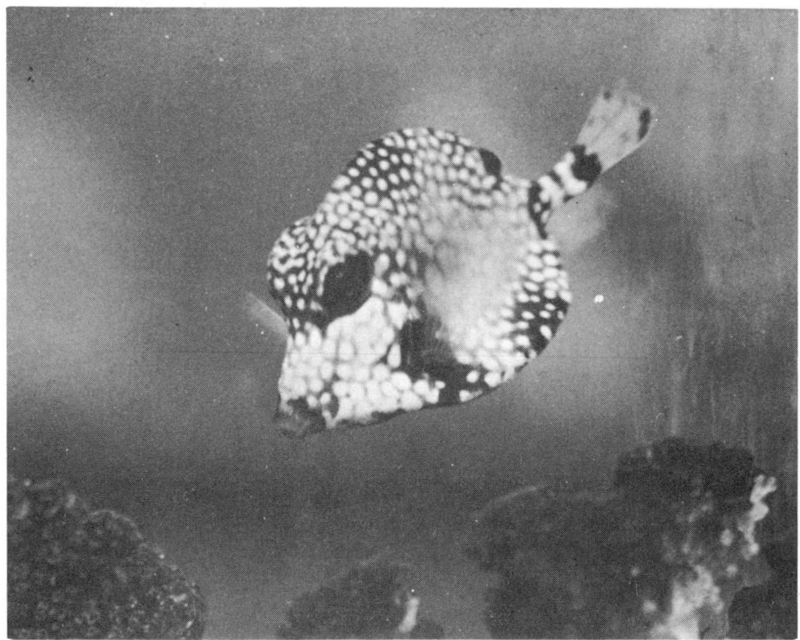

Fig. 226. *The comical almond-eyed Spotted Reef Trunkfish is a much desired marine fish. Despite its innocent appearance, if aroused or annoyed, it will give off a deadly poison that will kill every fish in the aquarium in a matter of minutes.*

Butterfly fish, including the famous Moorish Idol, and bizarre Trigger fish, have been imported and many more will come when the public shows a desire to keep them. Here we have a truly inexhaustible supply with thousands of square miles of untouched reef area waiting for the collectors. There are so many interesting creatures in the sea that can be kept in the aquarium that the figure is staggering and, while it is true that many of them can only be kept a short while in the aquarium, a lot can be learned about them even in a week's time. As the years go by and more people keep salt-water aquariums, the life span of even the most delicate creatures will be greatly lengthened in the home display so that eventually this may become the greatest hobby in the world.

Other interesting groups of fishes worth mentioning are the File-fish and Wrasses. This includes a wide assortment of shapes and sizes and includes the common File, the Frilled File, the Scrawled File, and the beautiful orange File fish. Most of these are very inexpensive and easily obtained from collectors. The Wrasses also include a wide assortment of shapes and sizes. Among the most colorful is the Bluehead which travels in small schools and is very active. These mature at about six inches and require a large aquarium of at least thirty gallons. Slippery Dicks, Clown Wrasse, Gold Neon Wrasse, and a large selection of highly-colored members of this group are also available and are interesting to observe. They range in size from two to ten inches and usually become extremely tame. Most of them have the peculiar habit of lying down on the sand to sleep which gives them the appearance of being dead. Also, they will burrow under the sand if it is deep enough so that at night when they go to sleep, the aquarium will seem to be empty and there won't be a fish in sight. This comes as a surprise to the unsuspecting aquarist. This is also true of the green or Pearly Razor fish. These long flat fish spend a great deal of their time under the sand and will disappear in a flash. It gives one quite a start to see a head suddenly stick out of the sand and then just as suddenly disappear. Strange things such as this only help to promote the tremendous interest found in keeping the creatures of the sea in our home.

14

Breeding Salt-Water Fish

This fascinating and challenging aspect of the hobby will undoubtedly be attempted by the serious aquarist. He will receive nothing but discouragement from his fresh-water associates who will maintain that it is difficult enough just to keep the marine fish alive, let alone spawn them.

The author first began keeping marine fish many years ago when very little was known about them. It was quite a challenge at first, and still is, but tremendous progress has been made. Today, keeping marine fish is not only feasible, but in most cases it isn't really too difficult. While it is true that all the salt-water fish problems have not been solved, a great many of them have. In future years when more is learned about the wonderful creatures of the sea, the spawning of them on a large scale will be inevitable. Even at this date, some marine fish have already been spawned, and a few of them are described on the following pages. Actually, the task is not as difficult as the pessimistic and envious fresh-water aquarist would lead you to believe. Some people feel that if they have tried something and failed, then it just cannot be done and they will discourage everyone else because they would not want someone to succeed where they couldn't. So, marine aquarist, stand on your own two feet and don't be afraid to fail. For who knows, you may succeed and then your fair-weather friends will flock to your door for a handout of baby Rock Beauties or something like that. Think of the tremendous rewards that will be yours, if you can successfully spawn and raise a tank full of baby Jewel fish, or Clown fish, or Dascyllus. Already both of the latter fish have been spawned. The next step is to raise them, and while you will often hear that it is impossible, don't you believe it! Look at the tremendous progress that has been made in the fresh-water hobby. It was all done by aquarists like you, the kind that wouldn't give up. Now you have a real challenge; for the marine fish can be spawned and raised in the aquarium. First you

Fig. 227. *Spanish Hogfish* (Bodianus rufus), *large slender fish at right, is dark yellow with a blue back and head. Sea fans used in aquarium here are specially cured for salt-water and have all exterior coating removed, leaving only the lacy skeleton. Note beautiful lettuce coral at left and large cluster coral at right. Aquarium is the new, experimental, all-glass type made especially for salt-water use.*

Fig. 228. *A mated pair of marine Clown fish.* (Amphiprion percula) *which the author attempted to spawn.*

Fig. 229. *The Rock Hind or Spotted Grouper* (Epinephelus adscensionis) *is an intelligent and interesting fish for the aquarium. It has large expressive eyes as do most members of its species. This handsome fellow lives for over two years in one of the author's aquariums.*

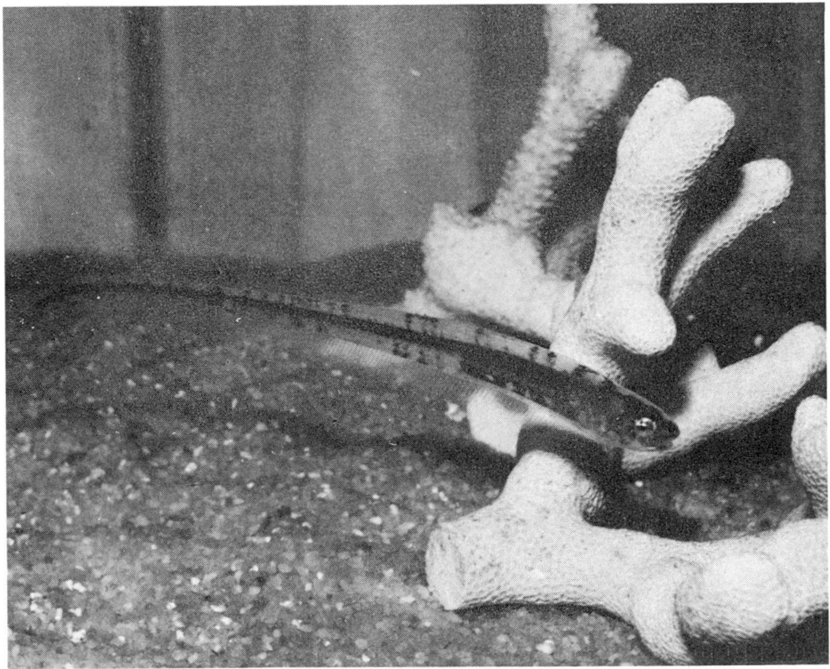

Fig. 230. *The Pearl Fish lives inside the body cavity of the lowly cucumber. It is an interesting experiment to keep both the sea cucumber and pearl fish alive in the aquarium.*

will have to learn how to keep them. Then, if you wish to tackle this problem, you should proceed in much the same way that you would in spawning the most difficult egg layers in the fresh-water field. Actually, marine fish are basically quite similar to their fresh-water relatives. They require similar foods, similar temperatures, and similar living conditions. The author has kept fresh-water aquariums nearly all his life and can speak from experience when he says that the marine and fresh-water fishes are quite similar in nearly every respect. The water they live in is the basic difference between them so that an aquarist who has had much experience with fresh-water tropicals, is almost certain to have better success with marine fish once he learns the few basic principles. The same will be true with breeding the salt-water fish. Basically, they spawn and reproduce much the same as their fresh-water relatives. Therefore, those attempting to spawn them should proceed along the same lines.

First, and this is the most important step, a mated pair of marine fish must be obtained. This is not too difficult a task, no more than selecting a mated pair of fresh-water Angelfish or similar species. Naturally you will have to know something about the fish and to obtain a mated pair, you will have to obtain several adult specimens of the fish you are attempting to spawn and observe them closely in the aquarium. With luck, you may find that two spend a great deal of time together and then the other fish should be removed from the aquarium. If it is a pair, the rest will be more or less routine, until an actual spawning is observed. Then you will be on your own, and heaven help you if you succeed. You will be the talk of your whole aquarium society and the people who discouraged you most will suddenly become your friends and will ask you many "casual" questions about your achievement.

Once a mated pair of marine fish have been obtained, they should be given an aquarium all to themselves. This should contain no hermit crabs, sea anemones, coral crabs, or any other living thing except the two fish and if possible, a good natural growth or marine algae, should be present. This can be started several months before the fish are placed in the aquarium, by keeping the light on for a good portion of the day. A few pieces of coral and shells should be placed about the aquarium in such a way that it affords the fish a completely dark retreat so that they can feel absolutely safe and free from observation when they finally build their nest. Fine sand should be used on the aquarium bottom, and it should not be deeper than a half inch, so that if necessary, it could be quickly siphoned from the aquarium without disturbing the inhabitants too much.

The fish should be conditioned with rich foods, like live brine shrimp, fish roe, enriched dry foods, baby guppies, adult brine shrimp, etc. and if they show signs of nesting, they should be dis-

Fig. 231. *Large cement blocks 15" x 15" x 6" known as column blocks are ideal for supporting a large number of aquariums. Simply set one block on top of the other and place plywood on top and you have a strong, level, rust, and maintenance free support. No nailing or bracing is required, and if you decide to move or re-arrange the tanks, it's simply a matter of taking them down. The fish breeder or laboratory will find this system useful.*

turbed very little. The main objective once a pair is obtained is to make them feel completely at home, and give them the aquarium to themselves. Keep the salinity down to about 1.022 and keep the water in good shape by removing uneaten food and cleaning the filter when it gets dirty. If the sand gets too dirty, take it out of the aquarium and wash it so that your tank will be in good condition. Then, it would be wise to start a growth of marine infusoria in an all-glass container so that if you do get a spawning, you will have something to feed the young when they hatch. Don't try to grow a culture of infusoria in an old aquarium. The foul condition of the water will react with the cement in the aquarium and it may poison your fish when you add it to your tank. Use an old two- or three-gallon fish bowl and fill it about two-thirds with sea water. Then set it in the sun and give it very gentle aeration. The water should turn a rich green and hair algae will usually grow. The infusoria which are tiny microscopic rotifers, and other "germs" will usually be present in this greenish water and their number may be greatly increased by setting up a little decomposition in the container. This can be accomplished by adding a small amount of yeast or well-mashed shrimp to the container, and allowing it to rot. As it decomposes in the greenish water, millions of the "germs" will form and these are to be used as food for your first hatch of marine fish. A simple check of the concentration of infusoria in your culture may be made by placing a few drops of the solution on a piece of glass, and looking at it with a magnifying glass or low-power microscope.

As stated before, it will only be the highly-skilled fresh-water aquarist, who has already spawned the difficult egg layers in his field, and who has learned the procedure for breeding and raising fish from babies, that can expect to successfully raise salt-water fish. It takes a lot of know-how and experience. Naturally, someone who has never even kept a goldfish, cannot expect to raise marine fish. They must first learn how to keep them before they can expect more. This has always been a constant irritation to the author for the first thing many people would ask about salt-water fish was, "Can you breed them?" Further questioning usually revealed that the interested party had never even kept any fish before, and yet this is nearly always a leading question.

Since salt-water fish have not been bred except in a few instances, the aquarist attempting it will be largely on his own. He must follow good aquarium procedure and learn by his own mistakes. If he is successful in obtaining a "spawn" and the aggs actually hatch, then the infusoria must be added several times a day, and the great experiment will be on. It will usually be best to remove the parents the same day the eggs hatch, but this will depend on the nature of the fish spawning, and whether or not it will bother the young. Some fish will not bother their young, while others will go around eagerly devouring their young as fast as they can catch them. The same applies to fresh-water fish. Some aquarists leave the adult fish in with the young, others shun this method and remove both parents immediately after the eggs have been laid and fertilized. Both methods are successful and many times it depends upon circumstances in the aquarium as to what is best. Marine fish usually spawn twice a year, in the spring and in the fall. During the spawning period which may last a month or two, they will usually lay several batches of eggs, so that if you "goof" on the first spawning, you will still have another chance. You will often have a chance to remove one spawning so that you can try to hatch it artificially, and the fish will spawn again so that you will have two chances at hatching the eggs. Then the rearing of the young can be attempted in the aquarium and in a separate container at the same time. Maybe one will be successful.

The hardest part in raising marine fish will be in getting them from the free-swimming stage which will be about three or four days after they hatch, to the size when they will be able to eat live brine shrimp. This will be the most trying and critical period. It will mean feeding them infusoria several times a day for at least two or three weeks and perhaps a month depending on the species. Some fish will be free swimming in a week, and then after about two weeks of heavy feeding on infusoria they may be large enough to eat other foods. If you get them past the critical two-week period, then with proper feeding and care, you will probably be able to raise them to maturity.

It might be wise to add here, that if you are using the sub-sand filter in the aquarium, it should be operated very slowly so that it creates practically no suction into the sand. Otherwise, it will draw all of the microscopic food into the sand and the baby fish will starve. The author once lost an entire hatch of over a hundred baby Neon Gobies by this mistake. The sub-sand filter had been allowed to operate normally and the fish were all drawn down into the coarse gravel. That is why fine sand is recommended for spawning. Also,

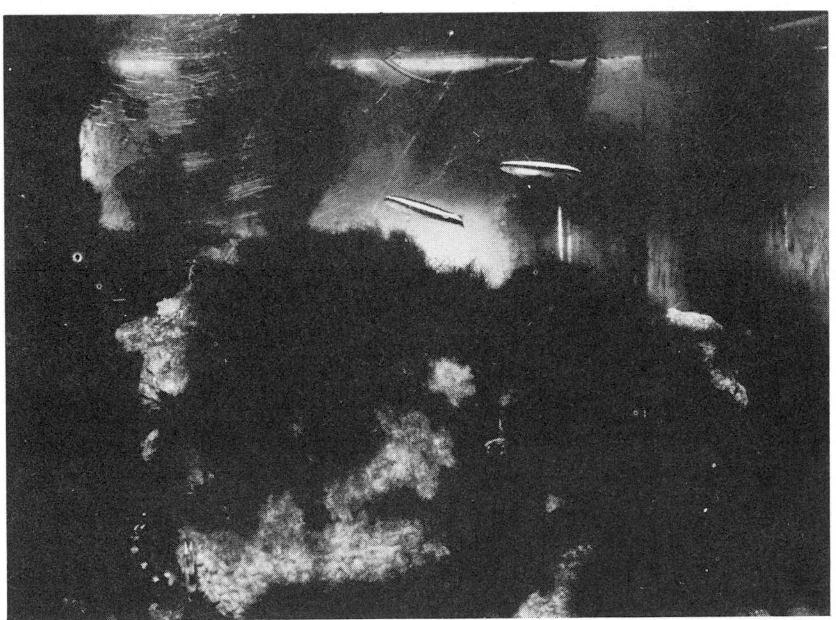

Fig. 232. *One of the author's experimental Green Algae Breeding tanks in which a heavy growth of algae was cultivated over a period of two years. A pair of banded coral shrimp spawned and hatched out their young three times in this aquarium, and at this writing are getting ready to spawn again. The Blue Neon Gobies have spawned at least twice and hatched out their young. The female at top right is again loaded with eggs. The tank also contained several large sea cucumbers, hermit crabs, several large anemones and other mollusks. It is a fifteen-gallon plastic tank.*

the outside filter should be run very slowly and the siphon tubes covered with fine cloth so that the babies will not be drawn into it. An air stone or two can be placed in the aquarium so that the fish will have plenty of aeration. This is important, since the other filters will now be running so slowly that the fish would suffocate unless additional air is supplied.

Common Toadfish. There is at least one marine fish that is rather easy to spawn and this is the common Toadfish. Pregnant fish can be collected in the shallow water by simply lifting old jars or cans into your net. The jars are better as they may be transferred to your aquarium without the danger of metal poisoning and also, because of their transparent nature, the toadfish can be observed without disturbing it. If aquarium conditions are right and the fish is contented you may awake some day to find many little Toadfish swimming about your aquarium. The parent fish will seldom bother the young and if they are all well fed, they may be reared to maturity. Usually,

Fig. 233. *Adult common Toadfish* (Opsanus tau) *with babies hatched and reared to maturity in the author's aquariums. There were over a hundred babies in all. This is perhaps the easiest of the salt-water fish to raise in the aquarium.*

when the jar and fish is collected, it is completely covered with mud so that at the time, it is difficult to tell whether the fish has produced a spawn. However, if great care is exercised, the mud may be gently rinsed from the jar and if there is a cluster of eggs, they will appear as a mass of jelly clinging to the inside surface of the container. It will somewhat resemble tapioca pudding and will be about the same size and consistency. Great care must be used if a spawn is noticed so that the fish will not become excited and destroy the nest in its frantic effort to escape. Never pick up the jars or cans by sticking your fingers in the openings. Toadfish have powerful jaws and teeth and will quickly grab your fingers.

The author has reared three hatches of Toadfish from the eggs and has found that the young are large enough to eat brine shrimp almost as soon as they are born. They will also eat very finely-chopped shrimp and this must be kept in motion with aeration or they will pay no attention to it. It seems that they like to chase their food for they will seldom pick up food which has been lying on the bottom. The large Toadfish will eat good-sized chunks of fresh shrimp and

Fig. 234. *Baby Octopus just one day old! Hatching out the little squirts is rather easy but rearing them is another matter. However, it will all come in time.*

can consume two or three tail sections at a meal. The food should be dropped a couple of inches in front of her so that she can see it fall to the bottom or she will pay no attention to it. If she is well fed, it is doubtful that she will eat any of her young, even if they climb on her open mouth which they often do. In addition to shrimp, the large fish may be fed earthworms and small minnows.

The average nest usually contains about one hundred to three hundred eggs and nearly all of these will hatch out. However, during the first few weeks, some of the young fish just do not seem to take up enough nourishment from the foods presented and slowly waste away, so that after about six months the brood is reduced down to about 60 per cent of the original hatch. After that, there is seldom any loss and the fish can easily be raised to maturity. Probably with more care and better foods the entire hatch could easily be reared to maturity without a single loss.

Although the author feels that large-scale breeding of salt-water fish will usually only be done in hatcheries near the sea, this should by no means discourage the hobbyist who wishes to tackle this great challenge. Certainly due to the great expense of salt-water fish at the present time, a successful hatching of one of the more costly species would be well worthwhile. Especially if they could be sold as tank-raised marine fish. The profits, both monetary and of self esteem, would certainly be worth the efforts.

Marine fishes which have already been spawned at present include the marine Clown fish, Sargassum fish, Dascyllus, Toadfish, Blenny, Dwarf Sea Horses, Neon Goby, and Banded Coral shrimp. No doubt others have been spawned by aquarists who have not made their findings public.

Marine fish which the author feels will spawn if a mated pair is obtained, and if a suitable aquarium is used in proportion to their size, include the marine Jewel fish, Royal Gramma, Rock Beauty, Queen, French and Black Angelfish, Beau Gregory, Cardinal fish, Sergeant Major, and Large Sea Horses. This list looks impressive and probably will draw laughs but it must be remembered that all of the above fishes are suitable aquarium specimens and with the exception of the Angelfish, they mate at a relatively small size. The fact that the Angelfish doesn't spawn until it is quite large, should not exclude it from the list for this can be an asset. The eggs will be larger and the young could probably eat brine shrimp after the first week or two, making raising them a cinch. The author has already heard of an unconfirmed report in which a pair of Angels spawned in a large plywood aquarium. It should be noted that this phase of the hobby has been practically untouched and that few people have ever even owned a mated pair of salt-water fish.

The next ten years should bring forth the successful hatching and rearing of many exotic salt-water fish. In fact one scientist, Dr. George Schumann of California, is said to have spawned and reared numerous salt-water fish of many different species. He visited the author in Miami and said that if an aquarist could get a pair of fish to spawn then the fish could be raised. He suggested large containers with an abundance of algae and a cultivation of protozoa for the first few days until the small fish grew large enough to eat newly-hatched brine shrimp. Clean, sterile aquariums apparently are a necessity, and of course as mentioned earlier, it takes experience to raise any fish, fresh or salt-water.

The author has hatched out numerous fish in various aquariums and indications are that fairly soon we will see some of the more exotic salt-water fish raised in the aquarium. The following is an account of the first hatching of the eggs of the Beau Gregory and also the hatching of squids, reprinted from *Salt Water Aquarium Magazine*.

Beau Gregory Eggs Hatched

"A milestone in the frustrating efforts to raise exotic salt water

Fig. 235. *First High Hat or Cubbyu* (Eques acuminatus) *to ever spawn in the aquarium is shown here. Free floating eggs may be seen at upper right. The fish were approximately five inches long when they spawned. Unfortunately they spawned in a community tank which is often the case, and although the mated pair of high hats were separated by a sheet of glass to protect the fish and eggs, many of the fish in the tank got by the glass and devoured the eggs.*

fish in the aquarium was at least nudged a little by the successful hatching and rearing of the eggs of the Beau Gregory *(Pomacentrus leucostictus)*.

This exciting event took place in our new experimental shop in Miami. The adult Beau Gregory and a large conch shell were collected in shallow water off Key Largo on a recent collecting trip. I had come across it while swimming in the shallow water. The shell appeared empty and I thought perhaps it might contain an octopus which often inhabit the shells but as I approached, I got a quick glimpse of a fish darting inside and knew from the flash of yellow that it was a large Beau Gregory. Thinking that perhaps it had a nest inside the shell, I carefully placed my net over the shell and carefully transferred both fish and shell to a collecting bucket. Upon returning to the boat and studying the shell in detail I noticed hundreds of tiny black specks on the outside of the shell and quickly surmised that they were eggs. It was an exciting event for it is always a challenge trying to rear any colorful salt water fish.

The shell and the adult fish were placed in an all glass aquarium with an under gravel filter and in a short while the parent fish

Fig. 236. *Eggs of the Beau Gregory* (Pomacentrus leucostictus) *were found by the author on a large conch shell. One of the parents was guarding them. Both eggs and the adult fish were carefully collected and transferred to one of the author's tanks. The eggs hatched out in about four days, which was probably the first hatching of Beau Gregory's eggs in a self contained aquarium. It was reported in Salt Water Aquarium Magazine, Vol. 2 No. 4, and although the young were not reared to maturity, it is a step in the right direction.*

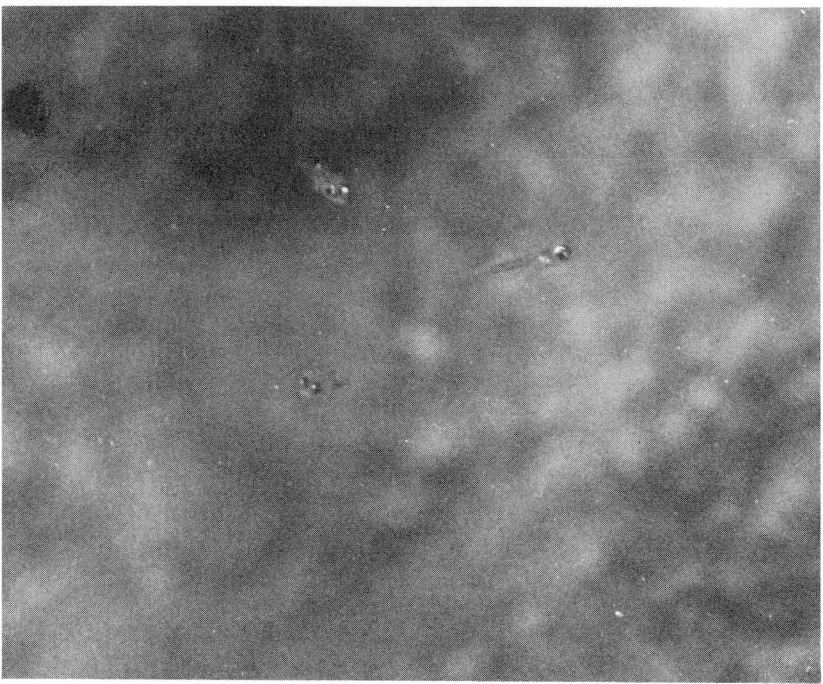

Fig. 237. *First photo ever taken of a baby Beau Gregory! These little fellows are just one day old and were hatched out in the author's aquarium.*

which I think is a female was swimming about the tank dashing madly inside the conch when anyone approached. However when things calmed down, she swam over to her nest and began fanning the eggs with her tail and body. She would swim over them vigorously making them ripple with the current of water she produced with her fins. The water in the tank was crystal clear and all seemed to be going well. In about four days the young fish began to hatch and soon the tank was filled with them. They were fed baby fish food and brine shrimp were added in case they would be able to eat them. Bob Austin, who had accompanied me on the collecting trip was over to see the young fish and took a baby fish home with him to see if he could rear it separately. The tank was darkened except for a corner as the fish seemed to shun bright light and they seemed to be thriving. Lest the mother fish eat the young, she was removed but later this was regretted for we found that there were hundreds of eggs which had not hatched out after she was removed and which would probably have hatched had she been allowed to remain in the tank. The young fish were of course very tiny, even slightly smaller than baby neon gobies and the number of eggs were estimated at between one and two thousand. They encompassed an area in the shell of about six inches around. The adult fish which I feel is a female is approximately four inches long and mostly devoid of color except for yellow on the tail and underside portion of the body. It has been reported that it is usually the male who guards the eggs but since this fish has none of the rich blues and yellows of the Beau Gregories it is assumed that it is a female until it is determined otherwise.

The young fry seemed to be eating, but alas after about four days of life their tank was nearly devoid of swimming fry and the little fish were no more. Why they succumbed remains a mystery and a challenge for those who would tackle this most rewarding aspect of the marine hobby. At least they hatched out and lived for a little while. Had they survived just a week more perhaps I could have reared them. I shall try it again and this time proceed a little differently, for I feel that it is only a matter of time that aquarists throughout the world will be breeding and raising even the most exquisite salt water fish. I would not doubt that Royal Grammas and Lionfish as well as clownfish will be among the first to be raised in aquariums and we hope that we can report the event to you readers in this magazine some day. Meanwhile let's hear from you readers who raise or may attempt to raise any salt water fish."

Fig. 238. *The eggs of Octopus briarius are easily hatched out in the aquarium. Note the empty egg cases and fully developed specimen still in the egg case. The author obtained the eggs under a rock on the reef and collected both the eggs as well as the adult octopus.*

Baby Squids Hatched

"The month of April proved to be a real bonanza for hatching out baby marine fish and crustacea. Everything seemed to spawn in one grand effort. At my experimental shop in Miami the following blessed events took place. A Beau Gregory nest complete with one parent was hatched out in a ten gallon tank. Neon Gobies spawned several times and the young were raised to free swimming stage but not to completion. In additional coral shrimp, nudibranchs, octopuses, whelks and squids were born in the aquarium. You'll hear about them in future issues.

However, the squid bears special mention for the hatching of baby squids from the egg case is not a common occurrence. In fact I doubt if it has occurred hardly at all in a small aquarium. The eggs were obtained far out at sea under a large rock. I had been collecting live specimens and found the egg case attached to the top inside surface of the rock and brought them back with me. At the time, I wasn't certain that they were squid eggs for I had seen the identical eggs pictured in a book and labeled Tulip Shell eggs. This I didn't really believe for Tulip Shell eggs have a different shape and construction. However, I was still somewhat taken aback when they finally began to hatch out.

Fig. 239. *Egg cases of the squid* (Sepioteuthis sepioidea) *which were collected by the author and hatched out in the aquarium. The eggs were identified in one book as that of a tulip shell. Imagine the surprise to find that they were squids.*

The eggs developed very slowly, and at first they showed no signs of life. They were placed in an eight gallon plastic tank with undergravel filter and given moderate aeration. The tank had been treated with a half teaspoonful of clorox as it had been badly infested with parasites and the water had been aerated about a week before the eggs were placed in it. After about two weeks, I noticed a movement inside one of the eggs and could clearly see the outline of a worm like creature wriggling within but I still did not guess that it was a baby squid. Then I noticed that other portions of the case were developing the same way and in fact nearly every section of the case appeared to be alive and healthy. Another week passed with slight change and then one morning when I peered casually at the tank, I caught a glimpse of something darting across the tank. At first glance I couldn't see what it was but then it swam out in the open and I gazed in surpise. It was a perfectly formed, newly born baby squid! I wondered where it came from and then I looked at the egg case which had changed shape slightly. Little squid were literally crawling from it. They swam about the tank, changing color as they moved along then they would settle to the bottom and crawl under a plant *(penicillus)* of which there were several in the tank. Many people who visited the shop saw the cute little fellows and they lived for a week or more and finally succumbed one at a time either from lack of proper food or too much light or chemical substance in the water. It would be interesting to raise them but unfortunately it would be a full time project as squid are notoriously poor aquarium residents and little is known about keeping them in a self contained aquarium. At least it's a first step. If one can at least hatch out a species then there is a chance to rear it, and we hope that this will all come in time. Just imagine the thrilling sight that a fifty gallon tank would make filled with live squids that were raised from mere eggs! There could hardly be a more interesting creature in the entire ocean except perhaps mermaids, and raising mermaids would likely lead to complications (especially when they matured)."

In addition to raising fish there is also the rearing of live sea shells and other invertebrates to consider. Already Japan has succeeded in raising shrimp from the eggs to marketable size. This major breakthrough is only a beginning. Beautiful banded coral shrimp, or the rarer and more expensive scarlet cleaner shrimp, will eventually be raised in the aquarium. The author has had one pair of coral shrimp spawn and hatch out their young several times in one year. Although the young were not raised, this will undoubtedly come in time. Live murex shells were hatched out from eggs and at this writing are over one-fourth of an inch long and growing rapidly. Raising live sea shells could prove an interesting

Fig. 240. *Young squid hatched out in the author's aquarium where they were seen by many visitors at the experimental store in Miami.*

project, especially if rare and beautiful shells are selected. One problem in raising live shells is that the young have a tendency to crawl out of the tank and die. This can be eliminated by placing a sheet of glass directly on the surface of the water as soon as the young shells hatch out. They will then crawl on the glass and back down into the tank. It will be necessary to cut a small hole on the edge of the glass for the plastic tubing but this is easily done with a glass cutter. The author has also raised live nudibranchs on various occasions which were hatched out from egg cases laid on the sides of the aquarium. This is accomplished by providing a natural diet of tiny anemones and algaes upon which the various nudibranchs feed. A large number of live rocks and corals usually provide a varied diet of both live and decayed matter that will support certain nudibranchs and shells if supplemented with feedings of live brine shrimp, very finely shredded shrimp and scallop, and occasional feedings of dry foods. Light is also essential as is good aeration and filtration. The new Dynaflo magnetic drive filter should prove useful here if run intermittently or continually with well-aged activated carbon. Of course it will take a great deal of experimenting. Too much filtration would remove all the food and not

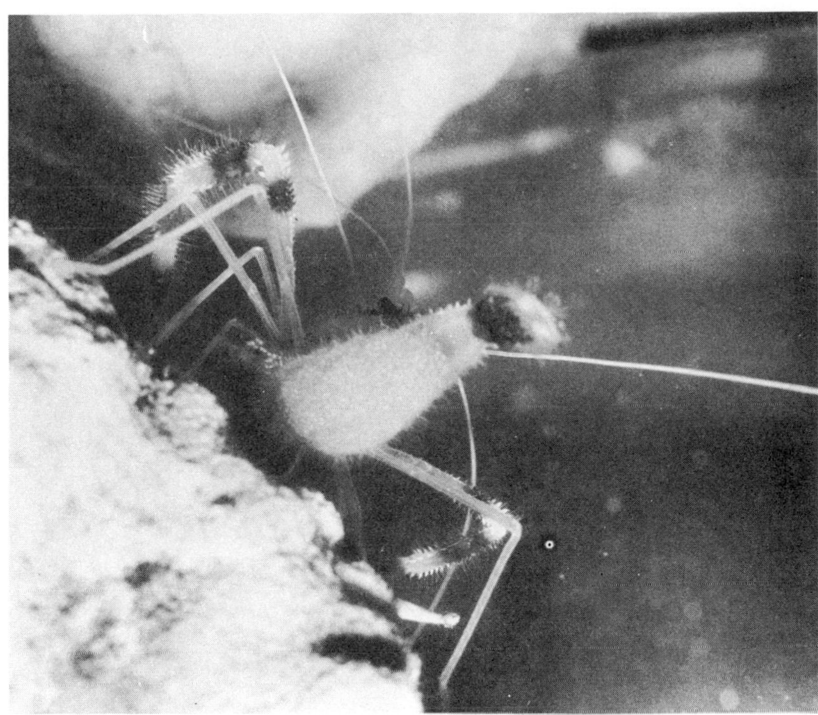

Fig. 241. *Banded Coral shrimp carries its eggs beneath its tail where they mature into tiny quarter-inch babies. The young are transparent but easily seen with the naked eye, for when they hatch out the aquarium seems full of them.*

enough would allow toxic gases or molds to build up under the corals. The proper amount of light is important, whether natural or artificial. Too much light will allow algae to take over the aquarium, which would kill off many of the desirable plants and corals. Not enough light would kill much of the anemone and coral growth. The author uses about ten to eighteen hours of light per day on the live coral tanks. It is especially important with anemones as most of them require considerable light. There are new, fluorescent lights on the market that are said to almost duplicate the sun itself and these should certainly be investigated for use as lighting, particularly on the breeding tanks were one would wish to duplicate nature as closely as possible.

Breeding of salt-water fish is an exciting field. Those who succeed at it first will be rewarded not only by their achievement, but financially as well. Simple arithmetic shows that a thousand of ANY colorful salt water fish would be worth a small fortune, even at a wholesale level. Remember, all you need is a mated pair of fish kept

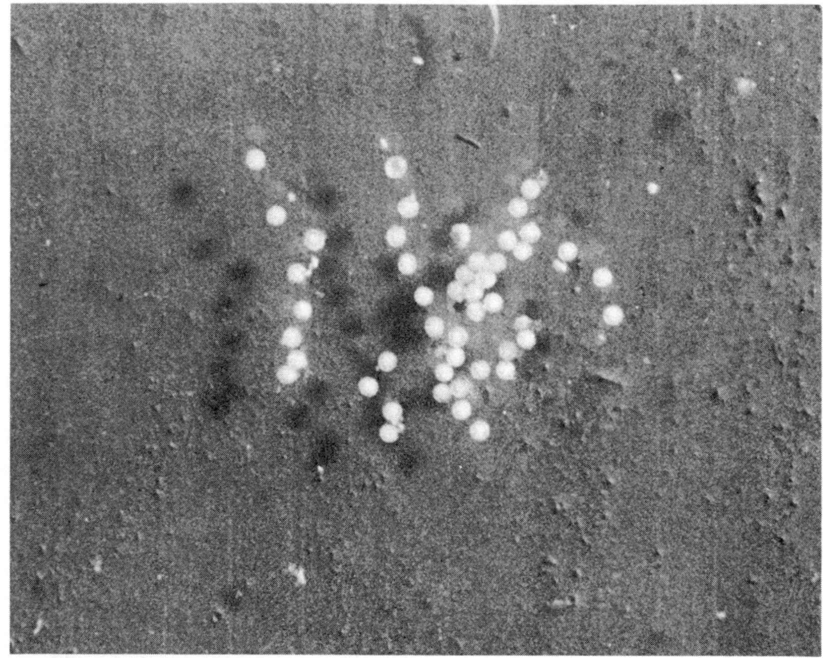

Fig. 242. *First photo ever taken of the eggs of a salt-water Black Angelfish* (Pomacanthus arcuatus), *which spawned in one of the author's tanks. Surprisingly, the female was only about four inches long. The eggs were scattered in the water rather than deposited in a nest.*

to themselves in a large, scrupulously clean aquarium and a good supply of protozoa raised in another equally large and scrupulously clean aquarium. When the young hatch out, leave half of them in the original tank and transfer the rest to the other tank, or try some system on your own. If you succeed in raising the young, who knows, you might become a millionaire. At any rate it would be an exciting event.

15

Projects for the Salt-Water Aquarist

Keeping salt-water fish is not a new hobby. History records that they were kept by the ancient Egyptians many thousands of years ago. Unfortunately little was learned from them about maintaining a successful marine aquarium and today, although we can keep many of the wonderful creatures of the sea in our home aquariums, there is still a great deal to be learned. The salt-water hobby is on the very threshold of discovery and maintenance so that we all have an opportunity to learn and discover new things about the living wonders of the sea. The author does not wish to imply that his findings arc the "last word" in aquarium keeping, and that his methods should be followed unerringly by other aquarists. All the information in this book is merely experimental, much of it based on general aquarium procedure and mostly by personal experience. It is liable to fault and is mcant as a basis for continued experiment in the salt-water field. The author has found that although salt-water aquariums have come a long way, they still have a long way to go and it is a challenge to the aquarist. However, they are definitely practical at this present stage, even for inland aquarist who must import their sea water as well as their fish. Below are a few experiments and problems that can greatly aid development of the salt-water aquarium hobby.

All Glass Aquariums

It will be up to hobbyist and dealers to encourage large glass manufacturers to turn out all-glass aquariums, especially for salt water. These should be in standard sizes and made of clear glass so that they give no distortion. Also, they should have a glass cover which fits down inside so that no salt water can drip down the outside of the aquarium. In addition, they should have a plastic or glass fluorescent light that will conform to their general appearance.

Fig. 243. *A large battery of plastic and glass tanks in one of the author's experimental shops. This one was at the Miami Serpentarium in a large building in the rear of the famous reptile exhibit. The drawers below the aquariums formerly held deadly reptiles. The shop was later moved to a location near the Miami airport.*

The whole unit should be corrosion free, and this will eliminate many present problems. This type of tank will positively keep marine fish healthier and longer and maintenance will be vastly simplified.

Salt-Water Plants

This is another field of exploration that is badly in need of expert attention. An interesting experiment presently being carried out by the author is a set of aquariums planted with a wide variety of fresh-water plants. The salinity of the water was raised to 1.010 and gradually the salt content will be increased so that eventually, when the plants send out new shoots, they may survive in a specific gravity of 1.015 or more. Then, Dwarf Sea Horses, Demoiselles, etc. will be brought down to this salinity and perhaps if the whole experiment is successful, it may lead to a balanced marine aquarium. There is such a wide variety of fresh-water plants that this experiment must be done on a wide scale to produce maximum results.

Regular marine plants and algaes have already been successfully grown as described in the chapter on plants. Here again, due to the variety of marine plants, there are many that may be tested. Perhaps over a period of time, specimens may be grown and reproduced in the aquarium so that a better strain is developed which is suitable to small home aquariums. Tank-grown plants are always best for aquariums even in fresh water and there is little reason why this cannot be done in the salt-water field.

Specific Gravity Tests

Although at present, the standard salinity for marine fish is 1.020 to 1.025, tests by the author have revealed that they can live under a wide range of hydrometer readings. The author has kept many marine fish in ranges from practically fresh water to water with a reading as high as 1.045. They seemed to live in apparent content although they certainly did not eat and swim as readily as in normal solutions. Dwarf Sea Horses seldom if ever reproduce in salinities higher than 1.030 in the natural state, a fact discovered by the author by testing the salinity at the collecting grounds over a period of several years. When sufficient rain had diluted the area so that salinity was around 1.020, there were many pregnant males per hundred specimens collected. Both males and females were large and healthy looking, but after a prolonged drought, when the salinity went up to 1.040 there would be extremely few pregnant males and all the horses would be very thin and undernourished. No doubt the higher salinity also affected their food supply.

Many aquarists have tried or entertained the thought of slowly converting salt-water fish to fresh water with the idea that it would help eliminate certain problems. Although this experiment has been tried many times, no conclusive results have been obtained that would benefit the hobby. The experiment is usually done on a small scale with one or two tanks and consequently the results cannot be accurately determined. No matter what happens to the fish over a period of time, little is proven. If they die at a salinity of say 1.010 perhaps they would have died anyway had the salinity remained normal. Therefore, this experiment is still a challenge to the aquarist and if accurately worked out, it may contribute something of value to the salt-water hobby. The author suggests a battery of all-glass aquariums, each set up with a sub-sand filter and no outside filter. Then sea water from the same area should be placed in each aquarium, and fish of one variety from the same area should be used in the experiment. No coral should be used and a flat shell provided for cover in each aquarium, so that the fish will feel secure. With a set-up of six such tanks, each with the same water to begin the experiment with, and each with the same size and species of fish, then if the same experiment is performed in each aquarium, and the results are the same, it will be a fairly accurate indication that your findings are significant. Then if the same experiment is performed several times, and the outcome still the same, an accurate statement could be made. In the salt-water field there are so many variables that it takes much time and research to determine definite facts.

pH in Salt-Water Aquariums

The importance of pH in the marine aquarium has not been determined and is another field of exploration for the advanced marine aquarist. Natural sea water usually has a pH of about 7.8 to 8.0 and the value of controlling this has not been accepted as being of major importance at the present time. Other factors such as feeding, general cleanliness, etc. are much more apt to cause serious trouble. Ordinary fresh-water pH test kits are of no value in salt-water tanks

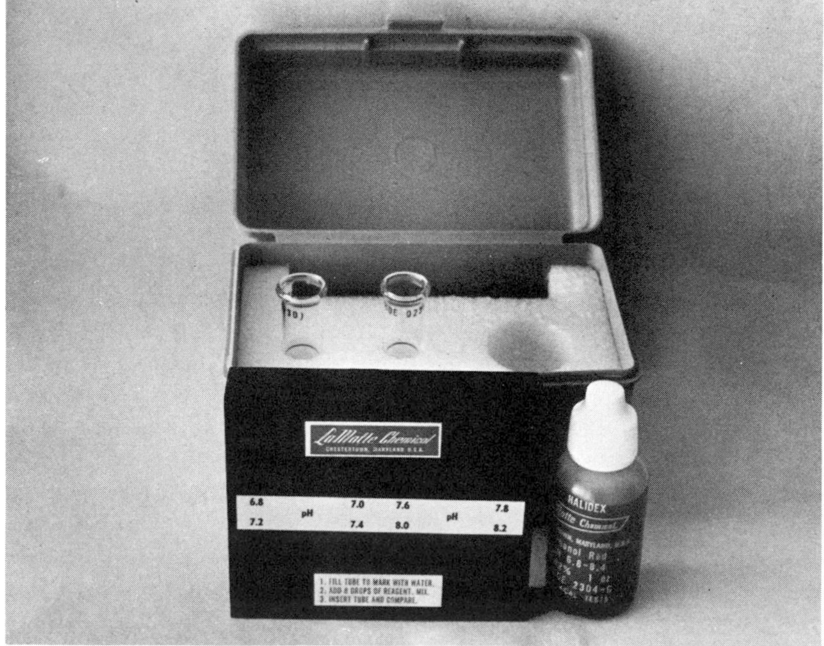

Fig. 244. *A pH kit for testing pH in the aquarium, manufactured by the LaMotte Chemical Company. There is a great deal of work needed in pH for marine aquariums. The author feels that the pH of the water should be checked, particularly when artificial water is used. It should be checked before and after the salts are added.*

and a special water solution kit which costs about $40 is the least expensive kit that will give an accurate reading. Even this is not completely accurate, but for practical purposes it is sufficient. A much more valuable tester, electronically operated is also on the market for about $150, but as stated before, the author has found little evidence at present that pH is of enough importance to worry about. The large aquariums who purchased the expensive test kits have had no better success with marine fish than those who never bothered with pH which bears out proof of the author's statement.

Nevertheless, those wishing to experiment with pH may find something of importance, especially in keeping the more delicate specimens. The salt water in the aquarium may go acid after a long period of time and if it is desired to bring it back to normal a buffer salt like Sodium Phosphate, mono-basic or di-basic may be used. Usually about one quarter gram of Sodium Phosphate per each two gallons of water in the aquarium will change the pH from 7.2 to 8.0, but since pH change is hard on fish, it should be done slowly. If the water gets too alkaline a drop of hydrochloric acid will help bring the pH back to normal. Often high salinity will make the water very alkaline and it may be brought back to normal merely by adding fresh water to the aquarium. Many aquarists use Sodium Carbonate to check pH and add this to the filter where it can be slowly introduced to the aquarium. It will take a great deal of time to really tell if pH is of such importance that the aquarist will have to worry about it, but it is a good field for experiment.

Feeding

Many marine fish die of starvation. Some eat well, but continue to lose weight and eventually waste away. The author has prepared a special food chart at the end of this book as a guide to proper feeding, but there are many fine foods which have not been mentioned merely because they were not tested. The marine hobbyist can experiment with a wide variety of foods and perhaps prolong the lives of some of the more delicate fish. Fresh frozen plankton from the sea may some day become available as a perfect marine fish food. Perhaps chopped and frozen algae would help the food situation for some fish. Another highly needed food is a live food for large Sea Horses. The brine shrimp eggs are fine for Dwarf Sea Horses and even the mediums, but the large must have live food. If someone could find a larger sized egg that is similar to the brine shrimp egg and put it on the market, not only would it alleviate this situation, but it could turn into a profitable business. There are several small fresh-water shrimp that mature at about an inch and if these could be propagated in the home aquarium in large quantities, they could also be used as a practical food for large Sea Horses and in addition they would be highly beneficial to many marine fish, especially the delicate feeders. The author has been experimenting with this project for some time and the results look promising. This type of live food would prove invaluable for breeders who need a larger food than the present-day brine shrimp.

Sea worms, sold in most coastal areas as fish bait are an excellent marine fish food and although they are difficult to obtain by the inland aquarist, perhaps some far-sighted individual will package them up for inter-state shipment. These worms are quite inexpensive and can easily be shipped alive as they are usually kept in damp sawdust before sale. They are ideal for feeding large Angelfish, and if chopped into small bit-sized chunks, most salt-water fish will relish them. Smaller sea worms are badly needed as food for the shy Butterfly fishes, and perhaps the salt-water aquarist living near the sea will discover a practical supply.

Although the feeding problem for most marine fish has been largely solved, there is still need for much experimenting for better foods, more nutritious foods, and foods with an ocean origin. These foods when perfected will not only lengthen the life span of marine fish, but will also keep them in maximum color, which of course is highly important.

Other Experiments

There are numerous projects in the salt-water aquarium field and anyone who keeps an aquarium any length of time may find out new and interesting things. For this reason, it is suggested that the marine aquarist keep careful records of his salt-water aquarium. A small "log" book giving the date the aquarium was set up, the kind of sea water (artificial or natural), types of specimens kept, feeding, longevity of fishes, appearance of diseases, etc. will prove invaluable to both the aquarist and perhaps other aquarists if the findings are significant. It will be the skilled aquarist that keeps records who will contribute to the advancement of the home salt-water aquarium. The help of everyone is needed.

Salt-Water Aquarium Societies

The nation's first salt-water aquarium society was formed in July 1955 by the author. It was given official recognition by Mr. Innes in *Aquarium Magazine* and created much attention. It was called the Greater Florida Marine Aquarium Society and was formed for the "propagation of the salt-water aquarium in the home, with hopes that free contributions from experienced members will better the success of the less experienced, eliminating repetition in research and pointing the way to those who wish to go ahead." The first meeting was attended by the author, Dick Boyd, Tom Reed, and Sam Heiss, all enthusiastic salt-water aquarists.

This was the nation's first exclusive salt-water aquarium society and was presided over by the author for its first year. Attendance grew rapidly, indicating the tremendous interest in home aquariums, and in October, 1956, it held its first marine aquarium show which was perhaps the first competitive aquarium show ever held any place in the world pertaining strictly to marine fish. Read the January, 1957 issue of *Aquarium Journal* for the full story.

Aquarium societies often promote greater interest in the hobby and each year, marine fish will enter the picture in stronger forces. Eventually there will be many salt-water aquarium societies and research in this fascinating field will progress at a much faster rate. If you have several fellow aquarists who are especially interested in salt-water fish, form your own society, either as a group of your main society or an entirely new group, for it is difficult to learn about marine fish in a fresh-water-minded society. Write to one of the aquarium or pet magazines for full particulars and if possible, give the matter much forethought. Don't have business meetings and aquarium meetings at the same time and try to donate nine-tenths of the entire meeting strictly to discussions and questions on marine fish. Too many societies are so formal with their "reading of the minutes" and other nonsense, that the actual purpose of the society is often neglected. The author recommends informal groups with just enough parliamentary procedure to make the meeting official and no more! A historian should be appointed to write down new discoveries and points of interest at such meetings and his findings should be typed into readable form and made available to those who may have missed a meeting, or who may wish to refer to a former program. Also, of course a president, vice president, secretary, and treasurer should be appointed.

16

Adventures in Collecting

Many salt-water hobbyists who vacation to the southeastern part of the country will have an opportunity to collect some colorful and interesting specimens for their home aquarium. Since collecting is a full time job that requires years of experience, the casual hobbyist must not expect to be completely successful during his short vacation stay. Nevertheless, there is always an occasional Angelfish or other highly-colored specimen that may swim in very shallow water and these should be considered a bonus rather than a commonplace thing.

Necessary pieces of equipment are a glass-bottom bucket, face mask, rubber sneakers, gloves, and a dip net. Then it will be a matter of covering much area to locate the prized specimens, before they can be netted. It will take practice to catch the elusive little fellows, but the more you try, the more proficient you will become, until soon you will be able to net your specimens in a few minutes. The author, who has been collecting marine specimens much of his life, finds that catching them is the easiest part. It's finding them that takes the time!

Old fishing piers, rockpiles that are partly submerged, and sponge beds offers the easiest collecting grounds for the novice and collecting should be done *only* in clear water. Large barracudas travel close to shore and will sometimes attack a wader in dirty water. It may see a part of your arm or leg flashing through the water and will strike with lightning speed mistaking you for a fish. Nearly every attack of this fish in this area has been under similar conditions, so collect accordingly.

The skin diver will find his most valuable collecting on the outside reef, where fish are abundant and the water is usually crystal clear. It is like diving into a strange new world and will fascinate you every time you go down. Fish will swim so close to you that you can almost reach out and touch them and your first impression of the

Fig. 245. *The author photographing marine life on a shallow coral reef. Some of the specimens portrayed in this book were collected on this same reef.*

colorful inhabitants will usually be that there are thousands of them. You will wonder why they are so expensive up North until you study the situation more closely. Then you will see that they are not as plentiful as you first imagined, especially when you approach the area with a collecting net. There will still be many highly-colored fish, but these will be mostly large Parrot fish, Angelfish, Porkfish, Grunts, and Snappers. They will all be much too large for a small home aquarium and the search will begin for a small specimen. When you finally locate a little fish that is highly colored, and you have successfully captured it in your net, only then will you realize why marine fish are costly. They cannot be collected in seines several thousand at a time, like their fresh-water relatives, but must be collected one at a time out on the reefs and it is dangerous work if done all year round.

Sudden tropical storms may catch you far out at sea. This can quickly prove disastrous. Dozens of boats are swamped every year out on the Florida reefs. The author has been caught in many bad thunder squalls and one in particular nearly cost him his life—as he describes it:

"I was collecting on the very last outside reef on a beautiful summer day and had made a good haul. Rock Beauties, Jewel fish, Neon Gobies, Blue Reef fish, and a variety of less spectacular fish were in my live well and I prepared to call it a day, and head for home. Suddenly, as I began to lift anchor, I realized that I no longer could see shore and that a tremendous storm was closing in. A cold wind blew steadily toward me and I realized that I could not make it to shore as the storm was already part way out, and advancing in all directions. I had spent so much time in the water collecting, that I had failed to notice formations of the storm and now I was definitely in for trouble. When a storm hits, the sky becomes so dark that vision is limited to just a very few feet so I had found out that the best procedure was to drop anchor and stay in one spot until the storm passed. I secured my gear, turned the air pumps on the fish, and made preparations to jump overboard. I have always been very cautious in thunder storms, and reason that it is quite dangerous to sit in an open boat during electrical storms. After securely anchoring the boat, over the side I went.

"I didn't have to wait long and the storm hit with a wild fury unlike anything I had ever seen before. Since I was collecting right at the edge of the Gulf Stream, the ocean here was specially rough and huge waves crashed down in the semi-darkness. Rain poured down in fantastic torrents and lightning and thunder crashed on all sides. Soon the sea became so rough that I could no longer see. The entire surface layer was lashed into foam. This presented a new peril for at this time of year, the sea was filled with large stinging jellyfish and when the water had been clear, I was able to dodge them successfully. Now with visibility impaired, I no longer could see them and they seemed to come from all directions. I was stung many times and in my agony I failed to notice that the boat had broken loose and was rapidly drifting away. When I finally did notice it, it was a long ways off and I could only see it through occasional flashes of lightning. I swam towards it through the heavy seas with all the speed I could muster. I never felt so alone and so small as I swam out into the Gulf Stream that stormy evening. I was over very deep water now and every few strokes, I turned half way around to be certain no sharks were inspecting me. The water was so dark that there could have been a hundred around me and I would not have seen them. Finally, after what seemed like a hundred years, I made it to the boat and climbed aboard. I started the motor, pulled in the frayed anchor rope, and headed back to the reef. Then I saw the most horrible danger of all!

"A giant water spout of tremendous magnitude was heading right towards me. The sky was a strange brilliant orange. Thunder and lightning crashed upon the water on all sides, and I was in such a state of mind after the harrowing swim that I felt I was doomed. I scrambled through my equipment for a pencil and paper so I could write my last words, explaining how I had met my fate. I couldn't find a pencil so abandoned that project. Now I concentrated on the water spout. I somehow had the feeling that I had been spared. The storm let up somewhat and the water spout which had been churning the ocean into a wild mass of waves, was dissipating before my very eyes! I had been keeping the boat out of its path and when it began to disappear I went directly underneath it and saw the strangest spectacle in the world. I saw it raining backwards! I saw a huge sheet of water from the ocean carried right into the sky, and then it was all over. The seas calmed down and I headed for shore. I looked up at the star-studded sky and watched the gentle sea break over the bow, and I wondered if I would ever be able to go out again. I had been so badly frightened that even as I write this story and recall that frightening day, I shake a little. This may sound like a tall story to some people, but I would swear it all on a Bible for it actually happened."

Such is a collector's life. Storms are actually a minor hazard compared to the dangers of the reef. The author would estimate that during his collecting career on the Florida reefs and in the Bahamas, he has encountered approximately 50,000 Barracuda, perhaps at least 15,000 Moray eels, and numerous sharks, and other giant fishes. The barracuda figure may sound high, but anyone who has dived the outer reefs on a cold winter day, can agree that these fish congregate by the hundreds on the outer reefs so they can soak in the warmer Gulf Stream water. Multiply this by a couple hundred trips a year and you will soon have a high total. It's a known fact that occasionally these creatures attack man, especially when he is alone, so that year in and year out, the collector is more likely to be attacked than the weekend swimmer. This is another reason why marine tropicals are costly and they will continue to be costly until you aquarists get busy and breed them. Only then will the price go down so that they compare with the fresh-water fish.

Long-spined sea urchins are the most common hazard to the skin diver and potential collector. These porcupines of the sea are everywhere and colorful fish often take refuge among their spines so that a serious collector will usually puncture himself at least a few times every day. Fortunately, although the wounds are very painful at first, and the needles break off and cannot be extracted, they seldom cause infection and will usually dissolve right in the flesh if left alone. It is useless to try to dig them out as they usually penetrate to the bone and the author who has been punctured well over a thousand times, can testify through personal experience. One especially bad encounter resulted in a needle penetrating completely through the finger of one hand. It was broken off on both sides and

Fig. 246. *The deadly Man-of-War jellyfish is one of the most potential dangers to swimmers or fish collectors in tropical waters. The author's last encounter with a large specimen nearly cost him his life, causing the most hideous pain imaginable, and according to experts, he probably would not survive another encounter.*

although the joint ached for several days, it gave no further trouble. The needles are extremely sharp and will easily penetrate rubber-coated canvas gloves. With a bad contact, it is usually necessary to remove the glove and break off the ends of the needles from your fingers. Rubber suits worn in winter for protection against the cold water are easily punctured by the ever-present "Porcupines." Often, depending upon the seriousness of the wounds, it may mean a trip back to the boat to remove the stubby ends of the needles which have broken off inside the suit. The most painful encounter with sea urchins by the author was on a shallow reef in rough weather. The author had surface dived and a large wave catapulted him onto a huge sea urchin head first! Not only was his skull painfully punctured, but several spines stuck into his face, one driving deeply into his lips. That same day, a customer told him he was charging too much for his fish and the author's comments were not pleasant.

Fire coral is another painful hazard to the marine collector. It can easily be recognized by its orange-yellow color and the comparatively smooth texture of its surface, in contrast to the other corals. Technically, it is not a true coral, but instead a "stinging hydroid," but it may be collected and treated similar to coral and some types are very beautiful in the aquarium. The serious collector can hardly avoid occasional contact with fire coral and it is rightly named for it feels as though you had suddenly brushed against a red hot stove. Bad contact may result in a serious burn which will often last many months and is usually followed by a severe itching in the affected area. Since many colorful fish make their home in this colorful formation, the collector who must work right up against this stinging coral, is often burned quite frequently at first, until he learns how to maneuver closely without contact. Beautiful Jewel fish as well as Rock Beauties and other highly-colored fish are found almost exclusively in the fire coral and extracting them is usually a lengthy and difficult project, which explains the high price they command.

Another extremely dangerous hazard to the collector is the Portuguese Man of War jellyfish, which can inflict such intense stinging, that the victim often goes into a state of shock and will drown if not removed promptly from the water. Fortunately, they are only present during certain winds, but occasionally a stray specimen will appear and attach itself to the unwary diver. As stated before, the chances of being molested by the various hazards of the sea are greatly increased for the full-time collector who must spend a great deal of time in the water, so that invariably, he can expect to swim into a Portuguese Man of War. After all, no one can lead a charmed life and the law of averages soon catches up with you. The author has been stung by the Man of War several times, once seriously and the scars from this dangerous encounter lasted nearly a year.

Huge Moray eels are present everywhere on the reef and since they live in holes and ledges, they are often encountered by the collector. Normally, they are quite placid and if left alone, will seldom disturb the diver. But there is always an occasional specimen who feels that he owns the reef and he will attempt to drive the invaders away, including men. These are usually fearsome green monsters which sometimes reach a length of six to eight feet. They can inflate their bodies to twice their normal size and are actually fearless, and capable of easily drowning a human. They may emerge from a large coral head and will sometimes swim straight for the diver, in an attempt to drive him from the area. Perhaps they are guarding a nest, when they behave this way. Normally, they will not leave their home and are only dangerous when working in the immediate area. Rather than shoot them, or take unnecessary chances, the author finds it best to leave them alone, and work in another area. Small Morays are usually not so brazen and can be driven out of sight with a few jabs on the nose with a stick.

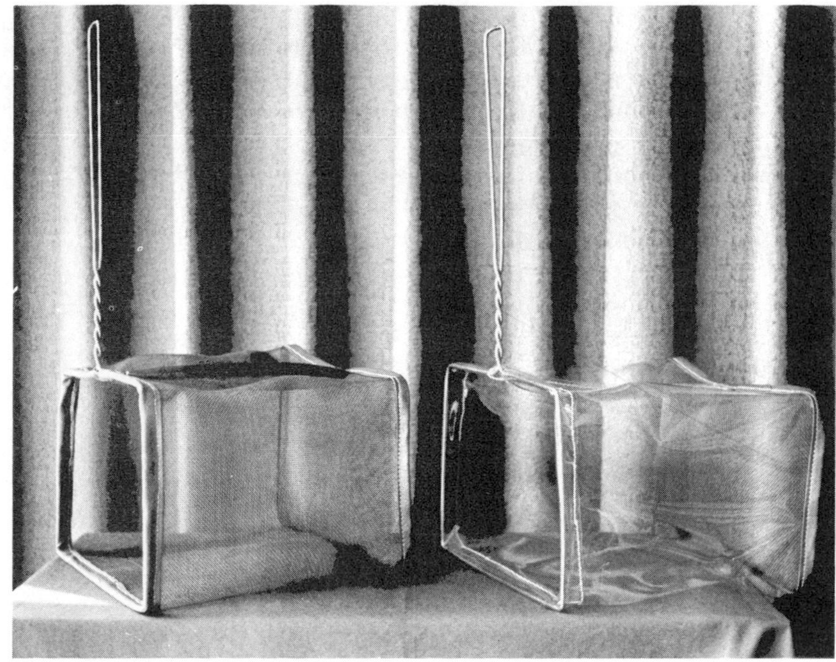

Fig. 247. *Fish collecting nets designed by the author. The net on the left is made of plastic screen and is best for general use. The clear plastic net on the right was first suggested by aquarist Rick Fried who collected with the author. It is made of clear plastic with a screen bottom. It works best in very clear water or on the outer reefs. The frame is a regular ten-inch aquarium net frame. The nets are fifteen inches deep.*

Collecting live Morays in a hand net is a thrilling experience and requires careful concentration. They can usually be driven out in the open and must be approached with much caution for without the protection of the coral, they have no other alternative, but to defend themselves. They will coil up on the bottom like a rattlesnake and strike out fiercely as you approach. When sufficiently frightened, they will make a wild dash through the water, so fast that the eye cannot follow. If no other escape route is offered, they will head straight for the diver who must raise his net to ward off the attack. The object in collecting them by hand is to get them in your net before they make this wild dash and once captured they must be brought swiftly to the surface before they become too excited. Like the other marine hazards, the serious collector cannot expect to spend his time on the reef without suffering an occasional bite from these vicious creatures. They have needle-sharp teeth and can inflict a very serious wound, quite often requiring hospital treatment. Although the bite is not as infectious as claimed by some authorities, it all depends upon the seriousness and nature of the wound as to the final outcome.

Sharks and Barracudas are an ever-present menace to the full-time collector who spends a great deal of time in the water. He will encounter many Barracuda and relatively few dangerous sharks in the Florida waters, but the number of sharks will increase sharply as he works closer to the Gulf Stream, or in the clear Bahama waters. Although they are a potential danger, neither sharks nor Barracuda will seldom bother the diver, especially when the water is clear, but there is always the exceptional specimen that doesn't adhere to the rules. Then the diver will silently disappear if he is by himself, or he may be rescued if accompanied by other swimmers. Most deaths by these predatory fishes have been attributed to the fact that the fish struck its victim believing it to be another fish, and upon realizing its mistake, the attacker usually swims away leaving its victim to bleed to death. A small two foot length of rope that could be applied as a tourniquet, should be carried about the waist of the collector for such rare emergencies. It could also be used to support a sharp knife which might also save your life if you should be suddenly held down in the vice-like grip of a moray eel, or if you should become entangled in rope or line under water.

Large Barracuda will often follow a diver for hours on end and each time he dives, they will usually swim to within a few feet of him, always approaching from the back. The author finds it extremely prudent to look behind him systematically every few minutes, especially when diving in deep water. Usually the commotion caused from a diver working in among the coral on the bottom, will draw any large fish in the area up close for a look, and they will nearly always approach from behind. Therefore, it is a wise practice to develop the habit of turning completely around automatically as you push up from the bottom. This will acquaint you with many large predators who may have been attracted to the area, and who may have thought you were struggling for your life on the bottom instead of merely collecting tropicals. As soon as they see your face, they will invariably swim a safe distance away especially if you appear alive and healthy.

Although Barracudas have a bad name, large sharks are mostly feared by the skin diver and underwater collector, for here is a cold-blooded killer who will attack man, not mistaking him for another fish, but as a tender meal. Most sharks are normally cowards, but some, like the Mako or Mackerel shark, attack so swiftly that they don't have time to be afraid and an attack from them is usually fatal. They sometimes grow to enormous proportions and the author has encountered several that would weigh well over a thousand pounds.

Their swiftness through the water is frightening, for it makes you realize that you wouldn't have the slightest chance if one decided to attack you. The author was once collecting tropicals in about twenty-five feet of water and encountered a fantastic brute who showed absolutely no fear. Here is the true story as he tells it:

"We had exceptionally bad weather for about two months and the orders were piling up when finally a decent day came and I enthusiastically headed for the reefs. The sea was calm and although the water was very dirty, I made a tremendous haul and caught dozens of Angelfish, many of them young Townsends, the most colorful of all. I had found a good spot and was rapidly making up for the bad weather days and hadn't given sharks a thought in the murky water. However, by habit, I would make a complete turn under water before swimming to the surface. On one of these turns, I surprised a Mako that had approached quite close as I was busy chasing a small fish out from under a ledge. The shark quickly swam away and I instinctively pursued it for a few feet which is my usual custom, and successfully chased it into the gloom before returning to the surface for air. Sharks are usually cowards, and once they show fear, they will usually retreat at the first sign of danger. This fellow behaved normally so I thought nothing more of the incident. I was in a good collecting spot and I was going to make the most of it.

"Everything went well for about a half hour until I noticed a long grey shape circling around beneath my feet. At first I thought it was the same shark and wasn't too alarmed as he had seemed quite frightened before, so I dove down to frighten him away again, but since he was down about twenty feet I had miscalculated the size and before I could stop myself, I had nearly landed on his back which was at least three feet wide! I quickly realized this wasn't the same shark and that I might be in for trouble. I did a back flip underwater so that I wouldn't be near his mouth. Then I yelled loudly and gave a tremendous kick with my flippers which usually sends a curious fish scurrying off at top speed.

"It didn't work this time for the giant creature didn't seem to notice it at all. Instead, it twisted its tail sharply to make a tight turn, and came straight for me! Its huge body cutting through the water caused small whirlpools that gave the impression of immense power. As it approached, I couldn't help but marvel at its ultra-streamlined body. It glided effortlessly, scarcely moving a fin and its huge tail wavered slightly now and then like a ship's rudder. I was by myself and at least a thousand feet from the boat and I realized that there was nothing I could do but face the creature and hope for the best. My only protection was a small hand net and a short piece of rod that I use for moving urchins out of the way. I knew that this fellow was definitely interested in me and that he was probably searching for food. It was almost high tide, and the time that most large fishes feed.

"My heart was beating loudly and I began to think of all the shark stories I had heard. Only recently a boy had been killed by a shark out in California and I remembered the lurid details of how he kept attacking the unfortunate victim even while onlookers were dragging him to shore. There weren't any onlookers here and I hated to think of ending up in a shark's stomach. Then I thought how foolish I was to be swimming in this murky water in the first place, especially after I had repeatedly warned many skin divers of the danger of poor visibility. If you've ever faced a large shark alone, far out at sea, without even a knife, you might have some idea of how badly frightened I really was. He came to within a few feet of me and stared at me with cold, merciless eyes. I knew that his small brain was functioning with only one thought in mind. That was food.

"I realized the most dangerous place for me was on the surface so I took a deep breath and dove slowly down to a depth of eight or ten feet, almost colliding with the brute on the way down. I expected to be bitten any second and could see the huge fish turn to follow me through the corner of my eye. I leveled off and turned in his general direction and he came at me again moving so close that the surge of his body obscured my vision for a few seconds.

"I was running out of breath so I gingerly swam back to the surface for more air. I noticed that the shark had followed me up, so I threw my iron rod up in the air so that it would fall down on his back. It didn't faze him and he apparently didn't even see it. I had once scared off a large shark that had been following me for hours in shallow water this way, but this time it didn't work. By now I began to realize that the shark wasn't going to eat me right at the moment, so I became braver and decided to make a few trial dives near him, and if he didn't act especially mean, I would continue my collecting. I was so badly frightened that I knew if I once got back to the boat, I would not go back into the water so I stayed there with that thought in mind for two whole hours in the same area and finished my collecting.

"My faithful companion stayed with me nearly the whole time, but was not quite as curious as he was at first. He would swim in and out of view every ten or fifteen minutes and his color blended so perfectly with the dull blue haze of the water that he would actually disappear when only ten or fifteen feet away. This made the whole situation especially nerve-wracking because I couldn't see him until he was almost on top of me. Many times when I was busy chasing a small fish down along the bottom, I would turn and he would be quite close, sometimes above me so that I would have to swim to the surface at an angle so that I wouldn't bump him.

"My collecting was seriously impaired by his presence when suddenly I noticed a change in his behavior. He began to swim very fast, in wide circles and came extremely close a couple times. I decided that I would give up collecting for the rest of the day. I headed for the boat, swimming slowly, and turning completely around every few strokes, and I made several dives each time working closer to safety. When I reached the boat, I was so nervous that I seriously considered taking up another trade and that's no joke."

But life under the sea is not always perilous and many people spend their entire life pursuing this fascinating hobby, collecting fish for their aquariums or taking pictures underwater of the wonders of the reefs and with the exception of an occasional Moray bite, or contact with the sea urchins, fire coral, and other pests, they suffer little permanent damage. When the sea is calm and the water is clear, the undersea world becomes a beautiful place and it is an unending thrill to dive and explore this wilderness fairyland. Skin diving or "snorkling" is the most enjoyable method of exploring the reefs. It is relaxing and requires little effort in contrast to the much publicized deep lung diving. The basic equipment needed for "snorkling" as the sport is called, is a good comfortable water-tight face mask, a pair of flippers, and a snorkle. The author has found that the straight-tube snorkle is by far the most practical and reliable. The popular version with the curved end and plastic ball is seldom used by professional divers as it is not dependable. Since the straight tube is not usually available, the author usually cuts off the curved part and discards it and many skin divers follow this procedure. A large three-quarter inch diameter tube should be used and it should be approximately fourteen to sixteen inches long. Three foot snorkles are about as useless and practical as an underwater bathtub and they could not possibly have been tested before being placed on the market, as they are useless.

No doubt many readers will visit the Florida waters to collect some fish for their home aquarium and fish obtained this way will mean much more to an aquarist for when he finally gets them up north, and the wind and snow is howling outside his door, he can relax in his living room to enjoy the beautiful creatures he caught on his vacation. Each specimen will bring to mind a small adventure and the salt-water hobbyist will plan for future trips to his newly discovered world.

Netting Marine Specimens

The most productive and practical method of collecting beautiful salt-water fish is to catch them with small, specially made hand nets. These are nets about a foot in diameter and they are made by sewing a bag about fifteen inches deep onto a net frame of the type usually sold as shrimp nets. The net frame may be purchased in commercial fishing stores, and a wooden handle about ten inches long should be firmly attached. Plastic screen makes the best netting material, as it does not damage the fish and is not too conspicuous in the water. The author has used it successfully for more than fifteen years, and it is far more durable than nylons and other nettings.

It is not too difficult to locate a suitable specimen out on the reef, but catching it is an entirely different matter. A person must be a good swimmer and diver to capture a colorful fish out on the coral reef. But, as pointed out earlier, a person's collecting ability will vastly improve with experience. The basic rule of collecting is to know where *not* to collect. This is probably the most important single factor in catching salt-water fish in hand nets. It is almost impossible to capture fish in dense coral reefs profusely overgrown with staghorn or elkhorn coral or on reefs with large brain or lump coral that is grown together in a honeycomb fashion. Staghorn or elkhorn reefs in particular are nearly impossible to work, as the net constantly catches on the sharp coral and is soon torn to shreds. Consequently, if a skin diver wishes to collect live specimens he should scan the reefs with a glass-bottom bucket and locate a small, isolated reef away from the main reef, and choose a coral patch with small coral heads or dead coral rock and Gorgonias. In areas like this, it is rather simple to net a delicate Butterfly fish or Angelfish, as it will not have the deep caves and overhanging corals in which to retreat when you pursue it with your net. Some divers use two nets, but the author prefers one, and a steel poker or rod is held in the other hand. This is used to move the needle-sharp urchins out of the way or to frighten the fish into the net. It is also useful as a means of protection against an aggressive Moray eel or shark. A piece of lead or galvanized pipe about eighteen inches long works best. One end should be flattened for probing into crevices or removing urchins; the other end should contain a six-inch spike which is held in place by flattening the pipe around it. This will be useful as a weapon and also is excellent for spearing urchins or gently chasing small fish from holes in the reef. It is an essential piece of equipment. The author has introduced it to many skin divers in South Florida.

When a suitable specimen has been located, it is best to observe it for one or two minutes before trying to capture it. Swim very slowly and do not frighten it, for if you do it will dart into a hole or swim rapidly away. Take a deep breath and dive to the bottom, keeping the net open and ready for use. Then set the net on the bottom near the fish, and with both hands and the poker, frighten the fish so that he will swim into net. Once he is inside, you must scoop up the net and bend it so that he cannot swim out again. This must be done very quickly. It is important that you observe the fish for a few minutes before you descend to the bottom so that you will be able to place your net properly. Most fish have little "paths" or routes they travel on the reef and these are used in getting from one section of the reef to another, and if you observe them for a few minutes you can easily see the path they will take when you pursue them. Then it is a simple matter to place the net in their path, preferably near a small coral head so it will remain upright, while you chase them. With this method, a skin diver can select his specimens and catch only what he desires. Also, the fish are collected with no damage to the reef. It is unfortunate that a few college professors of marine biology have mistakenly been led to believe that marine fish are caught on the elkhorn reefs by skin divers who tear up the entire reefs with crowbars to get at the specimens. Such misinformation has done considerable harm to the skin diver, and apparently the few bigoted professors who harbor these notions have spent too much time delving into ancient books and not enough time in the field. In actual practice, a skin diver collecting fish for his aquariums does less harm to the reefs than an angler catching fish from a boat. Nevertheless, a huge area in South Florida has already been banned to skin divers who want to collect fish for their home tanks, so that aquarists who wish to journey south for their vacation must now head to the Bahamas, where they may pursue their hobby in peace. There is no doubt that each year, as more of the nation's thirty million aquarium hobbyists convert their fresh-water hobby to salt water, more of them will want to come to the warmer waters and collect their own fish for their aquariums. It is a fascinating project, and there are trillions of colorful marine beauties abounding in the coral reefs of nearby Bahama and Florida waters. Collecting the little beauties by hand net will never deplete the supply even if half the nation's population went collecting at one time, as there are so many areas where it is impossible to collect and with this method of collecting, the fish will reproduce far more rapidly than they could ever be caught.

Skin-diving aquarists are welcome in most resort areas, but this will not always hold true if the diver aimlessly wrecks beautiful reefs to catch his fish. It is entirely unnecessary and behavior of this sort lends credence to those who feel this is the only way fish can be collected. Learn where *not* to collect, and you will catch far more. Dive on the isolated rocks, dead coral reefs, or tiny patches away from the main reef, and you will be able to collect without harm to the reef.

Underwater Conservation

Although at present, there is no danger of marine tropicals becoming extinct, they should not be collected aimlessly. Take only those which you can use and don't destroy their homes. When you visit the spot again, perhaps a year later, if you have been thoughtful, you will find a new hatch of pretty fish swimming about familiar coral. If you have ruthlessly destroyed their homes, the area will still be deserted and you will feel disheartened at your carelessness. Flat rocks which have been upturned, should be carefully replaced and coral should never be broken in an attempt to collect fish. A fine slender rod can be used to chase him out of a beautiful coral formation without damaging the coral, and you will be preserving his home for future generations. Sponges in particular, since they are easily broken, suffer the most damage by the collectors and since these are also temporary homes for colorful fish, they should be handled very gently. They are quite fragile. Unfortunately, this type of growth often grows close to shore in channels which are used by boats. During windy weather a small boat may uproot hundreds of sponges in a single day as the anchor is dragged along the bottom. At low tide, outboards frequently chop the sponges to shreds. Of course this is not done intentionally, but nevertheless it does destroy good collecting areas. The author recently visited some sponge beds down in the Florida Keys that had been favorite collecting spots for years. Now, due to the inroads of civilization, they no longer existed. In their place was a deep man-made channel, with dirt piled high on each side and although this no doubt increased the value of nearby property, it destroyed the homes of many colorful fish. Since the entire Keys area is being widely exploited, this same procedure has taken place on most of the shallow collecting areas so that in the future all serious collecting of marine fish must be done off the reefs.

Underwater National Park

Fortunately, there is such a tremendous reef area off the Florida coast and in nearby Bahama waters that the colorful reef fish are in no danger of becoming extinct or even scarce, so long as present methods of collecting are used. However, if dynamiting, poisoning, electrical shocking, or general wrecking of entire reef areas is employed, then the situation can quickly change. Since this is the only coral area in the entire country, conservation should be practiced by everyone, and the author joins other underwater naturalists in hoping that at least a part of this fascinating world can be preserved as a natural park so that future generations may enjoy it as we have. Such a project would cost nothing except for the salaries of a few conservation officers to patrol the area, and it should be open to skin divers, naturalists, and underwater photographers or explorers. Fish collecting, coral collecting, and even specimen collecting by

Fig. 248. *The author is preparing to dive on the coral reef. Heavy rubber suit is necessary during the winter months. Collecting net is made of plastic screen with foot-wide opening.*

students of biology, should be prohibited as there are many other areas where these people can work. It's a vast underwater world with plenty of room for all.

Collecting Coral

The marine hobbyist will often wish to collect a few pieces of coral for his aquarium while he is out on the reef. Again, he should use discretion and take only what he can use and no more. This should be selected with care and only those pieces that are to be brought home should be broken loose. They should be pried off the main stem with a piece of pipe or steel rod so that only the desired piece is removed. Done properly, a branch of coral can be extracted from the reef in such a way that its absence will have little effect upon the general beauty of the area, for if pried loose in the manner mentioned above, it will leave a small white scab which will be completely covered with new coral in a short while. Wholesale collectors of coral

Fig. 249. *Salt water will soon rust out even a brand new car or station wagon. The author devised a large plywood box of half inch plywood, which was made water tight and was placed in the wagon for collecting trips. All buckets of water, nets and equipment were placed in the box and any salt water that spilled out of collecting buckets was contained in the box where it could be sponged up. Two flaps of plastic cloth hang over the bumper when loading. This simple idea protected the auto from salt-water corrosion.*

would do well to heed this method for the destruction wrought by some is appalling. Huge areas of beautiful staghorn and elkhorn coral are often uselessly smashed and the more attractive pieces are gathered. The rest soon dies on the ocean floor and the area looks like a beautiful forest that had been ruthlessly exploited by lumberjacks with no conservation in mind. It reflects the greed and wastefulness of mankind even in the sea.

Many times, the skin diver and collector can find beautiful pieces of coral that have already been broken by storms or the heavy anchors of charter fishing boats which have been fishing in the area. These are often dead, and already partly cured, so that cleaning them is an easy task. The hobbyist who utilizes these detached pieces, will not only be beautifying the reefs, but will be aiding conservation of man's last heritage.

Collecting Techniques

The author, who has been one of the very few and sometimes the only full-time collector of salt-water tropicals in the country, has developed many methods for collecting marine fish and although there is really no great secret involved in catching the elusive creatures, it will take much practice for the beginner. The hobbyist or part-time collector will find that the first fish to catch is the hardest and after that, he will learn more about their ways and with much more practice, he will gradualy get more proficient. It is best to start with the Sergeant Majors and the Beau Gregories as these are quite common and after a good technique has been developed, you will have confidence and can go after the more elusive fishes.

A small minnow trap, baited with shrimp, will often yield a surprising catch and is one of the most popular methods used by the hobbyist who is not aquatically inclined. Also a small hand net or dip net can be employed around rocks and coral, especially out on the reefs where the fish are more plentiful. You may not get much at first, but when you do catch that first Angelfish or Rock Beauty, you will experience a thrill unknown to the landlocked hobbyist for you will have outsmarted a fish in his own element. When you finally place it in your aquarium, you will feel so proud of your accomplishment that you will encourage your friends to get a salt-water aquarium and bring the ocean into their living room.

17

Marine Fish Food Chart

Anemones. Feed small half-inch chunks of fresh shrimp once or twice a week. Drop food in center of Anemone directly on tentacles. Anemone will take food inside.

Angelfish. Up to one and a half-inch feed live brine shrimp several times a day so there are always some in aquarium. Also feed very fine chopped shrimp, dry food, green algae, fish roe, tubifex worms, etc.

Angelfish. Over one and one half inch feed same foods except larger chunks of fresh shrimp, and not so much brine shrimp. Chopped earthworms or whole earthworms are relished by the larger fish. Diet may be varied with lean beef or beef heart. Highly-colored specimens are helped with paprika mixed with their food.

Angler Fish. Small live minnows about a quarter the length of the Angler fish. These should be kept in the aquarium with no place to hide, so they can be easily eaten. Small grunts are good.

Barnacles. These gather their food from the water. A little clam meal or finc dry good, mixed will in the water, willl usually keep them alive. Also heavy concentration of live brine shrimp.

Barracuda. Small minnows, Guppies, etc. Should be small so they may be easily swallowed.

Batfish. Small live minnows, baby Guppies, etc. These should be fed in large numbers and introduced to aquarium slowly, so they will live well until eaten. They should be given no cover. Small Grunts are excellent.

Beau Gregory. Dry food, brine shrimp, chopped shrimp and nearly all other aquarium foods. An excellent feeder.

Bermuda Chub. Dry food, finely chopped shrimp, brine shrimp, tubifex worms, etc.

Bluehead. Chopped shrimp in half-inch size chunks, small earthworms, tubifex worms, chopped crawfish, crushed sea urchins.

Blue Reef Fish. Live brine shrimp, finely chopped shrimp, tubifex worms.

Blue Hamlet. Chopped shrimp quarter-inch chunks, small live minnows, earthworms, worms.

Boston Beans. Live brine shrimp, very fine chopped shrimp, fish roe.

Boxfish, Spiny. Chopped shrimp—pea-sized chunks, sometimes they prefer it with shell left on. Food must be dropped in plain sight so Spiny Box can see it fall. He will chase it to bottom. Also will eat live earthworms, small half-inch scallops and snails.

Butterfly Fish. Tubifex worms, white worms, micro-worms, very small earthworms. Will sometimes eat live brine shrimp, but this should not be main food.

Butterfly Fish, Painted. This specimen deserves special mention for it will eat dry food, brine shrimp, and most other aquarium foods, including chopped shrimp. It is also known as the Least Butterfly, and is one of the very few hardy members of its group.

Butter Hamlet. Chopped shrimp in fairly large bite-sized chunks. Small minnows, live earthworms. Food must be dropped so that fish will see it fall at first.

Cardinal Fish. Same as Butter Hamlet.

Catfish, Coral. Brine shrimp, finely chopped shrimp, micro-worms. This fish is highly poisonous and must not be handled.

Clingfish. Small chunks of fresh shrimp or crawfish. Dry foods, brine shrimp, live earthworms cut into small sections, tubifex worms.

Clownfish. Dry food, chopped shrimp, brine shrimp, chopped worms.

Clown Wrasse. Brine shrimp, dry food, chopped shrimp, worms, fish roe.

Conch Fish. Chopped shrimp, earthworms, tubifex worms, small live fish.

Coral Shrimp. Chopped shrimp, green algae.

Cornet Fish. Chopped shrimp, live adult brine shrimp, Sargassum shrimp.

Cowfish. Chopped shrimp, live Sargassum shrimp, very small minnows, tubifex worms, earthworms. Small cowfish under an inch will eat live brine shrimp.

Cowry. Green algae, lettuce, spinach, etc. Push food directly under shell.

Crabs. Most crabs will eat chopped shrimp, green algae, frozen brine shrimp, small minnows.

Crawfish, Spiny. Chopped shrimp, green algae, lean beef, chopped fish.

Cubbyu. Chopped shrimp, brine shrimp, small minnows, Sargassum shrimp, fish roe, etc. Occasionally will eat dry food.

Cusk Eel. Same food as above.

Dascyllus. Dry food, brine shrimp, live or frozen, chopped shrimp, tubifex worms, most other aquarium foods. Occasionally will eat green algae.

Demoiselles. Same as above. Good feeders. Very active.

Doctor Fish. Dry food, algae, brine shrimp, fish roe, tubifex worms, etc.

Dolphin. Dry food, brine shrimp, fish roe. Feed at the surface.

Dwarf Sea Horse. Live brine shrimp, freshly hatched.

Eel, Moray. Fresh shrimp. Usually the whole tail section will be eaten at once. Small fish are also eaten. Food should be dropped in plain sight at first so Moray can see it fall. Small fish should be killed before feeding and then pushed toward the Moray's mouth with a slender wooden rod. Do shrimp the same way.

Electric Ray. Small chunks of fresh shrimp. This should be pushed under its body towards the mouth. Use a wooden rod for this purpose, so you won't get shocked.

Electric Stargazer. Small live minnows which should be fed in large quantities and introduced to the aquarium slowly so they will live. No hiding places should be given for the live food.

Filefish. Brine shrimp, fish roe, small minnows, finely chopped shrimp, dry food, tubifex worms, etc.

Flame Scallop. Live brine shrimp, fine dry food mixed well with water. This mollusk filters the water to obtain food. Shrimp or clam meal mixed well in the aquarium will help it obtain food. Don't over-feed.

Flounder. Finely chopped shrimp, fish roe. May eat brine shrimp.

Flying Fish. Large continuous supply of live brine shrimp. Must be fed a great deal or it will die.

Frogfish. Small live minnows kept in the aquarium without any place to hide so they can be easily caught.

Gambusia. Live brine shrimp, chopped shrimp, dry food, fish roe.

Garibaldi. Live brine shrimp, finely chopped shrimp, fish roe, etc.

Goat Fish. Brine shrimp, chopped shrimp, Sargassum shrimp, Daphnia.

Gobies. Dry food, live brine shrimp, finely chopped shrimp, fish roe, Daphnia, etc.

Grass Porgy. Brine shrimp, fish roe, chopped shrimp, dry food.

Grouper. Small minnows, chunks of fresh shrimp, fish roe, earthworms.

Grunts. Dry food, brine shrimp, fresh chopped shrimp, fish roe.

Hogfish. Live brine shrimp, finely chopped shrimp, tubifex worms, fish roe.

Horseshoe Crab. Freshly chopped shrimp, or fish. Push it under the crab.

Jawfish. Fairly large chunks of fresh shrimp. Drop in plain view, so fish can see it fall.

Jellyfish. Live brine shrimp fed in large quantities, live plankton.

Jewel Fish. Dry food, finely chopped shrimp, brine shrimp, fish roe, and most other aquarium foods, including green algae. It is an excellent feeder.

Lion Fish. Small live minnows. These should be fed one or two at a time and should be given no hiding place so they can be easily caught. If the Lionfish has difficulty catching them, they should be partly stunned before placing in aquarium. Put them in plain view and remove them if not eaten immediately. May eat earthworms, chopped shrimp.

Lizard Fish. Small minnows, chopped shrimp, earthworms.

Lobster. Feed chopped shrimp or fish.

Lookdown. Small specimens will eat brine shrimp and finely chopped fresh shrimp. Larger specimens will eat Sargassum shrimp, and chopped shrimp. Sometimes will eat dry food.

Molly Miller. Dry food, chopped shrimp, brine shrimp, algae and most other aquarium foods, including tubifex and micro-worms.

Moon Fish. Same as Lookdown.

Moorish Idol. Tubifex worms, micro-worms, white worms, brine shrimp, etc.

Mousefish. Live minnows. Place several in aquarium at one time.

Mud Skipper. Very small grasshoppers, houseflies thrown into water, live insects, chunks of earthworm. Food must be dropped in plain view, so that Skipper can see it wriggle. Can be trained to eat chopped shrimp if it is dropped about an inch in front of Skipper. He will usually grab it as soon as it hits the water, but will seldom bother with it if he doesn't see it fall.

Nomeus. Live brine shrimp, fish roe, live plankton, Daphnia.

Nudibranch. Green algae, decayed vegetation.

Octopus. Whole fresh shrimp, small crabs, scallops, snails, conchs, etc.

Orange Demoiselle. Dry foods, brine shrimp, chopped shrimp, algae, and most other aquarium foods. An excellent feeder.

Parrot Fish. Natural food is live coral which the Parrot fish crushes with its powerful beak. Will also eat chopped shrimp which should be served with the shell left on. Very small Parrots will eat live brine shrimp.

Pipe Fish. Small specimens up to four inches feed on live brine shrimp. Larger specimens will need adult brine shrimp, baby Guppies and small live swimming crustacea.

Polyp. Obtains its food directly from free-floating particles suspended in the water. A little fine food, clam meal, etc. mixed with the water will provide it with enough nourishment. May eat brine shrimp.

Porcupine Fish. Small specimens up to one inch will eat earthworms and chopped shrimp, tubifex worms, Sargassum shrimp and small minnows. Larger fish up to six inches or more will eat large chunks of fresh shrimp which could be dropped in plain view so they can see it fall. They will also eat small minnows, Gambusia, small crabs, earthworms, etc. A stubborn feeder can usually be started eating by giving it a whole shrimp, the type used as fishing bait. This may be fed alive or stunned and dropped near your pet. It seldom fails to arouse a dull appetite.

Porgy. Live brine shrimp, chopped shrimp, chopped earthworms, etc.

Porkfish. Small chunks of fresh shrimp, fish roe, and small live minnows. Is especially fond of Neon Gobies and smaller fish. Porkfish under two inches will eat live brine shrimp, but the larger specimens cannot get enough food value from this tiny food. Also eats dry food.

Portuguese Man of War Fish. Brine shrimp, live plankton, Daphnia, fish roe.

Puffer Fish. Brine shrimp, chopped shrimp, dry food, fish roe, and most other aquarium foods.

Queen Angelfish. See Angelfish.

Queen Trigger Fish. Chopped shrimp, live earthworms, small minnows, crabs, etc.

Ray, Sting. Small chunks of fresh shrimp which should be pushed under the fish towards its mouth. It soon becomes tame and will come to the surface for food. Food may be served on slender pointed rod so that it can be placed almost in the Ray's mouth.

Razor Fish. Brine shrimp, fresh chopped shrimp, fish roe, dry food.

Reef Fish, Blue or Gray. Live brine shrimp, Daphnia, small live crustacea, fish roe, dry food, tubifex and micro-worms.

Remora. Chopped shrimp, or crawfish, live earthworms.

Ribbon Fish. Chopped shrimp, brine shrimp, small minnows, small live crustacea.

Rock Beauty. Green algae, hair algae, chopped shrimp, fish roe, brine shrimp, and dry food. A shy feeder, sometimes it is best to keep by itself or with gentle fish like Neon Gobies, Clownfish, etc.

Rock Hind. Chopped shrimp, small minnows, earthworms.

Rock Skipper. Dry food, brine shrimp, chopped shrimp, fish roe, earthworms, and most other foods. An excellent feeder.

Sargassum Fish. Small live fish about one half its body length. Also will eat live earthworms. May be trained to eat chopped shrimp by placing a chunk on toothpick and touching it gently against his nose. He will usually grab it.

Scallop. Filters the water to obtain food. A little clam meal or dry food mixed well with the water helps it obtain nourishment. May eat live brine shrimp also.

Schoolmaster. Chopped shrimp, earthworms, tubifex worms, etc.

Scat. Dry food, brine shrimp, chopped shrimp, algae, etc.

Scorpion Fish. Live earthworms, large chunks of chopped shrimp dropped in plain view so fish can see it fall. Also eats small minnows.

Sea Anemone. Feed once a week. Drop half inch chunk of fresh shrimp directly on tentacles. Anemone will take it inside.

Sea Horse, Large. Will eat only live food such as Sargassum shrimp, adult brine shrimp, mosquito larvae, Daphnae, baby Guppies and other tiny fish that may be easily swallowed. Seldom will eat newly-hatched brine shrimp as these are so small.

Sea Horse, Medium. Will eat live brine shrimp that are newly hatched. Also should be fed baby Guppies and Daphnae to supplement the shrimp.

Sea Horse, Small. Brine shrimp, live of course. Feed plenty, it's a growing horse.

Sea Horse, Dwarf. Live brine shrimp only. These should be freshly hatched and fed in good quantity so that there are always some swimming in aquarium.

Sea Robin. Small chunks of chopped shrimp, live Sargassum shrimp, earthworms.

Sea Slug. Green and brown algae. Cultivate this in aquarium. A few plants in the aquarium will provide plenty of foods.

Sea Spider. Chopped shrimp, green algae, fish roe, etc.

Sea Urchin. Chopped shrimp, which should be placed directly under center. Also eats algae and decayed plant matter.

Sea Turtle. Chopped shrimp and earthworms. Sometimes it is necessary to pry open its mouth and place food inside. Then put immediately in water. Once a week, food should be dipped in cod liver oil.

Sergeant Major. Dry food, brine shrimp, chopped shrimp, fish roe, and most other aquarium foods. An excellent feeder.

Shark, Mako. Fish collectors and distance swimmers. Also will eat unwelcome guests and in-laws. Shy Mako sharks may be tempted to eat by dangling a business competitor over their aquarium.

Shark, Nurse. Whole shrimp is a good basic food. Some specimens need force feeding at first. Grab shark firmly by back and push shrimp well into its mouth. Release gently so it won't become too excited. Usually they will eat if shrimp is dropped in plain view. Then it may be pushed towards them with a slender rod. Force feeding should only be attempted as a last resort. Be careful of their bite when handling them.

Shark, Sucker. Chopped shrimp, chopped fish, earthworms.

Shrimp. Chopped shrimp or fish fed in small quantities, green algae.

Slippery Dick. Chopped shrimp, small minnows, fish roe, earthworms, tubifex worms, etc. Small specimens up to two inches will also eat brine shrimp.

Spade Fish. Chopped shrimp, brine shrimp, fish roe, dry food.

Spanish Hogfish. Brine shrimp, chopped shrimp, tubifex, and micro-worms, dry food and fish roe.

Spiny Boxfish. Chopped shrimp cut into quarter-inch chunks with shell left on. Also will eat earthworms. Food must be dropped in plain view so that Spiny Box will see it fall. Also will eat small scallops, mussels and snails less than one inch. Baby Spiny Boxfish under an inch will eat brine shrimp in addition to the chopped shrimp. The shrimp should be very small so they can easily swallow it. Large Spiny Boxfish will seldom eat brine shrimp, no matter how hungry they become.

Spiny Lobster. Chopped shrimp, algae.

Squirrelfish. Chopped shrimp, small minnows, fish roe, brine shrimp, for the specimens under two inches. Also eats earthworms and tubifex worms.

Starfish, Basket. Exact diet unknown. It does gather food suspended in water. Suggest chopped shrimp which should be fed at night or when creature has its feathery arms extended. Mix shrimp well into water.

Starfish, Common. Chopped shrimp, algae. Place food directly under the center of the body. Will eat small scallops and clams.

Sticklebacks. Earthworms, tubifex worms, chopped shrimp.

Sting Ray. Chopped shrimp which should be pushed under the body where the mouth is located.

Surgeonfish. Dry food, algae, brine shrimp, chopped shrimp, tubifex worms.

Tangs. Same as surgeon fishes.

Toadfish. Good-sized chunks of fresh shrimp, small minnows. Especially fond of earthworms or marine worms. Young Toads should be fed fish roe and fine chopped shrimp. Food must be dropped in plain view so that fish will see it fall.

Trigger Fish. Chopped shrimp, earthworms, dry food, Sargassum fish, small aquarium fish, etc. Also Gambusia.

Tripletail. Chopped shrimp, brine shrimp, earthworms, tubifex worms, dry food.

Trumpet Fish. Small Sargassum shrimp and live crustacea. Chopped shrimp, adult brine shrimp, tubifex worms.

Trunkfish. Chopped shrimp, earthworms, tubifex worms, brine shrimp, live Sargassum shrimp.

Turtles. Chopped shrimp, earthworms, tubifex worms. Must be in water to swallow food. Once a week shrimp should be dipped in cod liver oil.

Wrasse. Chopped shrimp, earthworms, tubifex worms, brine shrimp for very small specimens under two inches.

Yellow Tang. Dry food, green algae, chopped shrimp, brine shrimp, worms.

18

Special Tips for Beginners and "Experts"

Perhaps here you will find the answer to a special problem not covered in the text.

If you have many salt water fish, it is wise to use a double air pump set-up, with duplication air stones in each tank. Most salt water fish won't survive overnight without air, especially if the fish are large or crowded. If a pump goes off or you forget to return an air stone to a tank, you could lose a lot of expensive fish but with a double set up, the risk is greatly reduced.

Don't put large mouthed fish like grouper, sargassum fish, scorpion fish, sea robins, lionfish, etc. in with small fish, even if the big fellows show no signs of aggression towards the little fellows. When the big mouthed fellows get hungry, your expensive little fish will disappear one after the other.

Live adult brine shrimp give indications that they carry salt water "ick" as well as oodinium and other parasitic infestations. If your tank becomes infested periodically, perhaps the brine shrimp are causing it.

Special to dealers . . . It is better to keep your fish in ten small tanks than in one large tank. When you get in new fish, place each bag of fish in a separate tank with the water in which they arrive. When the fish are sold from a tank, empty it out and dry it to kill any parasites or disease. This will cut your losses down to NIL.

Needless to say (but I'll say it) don't spray around your aquariums even if label says spray is harmless to fish. Don't keep activated carbon stored near chemicals or pesticides. The carbon will absorb the odors and can transfer poison to your aquarium.

Don't neglect the dip-tube, that ever handy aquarium tool. It is perfect for removing uneaten dry food which may settle to the bottom and which may fungus or cause pollution if it is not removed.

A common magnifying glass is useful in examining the fins of your marine fish. You can spot first signs of ick or parasites on the clear portion of the fins and on the eye covering and take remedial action before the situation gets out of hand.

If snow white coral develops a pink tinge after it is in the aquarium for a few weeks, remove it immediately and wash it well, then cure it by soaking it for at least a week in fresh water before returning to the tank. The pink tinge is usually caused from dead tissue which leeches out from the pores of the coral and it will pollute the aquarium unless promptly removed.

If a large aquarium is hopelessly infected with bacteria and parasites, and all the fish have died in it, the water need not be thrown away. Instead, clean up the bottom of the tank with a fine mesh nylon net and then put a cupful or two of clorox in the aquarium (one cupful for each 50 gallons). Let the aquarium set about a week and then filter with carbon and add a little chlorine remover. Filter the water a couple more weeks and usually it will be safe again for most or all fishes. It is best to try it with one fish before adding a number of costly specimens.

Pipe fish, dragonettes and cowfish all are great jumpers. Unless you wish to find their pitiful dried up bodies on your floor, you should cover their aquarium tightly.

Special for importers . . . In the winter months or during cold weather a lot of worry with ick, fungus and other disease problems can be reduced or eliminated by placing newly arrived fish in a separate aquarium with a heater and raising the temperature to 85 degrees for a week or more. This will help fish overcome chill received during transit and increase metabolism so fish will adjust better to new environment.

You can keep large sea horses, sargassum fish or other fish that might present a problem in your community aquarium by simply isolating them in a corner with a single sheet of glass placed across the corner about eight inches out from the end of the tank. This eliminates the need for a separate aquarium.

Pearly Jawfish and sharp nosed puffers are tremendous jumpers. Always keep their aquarium tightly covered. Even cover the hole around filter stems as they will jump through a very small opening.

If using an outside filter with activated carbon, make certain that the siphon tube reaches all the way to the bottom so that it will pick up uneaten food, fish droppings and debris. This will greatly prolong the length of time for tank cleaning.

If your fish stop eating, try increasing your aeration and filtration as much as possible. Check under coral for uneaten food or pollution. Also check pH and salinity. If none of this helps, check the fish with a magnifying glass for signs of ick or fungus, and change a portion of the water. If rapid breathing is noticed or signs of disease are evident, add a dose of copper.

Fine shredded scallop will often tempt a shy butterfly-fish to eat. Cut the fresh scallop into thin, wormlike pieces and drop them near the fish.

Always use a cover glass, either glass or plastic under your light. There is nothing quite as lethal to your fish as metal-poisoned water caused from spray or condensation which drips back into the aquarium from the light.

Use caution in selecting a light for your aquarium. Too much light will cause excessive algae to grow on everything making a great deal of maintenance necessary. Also it may blind the fish. The light should be strong enough so that it lights up the tank well but not so bright that it washes out everything with its brightness. A clean, carbon filtered tank will require less light and still offer excellent visibility.

Yellow wrasse (young Blueheads) and other wrasse will often eat neon gobies. If it is desired to keep the two together, obtain small wrasses and large gobies so that the gobies are nearly as large as the wrasse.

Live coral should be checked at least once a week for mold or fungus and also for decaying sponge material. This usually occurs along the sides near the bottom or beneath it. A visual check is alright but if you suspect decay, life up the coral and smell it. If decomposition is taking place a very foul odor will be present, in which case the coral should be promptly removed from the tank. The dead material may be brushed off and rinsed lightly to remove it and if it is not too extensive, the coral may be returned to the aquarium. If in doubt about it place it in a separate tank.

Special to dealers and aquarists who have a large number of aquariums! Hatch out live brine shrimp in artificial sea water rather than dipping up some water from one of your tanks. This way you can avoid the possibility of introducing any disease or harmful bacteria to your various aquariums. Also make sure that you thoroughly rinse your net before dipping brine shrimp from each tank to prevent the possibility of introducing disease from one of your tanks back into your brine shrimp tank.

Regular eating shrimp is one of the best staple foods for marine fish. Simple peel it and freeze it. Then when it is frozen solid, grate several of them through an ordinary food grater and you will have a food most fish will relish. You can freeze a scallop at the same time and mix a little in with the shrimp when you are feeding. CAUTION: Soak the shredded shrimp in fresh water and rinse several times to remove all milky juice. Feed SPARINGLY. Too much shrimp will quickly pollute an aquarium.

A plastic Back Scratcher is excellent for moving sand about the tank or removing chunks of food and other chores in the marine tank. Remember, the less you place your hands in the tank the better.

The two gallon drum type fish bowl makes an excellent hospital tank for small fish. Just equip it with the under gravel filter and silica sand and fill two-thirds full with sea water and it's ready for use. You can add medications to it which would otherwise discolor your main tank. It is also good for a temporary holding tank for new arrivals so you can check and observe them for disease before adding them to your tank.

Don't change water in your aquarium just for the sake of changing it. If fish are doing fine, salinity is proper and everything else is alright, a change of water may do more harm than good. Filtration with activated carbon greatly lengthens life of sea water in the aquarium.

Live Coral Buffs—If you want to keep live coral and fish in the same tank, set up the tank with the live coral first and let it operate three weeks before adding the fish. This seems to reduce chance of parasitic infestation.

Even the most fastidious of fishes that were formerly considered strictly live feeders, can be trained to eat chopped shrimp or chunks of shrimp or fish if it is presented to them properly. Robert Shaughan reports that he has even trained angler fish to take chunks of shrimp from a feeding stick. Also lionfish *(Pterois volitans)* have been completely weaned to chunks of shrimp rather than live food, living past the year mark at this date and growing fast! This may come as good news to those who have difficulty obtaining live foods. Also, feeding dead shrimp or fish may lessen the chance of introducing disease to a rare specimen. It would not be surprising that even the large sea horse could be trained to eat chopped shrimp or scallop presented to it on a toothpick in bite size.

Feed the new flake foods sparingly. Some of them dissolve very rapidly and disperse throughout the tank, eventually settling into the sand. This could lead to pollution of the water and also act as a nutrient solution causing an increase of micro-organisms in the water.

Beware of Drugged Fish! More than ever before, drugged fish are being placed on the market resulting in extremely high losses to both the dealer and the hobbyist. Results? Catastrophe! Some collectors wantonly use quinaldine, acetone, formaldehyde and rotenone or a combination of the above to obtain their specimens. The drugged fish look great when offered for sale and in fact look even better than fish caught with the conventional hand nets as they are "living high" on the effects of the drug. But a week or two later, they may die in wholesale lots with a mortality rate as high as ninety-five percent! Symptoms of over-drugged fish are ravenous appetites, extreme vivaciousness, and general listlessness. It is difficult to detect any of the above, even for a trained marine aquarist, but if your fish die shortly after you purchase them and for no apparent reason, you should strongly suspect drugs. Inquire through your dealer and shipper as to whether or not drugs were used in any portion of the handling of the fish and take steps to correct it by ordering completely undrugged fish so you can compare their longevity with the drugged fish.

If using a power filter or power pump as the sole filtering and aerating unit for your aquarium, make certain to add an air stone or two from a regular air pump so that they will have sufficient air, especially if the power filter clogs or stops filtering.

If your fish won't live in artificial sea water perhaps it's your tap water that is at fault. Some city water is lethal to most living organisms. Best bet in mixing artificial sea water is to use well water, pond or rain water or distilled water. Water softeners are also recommended if your water is hard.

Large Angelfish, particularly the exotic Pacific species such as the imperator or diacanthus apparently feed on small half inch long shrimp that live in the algae on the reefs. R. Straughan has noted many times that when the angelfish nibbled at the algae on the reefs, a close examination of the algae revealed many small shrimp living in it. While at first it appears that the angels were eating the algae, it had been suspected that they were also after the shrimp for they would often closely examine the algae before taking a bite. Recently these suspicions were confirmed when our large imperator who was eating poorly, savagely attacked small half inch shrimp when they were placed in the aquarium. It would search the entire bottom of the tank for the small shrimp which it eagerly devoured when it found them.

Don't shop around town for salt water fish. Buy all your fish at the same store. Then if you have problems with disease your dealer will be able to cope with them more intelligently. The hobbyist who buys his fish from a number of different stores stands a good chance of introducing a number of different diseases to his aquarium, in which case all a dealer can give him is sympathy when his fish all become diseased and die. You should not expect a dealer to help you with disease problems when you purchased fish from his competitor.

Keep ALL bay fish such as sea horses, cowfish, pipefish, filefish, spiny boxfish, porcupinefish, etc. in aquariums by themselves. These fishes are usually heavily infested with numerous diseases, parasites and bacterial infestation that will wreak havoc in your aquarium. Unless the bay fish have been sterilized and completely cleaned of all disease they should never be kept in the same tank with expensive coral fishes.

The large size wire framed aquarium nets with the weld at the top of the net may be easily repaired if the weld breaks by simply inserting a six inch length of aquarium plastic air tubing over the wire. Just work it half over one side and then slip it on the other side and work the wire frame back inside the tubing till they are joined together.

The efficiency of many power type filters may be increased a great deal if you insert a two-foot length of half inch plastic tubing into the outlet and place this at the bottom of the tank so that it stirs up dirt from the bottom enabling the siphon stems to pick it up.

Always check your large sea horses for external parasites, when you get them. The parasites are flat and usually colored the same as the horse so you must search for them carefully. Favorite hiding places for them are around the neck, under the chin, on top of the head or along the ridge of the back where they often nestle into the shallow cavity there. They can be picked off with tweezers.

Those new plastic milk bottles in gallon size now appearing throughout the country can have a multitude of uses for the marine hobbyist and dealer. Rinse them out well and cut off the top with a razor blade and you will have a fine container for floating new fish in the aquarium. They are also useful for dipping up sea water when emptying an aquarium, or isolating specimens which are aggressive. You can cut the bottom off them and use them for a temporary filter. Simply fill them full of nylon or orlon floss and pour water through them allowing it to fall back into the tank. Other uses are boat bailers, water jugs and possibly fish traps with a little adjustment.

Live coral seems to benefit immensely if you will dip up some water from the tank and pour it back from a height so that it really stirs up the water. You should pour quite close to the coral so that the water flushes the coral itself. Also, during heavy feeding of live brine shrimp, especially at night, don't forget to turn up the air stone and turn down the filters so that the food remains suspended in the water.

Many of the new aquarium nets are made of such extremely poor steel that the frames are dipped in oil so they won't rust before they get to the dealer. The galvanizing apparently is extremely bad. These nets should be wiped clean with a dry cloth and soaked in fresh water a few days before placing in aquarium. Or better yet, buy a good quality net that won't rust the first week you get it. All aquarium nets should be soaked in fresh water after use in the salt water tank to prolong their lives. Better yet, get the new all-plastic frame nets instead of wire frame.

You can make a giant filter for your large aquariums by using either the 2½ gallon or the eight gallon aqua-flair plastic tank. Set the tank up so that it is level with the top of your aquarium. Insert a Eureka under gravel filter and cover with three inches of sand. Then cover with several inches of activated carbon and you will have a large capacity filter. Let the bubbler stem from the under gravel filter pump the water back into your big tank. One or two siphon stems will be needed to siphon water into your giant filter. This is a slow filter but will filter water absolutely gin clear. If you want a faster filter you will have to hook up some type of water pump to it.

Use a separate aquarium net for every salt water tank. Nets are inexpensive and the use of a separate net for each tank will vastly reduce transmission of disease or parasites from one tank to another.

Always let your faucet run for a few minutes before drawing water to add to your aquarium, or to mix artificial sea water. Water which sets in the faucet itself may contain a lethal dose of copper if just a glass full is taken from the faucet without letting it run. This is also very important if you are using water from a garden hose, for the water laying in the hose could be very toxic if flushed into a small tank.

The large size wire framed aquarium nets with the weld at the top of the net may be easily repaired if the weld breaks by simply inserting a six inch length of aquarium plastic air tubing over the wire. Just work it half over one side and then slip it on the other side and work the wire frame back inside the tubing till they are joined together.

Quick relief from exterior parasites that are visible on the fins or body of the fish may be obtained by placing the fish in a container of fresh tap water and sea water (about a half and half mixture). We have noted that it would clean the fish completely of parasites. The fish should be left in the solution for fifteen minutes to a half hour or less if it shows signs of distress. Of course this is not a positive cure and it may work in some instances and not in others due to the fact that tap water varies so much in chlorine content in many areas but it is a good field for experiment. We examined the fish with a lens before and after treatment to determine results. A magnifying glass will prove helpful here.

Use distilled water or demineralized water to replace water which has evaporated from the aquarium to avoid chemical buildup in the tank. Distilled water should also be used when mixing artificial sea water if possible.

References

All Pets Magazine, Fond Du Lac, Wisc.

Aquarium Journal, Steinhart Aquarium, San Francisco, Calif.

Aquarium Magazine, Philadelphia, Pa.

Breder, C. M. Jr., *Field Book of Marine Fishes of Atlantic Coast.*

Chute, Walter H., *Guide to John C. Shedd Aquarium.*

Fisher, Ed, *Marine Tropicals,* All Pets Publication.

Mellen, Ida M. and Lanier, Robert J., *1001 Questions Answered About Your Aquarium.*

Morris, Percy A., *Field Guide to the Shells.*

Phillips, Craig R., curator, Miami Seaquarium.

Ray, Carleton and Ciampi, Elgin, *The Underwater Guide to Marine Life.*

Smith, Walton F. G., *The International Oceanographic Foundation.*

Wood, F. G., curator, Marine Studios, Marineland, Fla.

Zahl, Paul A., National Geographic Society.

Index